Human Services Online:
A New Arena
for Service Delivery

Human Services Online: A New Arena for Service Delivery has been co-published simultaneously as *Journal of Technology in Human Services,* Volume 17, Numbers 1 and 2/3 2000.

The *Journal of Technology in Human Services* Monographic "Separates" (formerly the *Computers in Human Services* series)*

Below is a list of "separates," which in serials librarianship means a special issue simultaneously published as a special journal issue or double-issue *and* as a "separate" hardbound monograph. (This is a format which we also call a "DocuSerial.")

"Separates" are published because specialized libraries or professionals may wish to purchase a specific thematic issue by itself in a format which can be separately cataloged and shelved, as opposed to purchasing the journal on an on-going basis. Faculty members may also more easily consider a "separate" for classroom adoption.

"Separates" are carefully classified separately with the major book jobbers so that the journal tie-in can be noted on new book order slips to avoid duplicate purchasing.

You may wish to visit Haworth's website at . . .

http://www.haworthpressinc.com

. . . to search our online catalog for complete tables of contents of these separates and related publications.

You may also call 1-800-HAWORTH (outside US/Canada: 607-722-5857), or Fax 1-800-895-0582 (outside US/Canada: 607-771-0012), or e-mail at:

getinfo@haworthpressinc.com

Human Services Online: A New Arena for Service Delivery, edited by Jerry Finn, PhD, and Gary Holden, DSW (Vol. 17, No. 1/2/3, 2000). *Focuses on the ways that human services are using the Internet for service delivery, social change, and resource development as more and more agencies can be found on the Internet.*

Computers and Information Technology in Social Work: Education, Training, and Practice, edited by Jo Ann R. Coe, PhD, and Goutham M. Menon, PhD (Vol. 16, No. 2/3, 1999). *Discusses the impact that recent technological advances have had on social work practice and education. Social workers and educators will discover ideas and projects that were presented at a week long conference presented at the University of South Carolina College of Social Work. This unique book covers a wide range of topics, such as different aspects of technology applied to assist those in helping professions, how computers can be used in child protective cases in order to practice more effectively, social services via videoconferencing, and much more.*

Information Technologies: Teaching to Use–Using to Teach, edited by Frank B. Raymond III, DSW, Leon Ginsberg, PhD, and Debra Gohagan, MSW, ACSW, LISW* (Vol. 15, No. 2/3, 1998). *Explores examples of the use of technology to teach social work knowledge, values, and skills across the curriculum.*

The History and Function of the Target Cities Management Information Systems, edited by Matthew G. Hile, PhD* (Vol. 14, No. 3/4, 1998). *"Essential Reading for anyone invested in improving the coordination and delivery of substance abuse services in large metropolitan areas." (Albert D. Farrell, PhD, Professor of Psychology, Virginia Commonwealth University, Richmond)*

Human Services in the Information Age, edited by Jackie Rafferty, MS, Jan Steyaert, and David Colombi* (Vol. 12, No. 1/2/3/4, 1996). *Anyone interested in the current state of the development of human service information systems of all types needs to read this book." (Walter F. LaMendola, PhD, Consultant, Wheat Ridge, CO)*

Electronic Tools for Social Work Practice and Education, edited by Hy Resnick, PhD* (Vol. 11, No. 1/2/3/4, 1994). *"Opens a new world of opportunities for readers by introducing a variety of electronic tools available when working with various clients." (Ram A. Cnaan, PhD, Associate Professor, School of Social Work, University of Pennsylvania)*

Technology in People Services: Research, Theory, and Applications, edited by Marcos Leiderman, MSW, Charles Guzzetta, EdD, Leny Struminger, PhD, and Menachem Monnickendam, PhD, MSW* (Vol. 9, No. 1/2/3/4, 1993). *"Honest reporting and inquiry into the opportunities and limitations for administrators, managers, supervisors, clinicians, service providers, consumers, and clients . . . A well-integrated and in-depth examination."* (John P. Flynn, PhD, Associate Director for Instructional Computing, University Computing Services and Professor of Social Work, Western Michigan University)

Computer Applications in Mental Health: Education and Evaluation, edited by Marvin J. Miller, MD* (Vol. 8, No. 3/4, 1992). *"Describes computer programs designed specifically for mental health clinicians and their work in both private practice and institutional treatment settings."* (SciTech Book News)

Computers for Social Change and Community Organizing, edited by John Downing, PhD, Robert Fasano, MSW, Patricia Friedland, MLS, Michael McCullough, AM, Terry Mizrahi, PhD, and Jeremy Shapiro, PhD* (Vol. 8, No. 1, 1991). *This landmark volume presents an original and–until now–unavailable perspective on the uses of computers for community- and social-change-based organizations.*

Computer Literacy in Human Services Education, edited by Richard L. Reinoehl and B. Jeanne Mueller* (Vol. 7, No. 1/2/3/4, 1990). *This volume provides a unique and notable contribution to the investigation and exemplification of computer literacy in human services education.*

Computer Literacy in Human Services, edited by Richard L. Reinoehl and Thomas Hanna* (Vol. 6, No. 1/2/3/4, 1990) *"Includes a diversity of articles on many of the most important practical and conceptual issues associated with the use of computer technology in the human services."* (Adult Residential Care)

The Impact of Information Technology on Social Work Practice, edited by Ram A. Cnaan, PhD, and Phyllida Parsloe, PhD* (Vol. 5, No. 1/2, 1989). *International experts confront the urgent need for social work practice to move into the computer age.*

A Casebook of Computer Applications in the Social and Human Services, edited by Walter LaMendola, PhD, Bryan Glastonbury, and Stuart Toole* (Vol. 4, No. 1/2/3/4, 1989). *"Makes for engaging and enlightening reading in the rapidly expanding field of information technology in the human services."* (Wallace Gingerich, PhD, Associate Professor, School of Social Welfare, University of Wisconsin-Milwaukee)

Technology and Human Service Delivery: Challenges and a Critical Perspective, edited by John W. Murphy, PhD, and John T. Pardeck, PhD, MSW* (Vol. 3, No. 1/2, 1988). *"A much-needed, critical examination of whether and how computers can improve social services . . . Essential reading for social workers in the field and for scholars interested in how computers alter social systems."* (Charles Ess, PhD, Assistant Professor of Philosophy, Morningside College)

Research in Mental Health Computing: The Next Five Years, edited by John H. Greist, MD, Judith A. Carroll, PhD, Harold P. Erdman, PhD, Marjorie H. Klein, PhD, and Cecil R. Wurster, MA* (Vol. 2, No. 3/4, 1988). *"Provides a clear and lucid perspective on the state of research in mental health computing."* (David Servan-Schreiber, MD, Western Psychiatric Institute & Clinic and Department of Computer Science, Carnegie Mellon University)

Human Services Online: A New Arena for Service Delivery has been co-published simultaneously as *Journal of Technology in Human Services,* Volume 17, Number 1 and Volume 17, Numbers 2/3 2000.

Cover Photo by Puja Telikicherla. ©P. Telikicherla, April, 2000.

Library of Congress Cataloging-in-Publication Data

Human services online: a new arena for service delivery/Jerry Finn, Gary Holden, editors.
     p. cm.
    "Has been co-published simultaneously in Journal of technology in human services, Volume 17, Numbers 1 and 2/3 2000."
    Includes bibliographical references.
    ISBN 0-7890-1010-0 (alk. paper)–ISBN 0-7890-1011-9 (alk. paper)
    1. Human services–United States–Computer network resources. 2. Social services–United States–Computer network resources. 3. Social work administration–United States–Data processing. 4. World Wide Web. 5. Internet (Computer network) I. Finn, Jerry. II. Holden, Gary.

HV29.5.U5 H85 2000
025.06′361973–dc21
                                              00-038880

Human Services Online:
A New Arena
for Service Delivery

Jerry Finn
Gary Holden
Editors

Human Services Online: A New Arena for Service Delivery has been co-published simultaneously as *Journal of Technology in Human Services,* Volume 17, Numbers 1 and 2/3 2000.

The Haworth Press, Inc.
New York • London • Oxford

Indexing, Abstracting & Website/Internet Coverage

This section provides you with a *chronological list* of major indexing & abstracting services. That is to say, each service began covering this periodical during the year noted in the right column. Most Websites which are listed below have indicated that they will either post, disseminate, compile, archive, cite or alert their own Website users with research-based content from this work. (This list is as current as the copyright date of this publication.)

Abstracting, Website/Indexing Coverage .... Year When Coverage Began

- *ABSTRACTS OF RESEARCH IN PASTORAL CARE & COUNSELING* **1992**

- *ACM GUIDE TO COMPUTER LITERATURE* **1992**

- *INFORMATION SCIENCE ABSTRACTS* **1992**

- *INSPEC* **1992**

- *PSYCHOLOGICAL ABSTRACTS (PsycINFO)* **1992**

- *REFERATIVNYI ZHURNAL (Abstracts Journal of the All-Russian Institute of Scientific and Technical Information)* **1992**

- *SAGE PUBLIC ADMINISTRATION ABSTRACTS (SPAA)* **1992**

- *SOCIAL SERVICES ABSTRACTS www.csa.com* **1992**

- *SOCIAL WORK ABSTRACTS* **1992**

- *SOCIOLOGICAL ABSTRACTS (SA) www.csa.com* **1992**

(continued)

(continued)

*Special Bibliographic Notes related to special journal issues
(separates) and indexing/abstracting:*

- indexing/abstracting services in this list will also cover material in any "separate" that is co-published simultaneously with Haworth's special thematic journal issue or DocuSerial. Indexing/abstracting usually covers material at the article/chapter level.
- monographic co-editions are intended for either non-subscribers or libraries which intend to purchase a second copy for their circulating collections.
- monographic co-editions are reported to all jobbers/wholesalers/approval plans. The source journal is listed as the "series" to assist the prevention of duplicate purchasing in the same manner utilized for books-in-series.
- to facilitate user/access services all indexing/abstracting services are encouraged to utilize the co-indexing entry note indicated at the bottom of the first page of each article/chapter/contribution.
- this is intended to assist a library user of any reference tool (whether print, electronic, online, or CD-ROM) to locate the monographic version if the library has purchased this version but not a subscription to the source journal.
- individual articles/chapters in any Haworth publication are also available through the Haworth Document Delivery Service (HDDS).

Human Services Online:
A New Arena
for Service Delivery

CONTENTS

ABOUT THE EDITORS

Jerry Finn, PhD, is currently a Professor at the Department of Social Work, University of New Hampshire. Dr. Finn has twenty years of teaching experience in social work that includes courses in Information Technology and Human Services at the Bachelors and Masters level. In addition he has published more scholarly articles, primarily in areas related to the impact of information technology on human services. He currently serves as a reviewer for the *Journal of Information Technology in Human Services, Journal of Baccalaureate Social Work*, and *Journal of Self Help Research*. In addition, he has given presentations and workshops in the area of information technology at international, national, and state conferences, including Human Service Information Technology Applications (HUSITA), Council on Social Work Education (CSWE), Association of Baccalaureate Social Work Program Directors (BPD), National Association of Social Workers (NASW) and the New York University Centennial Social Work Association of Baccalaureate Social Work Program Directors and the Council on Social Work Education. Dr. Finn has been provided training and consultation to human service agencies in the areas of database design, development of information and referral systems, web site design, and risk-management related to online activities. He received his doctorate from the University of Wisconsin-Madison in Social Welfare in 1980 and MSW from the University of Hawaii in 1974.

Gary Holden, DSW, is an Associate Professor and serves as Chair of Research at New York University's Ehrenkranz School of Social Work. He is a former faculty member in the Mount Sinai School of Medicine. Dr. Holden has published scholarly articles across a wide range of scholarly topics including the World Wide Web, computer network interventions, research methodology, self-efficacy and the relationship of psychosocial factors to health related behaviors. Dr. Holden is a member of the Health Summit Working Group–a national mutlidisciplinary effort to provide the public with a tool to assess the quality of health information on the Internet. He currently serves as a Consulting Editor for

Health and Social Work and is a member of the Editorial Boards of *Research on Social Work Practice* and *Social Work in Health Care*. Dr. Holden's primary community service activity has been the creation and maintenance of the Web site: World Wide Web Resources for Social Workers [http://www.nyu.edu/socialwork/wwwrsw/]. This site is currently the largest meta-index for social workers in the world. His research group just received funding to replicate and extend the research they report on in this volume. He received his masters in social work in 1987 and doctorate in social welfare in 1990 from Columbia University.

Introduction

Jerry Finn
Gary Holden

The Internet, once an esoteric communication channel for the military and academic researchers, is becoming part of the popular culture. The promise of the Internet is to create a society in which people have access to each other and to all information, producing synergy as people and organizations connect online in a global communications village to share ideas and resources. While that promise is yet to be realized, the Internet is increasingly used as an arena where people turn for interpersonal communication, consumer goods, and a myriad of information needs, including those related to human services. Not everyone, however, is enamored with the Internet. Human service professionals have raised concerns about loss of personal contact, use of unproven services, erosion of personal privacy, potentially negative outcomes for both children and adults, channeling of limited funds for technology, and lack of access for already disenfranchised consumer groups. And yet use of the Internet by human service organizations is increasing rapidly.

The exponential growth of the Internet has greatly exceeded the pace of scholarly analysis of the benefits and costs of using this new technology for human service agencies and consumers. Many questions are only beginning to be explored. To what extent are human

Jerry Finn, PhD, is Professor, Department of Social Work, University of New Hampshire, Durham, NH.

Gary Holden, DSW, is Associate Professor, New York University, Ehrenkranz School of Social Work.

[Haworth co-indexing entry note]: "Introduction." Finn, Jerry, and Gary Holden. Co-published simultaneously in *Journal of Technology in Human Services* (The Haworth Press, Inc.) Vol. 17, No. 1, 2000, pp. 1-5; and: *Human Services Online: A New Arena for Service Delivery* (ed: Jerry Finn, and Gary Holden) The Haworth Press, Inc., 2000, pp. 1-5. Single or multiple copies of this article are available for a fee from The Haworth Document Delivery Service [1-800-342-9678, 9:00 a.m. - 5:00 p.m. (EST). E-mail address: getinfo@haworthpressinc.com].

service programs actually up and functioning on the Internet? What agency services are being provided in this medium? To what extent are they successful in meeting agency and consumer needs? How are traditional services enhanced or changed through online collaborations? Can psychotherapy be done online? What policies and procedures must be initiated and/or changed to accommodate online services? What ethical, legal, and financial risks do agencies take in providing online services? How safe is the giving and receiving of services and support in cyberspace? Some of these questions would be raised by the adoption of any new service provision medium (e.g., Does it increase effectiveness?) and some of these questions are specific to the Internet itself (e.g., Does my professional license cover me if I am providing service to a client in another state?).

This special volume focuses on the impact of the Internet on human services and on ways that human services are using the Internet for service delivery, social change, and resource development as agencies increasingly come online. The articles include theoretical discussions of issues that impact human services, descriptions of demonstration programs, and evaluations of Internet-based services. This series of articles does not attempt to predict where we are headed, but rather presents a snapshot of where human services on the Internet are now. Our goal is to provide a view of the current state of service provision on the Internet and a preview of the issues that mainstream human services are likely to encounter in the very near future. We have loosely grouped the contributions into the categories: Demonstration Programs, Trans-Agency Issues, Promoting Collaboration, and Online Self-Help.

DEMONSTRATION PROGRAMS

This section focuses on specific programs that provide online services. Henrickson and Mayo provide an overview of the HIV Cybermall, a combination of a wide area network connecting 18 California agencies and a World Wide Web site serving individuals living with HIV. Holden, Bearison, Rode, Kapiloff and Rosenberg describe the only randomized controlled clinical trial in our collection. The authors attempt to determine if a technological intervention (in this case a network for hospitalized children) can produce meaningful change in key health variables. The remaining demonstration program in this collection is more closely related to professional education. Zipper, Broughton and Behar describe a training program that serves a group of local initiatives funded by the North Carolina Department of Health and Human Services, Child and Family Services Section. Training includes workshops and classes conducted by outside experts for the local sites. The Social Work Access Network (SWAN) is one of the more popular meta-sites for social workers on the Internet. Wright's contribution provides us with a view of SWAN users and their perceptions of this site through the use of an online survey. The study provides one model of obtaining online consumer input to enhance services development.

TRANS-AGENCY ISSUES

This section presents research that has implications for multiple agencies and programs engaged in service delivery over the Internet. Finn provides an empirical overview of domestic violence agencies on the Internet, finding that these agencies provide a wide variety of intervention and educational services while also achieving limited success in securing resources through the Internet. Many human service agencies wanting to go online face challenges related to their websites such as Web-based sources of client victimization, agency legal liability, agency vulnerability to online disruption, the need to create access for low-income clients, and difficulties in evaluation of Web services. Cameron, Graham, and Sieppert explore the computer utilization patterns of community-based HIV/AIDS organizations and consumers using these organizations in Canada. They find significant resource and access barriers to the use of technology among both agencies and consumers, and discuss future steps that need to be taken by community-based HIV/AIDS organizations. Cravens describes a website to match a new type of agency volunteer, the "virtual volunteer" with human service agencies. She provides preliminary research about successes and problems faced by online volunteers and the agencies that use them. Marx describes a range of successful online fundraising activities by human service agencies. He also notes that online fundraising may not be appropriate for all agencies, and examines cases where use of the Internet may not be a good match for the organizational context, whether in terms of ethics or dollars raised.

These Internet activities and others not described here, or even envisioned yet, will be subject to ethical and legal strictures. Banach and Bernat discuss dilemmas that arise when agencies and private practitioners offer direct services on the Internet without fully understanding the legal and liability issues that must be considered in order to provide ethical treatment to clients and risk management for service providers. As more human service providers seek to use the Internet, these issues will increasingly shape the nature and quality of the services provided. Levine describes the ethical issues involved in providing online practice with a focus on privacy, security, and confidentiality. She offers a model for analyzing and resolving ethical conflicts in clinical cases from the use of electronic information technologies.

PROMOTING COLLABORATION

This section provides examples of online services in which the expansion of communication opportunities via the Internet has promoted greater collaboration among human service organizations. Schultz, Fawcett, Francisco, Wolff, Berkowitz and Nagy describe the conceptualization and implementation of the Community Tool Box, an Internet based resource for community development. Dezendorf and Green provide a review of the literature on computer-mediated communications and results from a study of their adoption.

ONLINE SELF-HELP

Finally, a section of self-help is provided because self-help continues to be a major activity on the Internet. Meier presents an evaluation of a listserv-based self-help group for social workers dealing with work-related stress. It serves as a model for others seeking to successfully provide online social support. Even though the motivation of self-help participants generally seems positive, cyberspace is not always safe space. Waldron, Lavitt, and Kelley theorize about the potential harm that may arise in online self help groups, and provide examples from a variety of groups that indicate that human service professionals must exercise caution before referral to such groups.

We have sought to provide a snapshot of the use of technology in our profession. Any snapshot of a moving phenomenon runs a large risk of leaving subsequent viewers with a limited view. Beyond this caveat, we believe that this collection offers a good reference point for those attempting to understand the potential of the Internet for supplementing and enhancing human service practice.

The HIV Cybermall:
A Regional Cybernetwork
of HIV Services

Mark Henrickson
Judith R. Mayo

SUMMARY. The HIV Cybermall is a computer network and transportation system designed to link case managers at 18 partner agencies. The purpose of the project is to enhance and evaluate HIV-related medical, dental, drug treatment and psychosocial service delivery to people living with HIV in northern Los Angeles County. Participating agencies decided that the most important aspects of any linkage computer system were user-accessibility, cost-feasibility, and security of information. The investigators then designed a password-controlled wide-area network with a shared intake template and layered access to information. This network was combined with training sensitive to the particular needs of the agency worker, technical support, shared governance, and an integrated transportation system. The project intranet has two elements: (1) a closed, private network for confidential communication and information exchange, and (2) access to the public Internet. A key element in the project was the need to work closely with agencies in order to develop staff confidence and investment in the project. The paper describes the organizational processes that were

Mark Henrickson, MDiv, MSW, PhD, is Director, HIV Division, Northeast Valley Health Corporation.

Judith Mayo, PhD, is the Project Manager, HIV Cybermall, Northeast Valley Health Corporation-HIV Division.

Address correspondence to: NEVHC-HIV, 8215 Van Nuys Blvd., Suite 306, Panorama City, CA 91402.

[Haworth co-indexing entry note]: "The HIV Cybermall: A Regional Cybernetwork of HIV Services." Henrickson, Mark, and Judith R. Mayo. Co-published simultaneously in *Journal of Technology in Human Services* (The Haworth Press, Inc.) Vol. 17, No. 1, 2000, pp. 7-26; and: *Human Services Online: A New Arena for Service Delivery* (ed: Jerry Finn, and Gary Holden) The Haworth Press, Inc., 2000, pp. 7-26. Single or multiple copies of this article are available for a fee from The Haworth Document Delivery Service [1-800-342-9678, 9:00 a.m. - 5:00 p.m. (EST). E-mail address: getinfo@haworthpressinc.com].

7

essential for the successful design and implementation of this network. The article also outlines system hardware, software, security specifications and evaluation process. A website was also published at *www.HIVCyber-mall.org*. *[Article copies available for a fee from The Haworth Document Delivery Service: 1-800-342-9678. E-mail address: <getinfo@haworthpressinc.com> Website: <http://www.haworthpressinc.com>]*

KEYWORDS. HIV/AIDS, interagency linkages, Intranet, program evaluation

INTRODUCTION

In an era of expanding demand on available resources, linking existing community service agencies and coordinating care has become an essential component of HIV disease management. This is an understudied phenomenon. The HIV Cybermall is a computer network and transportation system designed to link 18 partner agencies in the San Fernando and Antelope Valleys, California, in order to enhance communication and referral among agencies providing HIV-related medical, dental, drug treatment and psychosocial services. The project is federally funded as a *Special Project of National Significance* (SPNS) for five years, beginning in September 1996. The requirements for an SPNS project are that the concept be both innovative and replicable in other communities. This paper offers an overview of the genesis of the project, an outline of the system specifications, and some of the early findings and initial learnings from this project.

Since the earliest identification of this "strange disease of unknown origin" (Leibowitch, 1985) impacted communities have struggled with appropriate ways to plan for and manage the impact of acquired immune deficiency syndrome, or AIDS. In the United States the earliest cases, then known as GRID (Gay Related Immune Deficiency) were first identified in gay communities in the east and west coasts in the late 1970s and early 1980s, although the disease was identified in other communities as early as 1982 (McLaughlin, in O'Malley, 1989). Shilts (1987), O'Malley (1989), Mann, Tarantola and Netter (1992), and Mann and Tarantola (1996) among many others document the emerging global and national impact of this new disease. As a result of the inability or unwillingness of many traditional social service and medical care agencies to care for the needs of people with HIV, what amounts to a parallel system of care developed to address the needs of people impacted by the pandemic. Jonsen and Stryker (1993) describe the social impact of what became known as AIDS, or HIV disease (the more inclusive and now more widely accepted term, from the virus that causes AIDS). They outline the development of community based service and advocacy organizations that arose to address the particular challenges presented by HIV disease in overimpacted communities; they note that the involvement of volunteers and dedicated AIDS service organizations has been one of the defining characteristics of the AIDS epidemic.

HIV disease impacts many different aspects of the ecology of an individual, and many different aspects of community service delivery systems. Aronstein and Thompson (1998) outline some of the particular challenges to social work practice presented by HIV, and some social work responses appropriate to address the needs of traditionally stigmatized populations and communities. Shernoff (1988) writes that serving people with AIDS encompasses the traditional social work role of advocating for underserved client populations. Evaluating HIV services is a complex undertaking and has focused more on primary prevention (e.g., Coyle, Boruch & Turner, 1991, Bolton, 1994), rather than on service delivery to infected persons. Program evaluation in AIDS service organizations has been perceived by those organizations as a kind of esoteric luxury for which there has been little time or money to perform.

As of December 31, 1998, 665,357 cases of AIDS had been reported throughout the United States, with a cumulative case-fatality rate of 60% (LAC DHS, 1999). Even this large number does not reflect the number of people who are infected with HIV but who have not progressed to an AIDS-defining condition. Many of these people are benefiting from aggressive new anti-HIV pharmacotherapies, and are living longer and more productive lives with HIV. Paradoxically, these new therapeutic advances require HIV service organizations to rethink their missions, scopes of service, and collaborations with other agencies. Agencies now must accommodate both the needs of highly vulnerable, traditionally underserved populations, and infected people returning to more normal lives who are experiencing more traditional lifecycle needs rather than the more acute demands of an inevitably terminal illness. At the same time evaluation of HIV service delivery programs has become more of an expectation by public and private funders. The HIV/AIDS Bureau of the Health Resources and Services Administration, which is responsible for funding most of the public HIV/AIDS care in the U.S., has identified specific areas of HIV/AIDS program evaluation in their grant announcements using clinical and program outcomes. Outcome evaluation is a new way of thinking for many HIV/AIDS programs more used to functioning in a crisis response mode.

It is in this dynamic public health and social services environment that HIV planners and service providers have worked for almost two decades. The HIV Cybermall was designed to meet the particular service delivery, research and program evaluation challenges presented by the evolving HIV pandemic in the United States. It is also our belief that this model can be exported to other service networks and applied to other health challenges in our communities.

Regional Overview: Needs Assessment

The San Fernando and Antelope Valleys are located in northern Los Angeles County, California. Over 1.6 million people live in the vast geographic area which makes up the Valleys (as they are called); it is an area that includes both sparsely populated high desert and mountains as well as densely populated urban sprawl. These regions are separated physically, politically, psychologically and culturally from the numerous HIV services located in downtown Los Angeles and Hollywood. Because of its distinctiveness as a region, a distinct array of region-specific services best meets the HIV service needs of the population; travel out of the region for service can be prohibitively expensive in both time and money. While in many localities across the country a one-stop model may be the ideal of HIV service delivery, in such a geographically and culturally diverse region as the Valleys, a one-stop model is neither feasible nor desirable. The HIV Cybermall uses a model of services that addresses the needs of clients in a comprehensive way as well as coordinates the existing array of services. The HIV Cybermall creates an electronic mall of services in which each agency becomes both a virtual and actual storefront and access point to all of the services available throughout the region. Since the San Fernando Valley has the dubious distinction of being the birthplace of the mini-mall, this model of services has all the cultural distinctiveness appropriate for this region.

In assessing the needs of a community for a project of this kind it is crucial to examine the demographic profile of the population. In addition to the topological diversity, the service region is culturally diverse. It is home both to the family attraction Universal Studios' theme park, and also serves as the informal headquarters of the nation's film pornography industry. The population of the region is also very diverse: Latinos/as constitute 27.6% of the Valley's population; Asian/Pacific Islanders account for 7.8%, African Americans, 3.2%; American Indians 0.04%; whites are 60.7%, and 0.2% are "other." Only 60.1% of all residents speak English at home as their first language (United Way, 1994). An estimated 15,000 homeless persons live in the Valleys (derived from United Way, 1994). The Valleys account for 5,948 (15.32%) of the 38,810 AIDS cases reported in Los Angeles County reported through December 31, 1998, (LAC DHS, 1999); this number does not take into account the County-wide number of living HIV infected persons, estimated to be as high as 54,000. The majority of reported AIDS cases (64.07%) have been reported in men having sex with men as the transmission risk. Case rates for women in the Valley, however, have increased markedly in the last four years; while women account for just 4.81% of cumulative cases, they account for 9.27% of recent cases (calculated from LAC DHS, 1999). HIV infection is not a reportable condition in California; therefore service planners must project demands on services based on available data. From Los Angeles County Department of Health Services, Centers for Disease Control estimates, and current project findings, we estimate that there are between 6,249 and 8,391 people with HIV in the Valley. Some of these people have been tested and know their HIV status, but presumably all of them will require HIV-related services within the next few years. (Henrickson, 1998).

The regional and population variations make it clear that any HIV intervention or service delivery system must be designed (1) to deliver or coordinate a wide array of services to a population scattered across a large geographic area; (2) to ensure that services are accessible to culturally diverse communities, in at least two primary languages. Because of competition for limited resources, any new system had to coordinate existing services rather than create a new entity that would be perceived as competing for those resources. In addition, we knew that any system had to be more than simply user-friendly. Several agencies had experience with a previous interagency data management and reporting system that had been required of many County-funded grantees. This existing system was designed as a reporting system, was County-driven, and was intended to monitor and discourage duplication of services by clients. It may have been prematurely implemented, since the initial experience reported by agency users was highly negative because of technology problems and because it was mandated by the public funder. Indeed, it was this negative experience that led one agency to decline to participate in the HIV Cybermall project, and contributed to a high level of initial mistrust by participating agencies. Since agency case workers frequently work in under-resourced community-based organizations, our experience was that they were not interested in being required to learn yet another reporting or usage-policing system. Unless the intervention both *actually* reduced the caseworker load, and was *perceived* to reduce the caseworker load, the intervention simply would not be used. In addition, because of the historical mistrust of the HIV service community of centralized databases and reporting, any intervention seeking to enhance linkages among agencies had to be client-driven: that is, the client had to maintain control of his or her information and who had access to his/her information. Security was a paramount consideration: the system had to have the highest feasible level of actual and perceived security. The history of the epidemic includes incidents of significant harm done to individuals simply because they were publicly identified as HIV positive.

With these parameters shaping the design, we decided the optimal linkage intervention would include a password-controlled wide-area network with a shared intake template and layered access to information, combined with supportive training, technical support and shared governance. In order to ensure that clients would actually get from the home agency to the referral agency, a blended transportation component was structured into the intervention; this component included bus, rail, taxi, and door-to-door van transportation staffed by a project driver. The goals of the project are to decrease negative client outcomes such as homelessness, hospitalizations, wait times for appointments and broken appointments, and to increase positive client outcomes, such as access to care, kept appointments and improved health outcomes.

Participating Agencies

Eighteen agencies offer the majority of services to people with HIV disease in northern Los Angeles County. Since no single agency offers all services interagency referrals are common. Agencies were selected into the project by invitation of the lead agency based on (1) at least partial not-for-profit status; (2) a strong history of serving people with HIV disease; (3) a history of informal collaboration with other project agencies; (4) geography; and (5) the need to create a linked, comprehensive yet non-redundant system of care, from case-finding by HIV antibody testing through street drug treatment, medical and psychosocial management, to home infusion and hospice care. At the same time, the system had to retain an element of consumer choice. Only one agency invited to participate by the lead agency declined to participate (reportedly based on their prior experience with interagency computer linkages). Since the initiation of the project some agencies have closed or changed service delivery sites for reasons unrelated to the project. Participating agencies include five medical outpatient clinics, a dental clinic, three substance misuse treatment agencies, several HIV-dedicated social service/case management agencies, including culture-specific groups, two home care and/or home pharmacy agencies, a homeless services agency, and a hospice and shelter. In order to ensure that lack of hardware was not a barrier to agency participation in the project, agencies were offered appropriate computer hardware and software. Training and technical support were provided as part of the project design. Ownership of the computer hardware and software will revert to the agency at the conclusion of the formal funding period for the project, September 2001.

At the outset of the project there were very few formal linkages among any of the agencies, and none that included more than a few agency clusters. Despite the fact that clients frequently accessed services at more than one agency, and there were frequent referrals among agencies, there was no common intake format, and clients had to reiterate intake information at entry to each new agency. Case managers making referrals reported often engaging in phone tag. Referrals could take several days or more, and there was no simple way to determine whether or not a client had actually successfully completed a referral (an important outcome evaluation measure). Both case managers and clients identified lack of transportation as an important barrier to receiving services.

One simple example illustrates how the HIV Cybermall may help clients. Many clients enter the region as they transition out of the correctional system. Prior to implementing the HIV Cybermall, HIV infected inmates who were discharged from jail returned to their home communities without adequate discharge planning or connections for their HIV care. Since they are released without medical records, they frequently had periods of one or more months without medications, a serious problem in HIV treatment. They often were unable to obtain such basic services as adequate housing, health care, drug treatment, transportation or employment services on their own. We know anecdotally that ex-offenders in such circumstances frequently return to the behaviors that originally landed them in jail. By interacting with any single agency in the HIV Cybermall network, clients can be directly linked to the array of available services almost instantly. For instance, if an inmate is released to a halfway house, with the client's permission the case manager at the house can enter the client into the network, schedule an appointment at an HIV primary care clinic and simultaneously book a van ride to the appointment on the network. The network can then be used to schedule an appointment with other service providers who will develop a care plan to address the client's housing, employment, mental health, dental or other needs, and schedule transportation to the necessary agencies for these services.

PROJECT DESCRIPTION

System Specifications

We decided that the most important aspects of the computer system were (1) user-accessibility; (2) cost-feasibility; and (3) security of information.

- Users were envisioned as case managers, who are usually overworked paraprofessional human service workers in understaffed agencies. They had minimal computer experience and little time or interest in learning another task-specific system. For this reason, the system had to be both genuinely useful in managing HIV cases and easy to use. Because case managers are busy and because they change jobs fairly often, training time and system complexity needed to be kept to an absolute minimum.
- Since participating agencies were principally not-for-profits with low overhead, cost was a major consideration; indeed for some

agencies the HIV Cybermall would provide their first computer. Costs for hardware, software, staff training and operating the system all required careful scrutiny and vendor selection.

- Security of information was a concern from the beginning of the project, and remained a foreground issue. Both case managers and clients had lived with the serious life consequences of disclosure of HIV positive status, or disclosure of other stigmatizing information. Both groups were extremely cognizant of the special importance of information security in providing HIV/AIDS care.

- For these reasons, a frame-relay wide-area network design was selected after reviewing a number of different options. Frame-relay is a wide-area technology that provides high-speed, high quality digital transport at low cost.

Hardware

The HIV Cybermall design is a state-of-the-art Intranct. An Intranet is a private network with Internet technologies used as the underlying architecture (Gralla, 1996). Our Intranet has two elements: (1) a closed, private network for confidential communication and information exchange, and (2) access to the public Internet for our case managers. The private network is a high-speed, high-quality digital wide-area network (WAN) creating an electronic link among the eighteen agencies that can be used for many different types of on-line communication and information exchange. The network operates on Pacific Bell's frame-relay infrastructure utilizing 56K connectivity to remote sites and bursting to 112K at no additional charge. The only static connection is a direct 128K connection to the Internet. The workstations that the case managers use are standard PCs with 233 MHz processors, 32 megabytes of RAM, 3.2 gigabyte hard drives, color monitors, video cards, cameras, mikes and ergonomic mice. The servers are two PCs with 333 MHz processors, 256 megabytes of RAM and 9 gigabyte hard drives each. Each agency is connected to the WAN by a Cisco 1601 router and Kentrox CSU/DSU monitoring unit. Speed and quality of the network are important incentives to the busy case managers to make use of the network. Slower networks with poor-quality engineering are frustrating to users and discourage them from using the network. The agencies have chosen to use the private network primarily as a referral network and for on-line conferencing and meetings.

Software

While initially we believed that it would be necessary to design our own custom software, we found that Microsoft's Office Suite®, an inexpensive, off-the-shelf software, could be easily customized for use on the WAN. Microsoft's Outlook 98®, a part of Office Suite®, is used to e-mail, to schedule appointments and transportation among the agencies, and to track clients to see if they keep the appointments. The referral network utilizes a common intake form as the primary client record. The intake form is a template in Outlook 98® and standardizes and eliminates repetition in the intake process among the eighteen agencies. All records are maintained as up-to-date and complete; thus phone tag is largely eliminated. Microsoft's NetMeeting® (also a part of Office Suite®) allows the network to be used for collaborative work such as on-line case-conferences, monthly staff meetings and joint document production. On-line meetings can be by chat (typing messages in real-time), and eventually by voice or video. The voice and videoconferences are possible because of the end-to-end quality of service on the closed network (not yet available on the Internet) and Pacific Bell's allowance for occasional bursting outside the usual bandwidth at no extra charge. Microsoft's Office Suite® is extremely user-friendly and has been used by millions of people worldwide, and so is largely bug-free. Training materials are plentiful and inexpensive. Office Suite® has a programming interface so that the calendar for scheduling, the forms that the case managers use every day (particularly the shared common intake form), and the report-generation function can be customized to suit the needs of the agencies exactly. This limited customization is important to make the software truly fit the needs of the case managers. Programs that are not quite right for the purposes they are purchased to accomplish are not used as much as programs that suit users' needs exactly. Programs that are over-customized, however, are expensive and frequently have too many bugs to appeal to busy staff. They also tie the purchaser to one software company for maintenance and technical support and require expensive, custom training.

Although not part of the original design, the creation of an HIV Cybermall website was recommended by the project's Client Advisory Board (CAB) and the Interagency Advisory Board (IAB). The purpose of the website is to create an on-line resource directory and to offer some services on the Internet as well. In order to provide input to the website design group and to the webmaster on content, links and design, a Website Advisory Group (WAG) was formed. This group was recruited from the IAB, the CAB, and from the technical support offered by the Columbia University School of Public Health (the organization selected to oversee the multisite collaboration and evaluation of the SPNS cohort, and to provide technical assistance on research aspects of projects). The WAG met by telephone conference call on an ad hoc basis. The website is a very popular HIV site on the Internet, with an average of over 5,000 hits per week, and has received national media attention.

Cost containment for the project was accomplished primarily by (1) selecting a virtual private network (the frame-relay design) rather than a set of permanently open static lines connecting agencies; (2) using off-the-shelf software, rather than paying a programmer for custom software; (3) using standardized training materials, including free Microsoft on-line training rather than paying for training in a customized program; (4) using a competitive bidding process for infrastructure needs (the backbone provider, computers for case managers and servers for the client-server WAN); and (5) using standard equipment (routers, cables, hubs, monitors, etc.) for the WAN and leasing it over a three-year period to deal with obsolescence. Obsolescence is a problem characteristic of information technologies. A virtual private network such as our frame-relay cuts costs by allowing the customer to pay only for the bandwidths that is used; that is, only when a message is being transmitted rather than paying full price for static lines that are always open, even when no information or communication is being transmitted. Using off-the-shelf software is approximately 10% of the cost of custom software for initial purchase and licenses. Savings in technical support and training for standard software are also of this magnitude. Careful selection of a vendor reduced our costs by approximately 50% for the backbone price we would have paid by taking the first suggested vendor; this suggests that anyone seeking to replicate this system would do well to shop carefully.

Security needs were met primarily by hiring a computer consultant with extensive background in network security, including Department of Defense background. The consultant, TeraTechnologies Corporation, configured the server for maximum security, trained the on-site systems maintenance specialist in server-based security procedures and configurations, provided trainings and training materials for security training of the case managers, and worked with the case managers to set up password systems and site-security procedures in the eighteen agencies. Security features include separating the public Internet from the private network by locating the Internet service on a different computer than the network, and by the use of firewalls (filtering hardware and software) and maximum encryption (sending coded messages rather than plain English ones and using a 128-bit key). These precautions were added to the more standard password protection and audit trails to trace security breaches. Configuring audit trails and planning system monitoring require a high degree of technical expertise (Sutton, 1997). Since network security is primarily a people problem rather than a technology problem, the security training and consultation in best practices for security-related policies and procedures were a crucial part of creating a secure system.

Project Governance, Authority and Decision-Making

The project originated as a collaborative proposal by the 18 agencies to the Health Resources and Services Administration. The five-year demonstration project was funded as part of the SPNS program created by the federal Ryan White CARE Act. The agencies each selected a representative (generally a case manager) to attend monthly IAB meetings. A key to the success of the project so far has been the leadership of the IAB, which meets on a regular basis. The IAB was chaired by project staff, but was immediately vested with the responsibility of making all major decisions related to the project, including: interviewing and recommending staff and consultants, forming evaluation questions, designing the implementation components of the transportation arm of the project, making decisions about inviting additional agencies to participate, and even devising the name for the associated website. (Not surprisingly they chose www.HIVCybermall. org.) IAB meetings are hosted by participating agencies on a rotating basis, so that participants have the opportunity to become familiar with the range of services available at participating agencies. There is little doubt that meeting together regularly, physically seeing other agencies, and meeting agency staff have contributed significantly to an increased understanding of programs, increased comfort with the agencies and their scope of services, and to an increase in interagency referrals apart from the specific computer-linkage designed as the intervention.

A CAB of HIV agency clients interested in the project meets more intermittently, but also has played a significant decision-making role in the design of the network. It is important to note here that there is no value, indeed it is deceptive, in creating a CAB if consumer input does not have a real impact in program decisions. For this reason and because consumer expertise is unique and valuable, the development of the project incorporated CAB suggestions into (a) a consumer information system (including the website), (b) the baseline client survey, and (c) an assessment of unmet client service needs.

HRSA supervision and support occur primarily through a Project Officer and three annual SPNS multisite project meetings, coordinated by Columbia. Finally, in addition to the contracted design consultants, dedicated on site project staff include the principal investigator (20% FTE), a project manager (100% FTE), a computer network administrator (25% FTE), a van driver (100% FTE), and clerical support and dispatcher (50% FTE). All other staff time has capitalized on existing staff at participating agencies.

The role of participant agencies has been absolutely vital. In our opinion it would not be possible to export the HIV Cybermall system as a turn-key operation, even with precisely the same hardware and software specifications, because community and agency buy-in is crucial to the success of the intervention. The native mistrust of technology that exists among some human service workers, the mistrust of information sharing by HIV care providers, and the common mistrust of anything new and different means that the more agency staff have an opportunity to shape an intervention, the more they will trust it and eventually use it.

Program Evaluation

Because it funds development of model programs, the SPNS initiative requires a strong evaluation component to determine which aspects of a model program work well for which populations and which do not work well. The HIV Cybermall project uses a true field experiment design that is planned to be both powerful enough and sensitive enough to allow program evaluators to determine how much impact the WAN and transportation systems have on (1) the number and types of services used by clients, and (2) client health status and quality of life (Lipsey, 1990). The success of the evaluation depends on the same two factors as the success of the network implementation: (1) agency and client buy-in and (2) technical expertise. Agency and client buy-in were assured by using participatory evaluation methodology (Whitmore, 1998). Technical expertise was provided by two PhD level researchers on the project staff who had training and experience in evaluation and by consultation from the Columbia School of Public Health. Last year the HIV Cybermall completed a baseline data collection consisting of surveys of clients and staff. The first-ever survey of the Valley HIV+ client population used a survey instrument that measured quality of life of HIV agency clients, health and mental health status, provided a needs assessment, measured service utilization and evaluated services. This evaluation instrument included standardized and validated assessment tools for addiction severity (Fullilove, 1997), diagnosable mental disorder (Spitzer et al., 1994) and general health functioning (Ware, Kosinski, and Keller, 1996). In addition, the remaining items in the survey instrument were field-tested and voted upon for inclusion by the cohort of twenty-seven funded projects in the SPNS program from around the country.

A survey research firm was contracted to administer the one-hour survey using a preprogrammed computer-assisted telephone interviewing (CATI) system in order to minimize errors. Interviewers were available in English and Spanish. Clients were recruited from participating agencies by letter and personally by case managers over a period of six months, and offered a $20 grocery coupon as an incentive to call the toll-free survey number. Each client was assigned a kind of case number by the researchers using an encrypted algorithm of their name and date of birth, and provided that number to the contracted interviewer at the time of the call. The interviewer did not have access to the encryption algorithm; client anonymity was preserved at this level. Some clients chose to call in from participating agencies so that they would not need to disclose personal information from home. It was felt that this passive interview system would be the least intrusive and the most sensitive to the privacy needs of clients. Epstein and Gfroerer (1995) also suggest that information obtained via anonymous telephone interviews may be more accurate for this population. The survey results show no reluctance to report socially proscribed behavior: 75.8% of the respondents reported that they had used some illegal drug at some time in their life, for example. In all, 310 clients out of a possible 1,029 (30.1%) completed the entire interview; characteristics of the survey population were compared to agency data on gender and ethnic composition of their clientele. There were no significant differences in race/ethnicity detected between the respondent sample and the overall client population, although women were slightly over-represented in the survey sample. The survey data will be used not only as the baseline for the project, but also for HIV program planning throughout the region.

The separate staff survey measured existing patterns of interagency contact and staff evaluation of services and communication systems. Both surveys were designed to provide the pre-test measurement in a pre-test/post-test control group quasi-experimental evaluation design. The post-test measurements will be taken after the network and the transportation systems have been operational for one year. After the first wave of nine agencies has completed a year of the system, the second wave will then be implemented. The impact of the intervention on both client outcomes and agency linkages will then be assessed.

Implementation

The implementation process was unexpectedly slowed by three types of unanticipated delays: (1) negotiating specific agreements among the inter-agency collaboration, the computer consultant and Pacific Bell (the primary system vendor) took more time than expected; (2) organizational changes within the 18 nonprofit agencies such as loss of trained staff, change of organizational leadership, change of organizational mission, closing of one service provider, and relocation to new offices occurred more frequently than expected; and (3) technical time and effort required for installation was underestimated. Although the implementation was slower due to these delays, it was steady and successful. Care was taken to minimize the impact of the new network on agency time and operations so that it would be experienced as an enhancement of personnel time and ability to provide services to clients, rather than an additional demand on time and an impediment to agency functioning. The HIV Cybermall staff attempted as far as possible to absorb the impact of delays or modifications themselves, rather than passing that time demand and stress onto the case managers and their agencies. For example, when four co-located agencies decided the day before they were to be connected to the WAN to relocate to four separate sites, we simply notified Pacific Bell of the installation delay (it was a delay of several months), uninstalled and picked up our four computers at the old site, waited until they decided what they wanted organizationally, reinstalled the computers and routers at the new sites and applied to HRSA for approval for the changes in the timeline and costs of the move, which were approved. None of these actions affected the agencies and all represented actions on the part of the HIV Cybermall staff to accommodate the needs of the agencies as a group and the long-range implementation goals of the network. A second example of absorbing delays and stresses in network installation is our ongoing policy of training agency staff at agency request and accommodating to their staff schedules. In this way, we have adapted to staff turnover without making any demands on the agencies themselves.

Agency case manager time for this project has been solicited on a voluntary basis according to the interests and availability of individual agency case managers. Agency feedback has been actively solicited throughout the implementation. Case managers at each agency who are using the HIV Cybermall are now communicating on the WAN, using a common intake form, and scheduling appointments and transportation on the WAN. Monthly reports on network utilization and cost-effectiveness are produced for review by the case managers so that they can evaluate the effectiveness of the network in improving agency operations and client services.

IMPLICATIONS FOR INTEGRATION
OF SERVICE DELIVERY

It is important to understand that the HIV Cybermall is a work in progress, and that all observations here are preliminary; an outcome evaluation is not possible at this point. It is our belief that a linked electronic system, with the training and security safeguards outlined above in place, combined with a blended transportation system, can be an efficient and cost-effective communications and care coordination tool for provider agencies sharing clients over a large geographic area. It is also quite possible that such a system may be feasible for more geographically concentrated agency clusters that share many clients. Such a system should be exquisitely sensitive to client and agency concerns. Our system, as technologically advanced as it is, relies entirely on the client's permission to access his/her information; the client retains complete control over his/her information. Our pilot studies prior to implementation found that clients were quite good at remembering passwords over time; we did, however, also investigate the possibility of using a swipe card system coupled with a password and chose to use the client's password only, since the loss or theft of a swipe card would complicate access. Systems that serve more complex client populations, such as multiply diagnosed or psychiatrically involved clients, may have additional considerations about how to balance client privacy rights and agency utility.

We wish to emphasize again that it is highly unlikely that simply exporting the system we have developed and dropping it into an agency network would result in its acceptance and use by agency staff. Our experience suggests that in addition to outlay for hardware and software, a considerable initial investment of time and project resources should be devoted to:

- ensuring that the project is completely transparent, so that neither agencies nor clients will find evidence to support negative suspicions about information sharing;
- developing and empowering advisory boards of both agency users and consumers, so that local and agency-specific issues will be incorporated into the design, and so that agencies have actual control over the intervention. Consumers will talk about the project; if they have been a part of its design it is much more likely that suspicion about the project and resistance to interagency information sharing will be allayed;
- assuring agencies that neither their individual independent resources nor their autonomy will be challenged by this project;
- responding to problems, concerns about the project, and requests for training and technical assistance in a timely way;
- choosing the best consultant to work on the particular system being developed; this means a consultant with the necessary experience for the project (e.g., one with experience in multi-site implementation, the healthcare environment, and in high-security networks) and a compatible working style for the group;
- taking the time to develop the optimal solution to meet the needs of all involved, which is primarily a matter of taking the time to

fully communicate the real system needs of the human service providers to the technology experts, and then following those experts' advice;
- taking the time to communicate thoroughly to case managers the aspects of the technology that must be understood for the network to function well; aspects of the technology that are of interest and which will excite may be offered to case managers with a deeper interest in technology.

We are entering an era where HIV services agencies are re-evaluating their missions and services, where organizations are faced with the hard decisions of retooling, realigning their services, laying off staff, or possibly even closing altogether. We believe that agency collaboration and creating computerized linkages among agencies can be an effective, efficient and compassionate alternative to these dire options. Individual agency resources can be maximized while clients are served with a minimum of duplication of services. In our region the HIV Cybermall serves as the technological infrastructure for region-wide case management services. In a recent round of grant applications the regions served by the HIV Cybermall submitted only one comprehensive application: all agencies that offered HIV case management or related services were included as part of that omnibus proposal (the proposal was funded). While these initiatives have not yet reached their full potential, we believe that our successes to date, in the implementation of the HIV Cybermall and in encouraging agency collaborations, are clear signals of a hopeful future for our agencies, and for our clients.

The solution we have proposed here is feasible: neither of the professional staff of this project had particular training or experience in computer systems prior to this project. Yet as the project developed we have become increasingly convinced that we are helping to shape not only the future of interagency collaborations. Even more important, we believe we are helping to improve service delivery for some of our most vulnerable clients.

ACKNOWLEDGEMENTS

Our thanks to the San Fernando and Antelope Valley agencies that have actively participated in the HIV Cybermall project. They are: AIDS Healthcare Foundation's North Hollywood Clinic, Being Alive, Bienestar Latino AIDS Project, Home Pharmacy of California, Cri-Help, El Proyecto del Barrio, Hands United Together, High Desert Hospital, Homestead Hospice and Shelter, Northeast Valley Health Corporation's HIV, Dental, and Homeless Divisions, Olive View Medical Center, Tarzana Treatment Center, Trinity Care, Valley Community Clinic, and Western Pacific Rehabilitation.

This publication is supported by the HIV/AIDS Bureau's Special Projects of National Significance Project 5H97HA00065 from the Health Resources and Services Administration, Department of Health and Human Services. This paper's contents are solely the responsibility of the authors and do not necessarily represent the official view of the funding agency.

REFERENCES

Bolton, M. (Ed.). (1996) *Challenge and Innovation: Methodological Advances in Social Research on HIV/AIDS*. London and Bristol PA: Taylor & Francis.

Coyle, S., Boruch, R.F., and Turner, C.F. (1991). *Evaluating AIDS Prevention Programs*. Washington D.C.: National Academy Press.

Epstein, J., and Gfroerer, J. (1995). A Method for Estimating Substance Abuse Treatment Need from a National Household Survey. Paper presented at the 37th International Congress on Alcohol and Drug Dependence, August 20-25, 1995.

Fullilove, R. (1997). *The Strengths and Weaknesses of the Addiction Severity Index in Assessing Substance Use*. Paper prepared for Special Projects of National Significance.

Gralla, P. (1996). *How Intranets Work*. Emeryville, CA: Ziff-Davis Press.

Jonsen, A.R., and Stryker, J. (Eds.). (1993). *The Social Impact of AIDS in the United States*. Washington, D.C.: National Academy Press.

Henrickson, M. (1998, October). San Fernando Valley HIV Estimates. Van Nuys, CA: San Fernando Valley HIV/AIDS Consortium.

Leibowitch, J. (1985). *A Strange Virus of Unknown Origin* (R. Howard, Trans.) New York: Ballantine Books. (Original work published 1984)

Lipsey, M. (1990). *Design Sensitivity: Statistical Power for Experimental Research*. Newbury Park, CA: Sage Publications.

Los Angeles County Department of Health Services, HIV Epidemiology Program (Jan. 15, 1999.) *Advanced HIV Disease (AIDS) Quarterly Surveillance Summary*. Los Angeles.

Mann, J.M., Tarantola, D. (Eds.). (1996). *AIDS in the World II*. New York, Oxford: Oxford University Press.

Mann, J., Tarantola, D.J.M. and Netter, T.W. (Eds.). (1992). *AIDS in the World*. Cambridge, MA, and London: Harvard University Press.

O'Malley, P. (Ed.). (1989). *The AIDS Epidemic: Private Rights and Public Interest*. Boston: Beacon Press.

Shernoff, M. (1988) Getting started: Basic skills for effective social work with people with HIV and AIDS. In D.M. Aronstein & B.J. Thompson(Eds.), *HIV and Social Work: A Practitioner's Guide*. New York: The Haworth Press, Inc.

Shilts, R. (1987). *And the Band Played On: People, Politics and the AIDS Epidemic*. New York: St. Martin's Press.

Spitzer, R., Williams, J., Kroenke, K., Linzer, M., Verloin deGruy III, F., Hahn, S., Brody, D., Johnson, J. (1994). Utility of a new procedure for diagnosing mental disorders in primary care: the Prime-MD study. *Journal of the American Medical Association. 272(22)*, pp. 1749-1756.

Sutton, S. (1997). *Windows NT Security Guide*. Menlo Park, CA: Trusted Systems Services, Inc., Addison-Wesley Developers Press.

United Way (1994, June). *Los Angeles 1994: State of the County Databook. Los Angeles.*

Ware, J., Kosinski, M, and Keller, S. (1996) A 12-Item Short-Form Health Survey: Construction of Scales and Preliminary Tests of Reliability and Validity. *Medical Care. 34(3)*, pp. 220-233.

Whitmore, E. (ed.) (1998, Winter). *Understanding and Practicing Participatory Evaluation*. No. 80. New York: Jossey-Bass.

The Effects
of a Computer Network
on Pediatric Pain and Anxiety

Gary Holden
David J. Bearison
Diane C. Rode
Merri Fishman Kapiloff
Gary Rosenberg

SUMMARY. The objective of this study was to test the impact of an enhanced version of STARBRIGHT World (SBW2)–a private computer network for hospitalized children. The impact of SBW2 was assessed with a series of 44 replicated single system designs. Utilizing an ecological momentary assessment approach, self-reports were obtained regarding children's perceptions of their pain intensity, pain aversiveness and anxiety. The results from the single system designs were aggregated using meta-analysis. Children experienced significantly less pain intensity, pain aversiveness, and anxiety in the SBW2 condition. These findings provide evidence regarding the effectiveness of SBW2

Gary Holden, DSW, is affiliated with New York University, Ehrenkranz School of Social Work.

David J. Bearison, PhD, is affiliated with The Graduate Center, City University of New York, and Mount Sinai-NYU Medical Center and Health System, New York, NY.

Diane C. Rode, MS, Merri Fishman Kapiloff, MS, and Gary Rosenberg, PhD, are all affiliated with Mount Sinai-NYU Medical Center and Health System, New York, NY.

Address correspondence to Gary Holden at New York University, ESSW, Room 407, 1 Washington Square North, New York, NY 10003 (E-mail: gary.holden@nyu. edu).

[Haworth co-indexing entry note]: "The Effects of a Computer Network on Pediatric Pain and Anxiety." Holden, Gary et al. Co-published simultaneously in *Journal of Technology in Human Services* (The Haworth Press, Inc.) Vol. 17, No. 1, 2000, pp. 27-47; and: *Human Services Online: A New Arena for Service Delivery* (ed: Jerry Finn, and Gary Holden) The Haworth Press, Inc., 2000, pp. 27-47. Single or multiple copies of this article are available for a fee from The Haworth Document Delivery Service [1-800-342-9678, 9:00 a.m. - 5:00 p.m. (EST). E-mail address: getinfo@haworthpressinc.com].

and demonstrate the utility of employing meta-analysis with single system designs. *[Article copies available for a fee from The Haworth Document Delivery Service: 1-800-342-9678. E-mail address: <getinfo@haworthpressinc. com> Website: <http://www.haworthpressinc.com>]*

KEYWORDS. Pediatric, computer, pain, anxiety, network, randomized controlled clinical trial

INTRODUCTION

The use of a variety of technologies to enhance self-help groups and deliver human services is increasing. For instance, Hawker, Kavanagh, Yellowlees and Kalucy (1998) report that their telepsychiatry program has performed nearly 2,000 patient assessments during the 1994-98 period. This phenomenon of technologically enhanced services is increasingly discussed as well (e.g., Finn, 1999, Galinsky, 1999; Lebow, 1998; Madara, 1997; Miller, 1997; Schopler, Galinsky & Abell, 1998; Schopler, Abell & Galinsky, 1998; Zaylor, 1999; www.uta.edu/cussn/cussn.html; www.ismho.org).

Whether the intervention involves peers who are defined by some special need communicating and supporting each other or professionals who are delivering a service, technology is forcing us to re-evaluate our understanding of these service activities. This paper reports the first replication in a series of studies that are assessing the impact of a computerized network for hospitalized children.

STARBRIGHT WORLD

Among all the newest therapeutic technologies employed at pediatric centers across the country, STARBRIGHT World has attracted considerable media attention (e.g., Bennet, 1998; Essick, 1999; Greenman, 1998; Makris, 1998). STARBRIGHT World is a private computer network for hospitalized children that enables them to interact with other hospitalized children in an on-line community and share their experiences.

STARBRIGHT World is one of the many interventions currently being developed by the STARBRIGHT Foundation, a non-profit organization formed by leaders in the entertainment, technology, and health care industries. The Foundation's mission is to improve the quality of life for ill children and their families, by designing computer-based, interactive, therapeutic interventions. The STARBRIGHT World project began in the fall of 1995 with five hospitals: Mount Sinai Hospital; Lucille Packard Children's Hospital; UCLA Children's Hospital; Pittsburgh Children's Hospital; and Dallas Children's Hospital. As of August 1999, there were 43 hospitals participating on line.

STARBRIGHT World has been modified over the last three years, but its basic principles and uses remain the same. The original version will be referred to as SBW, while the more recent enhanced version will be referred to SBW2. SBW2 is a private computer network that allows children in hospitals throughout the United States to interact with one another in both synchronous and asynchronous modes. SBW2 includes a wide array of interactive programs focused on communication, distraction, information, self-expression, and social support. Using SBW2 children can access answers to medical questions or learn about procedures. SBW2 users have access to a variety of ways of communicating with other hospitalized children such as video-conferencing, chat rooms, bulletin boards, and e-mail. A key SBW2 feature, "find a friend" enables children locate friends within the SBW2 system, or meet children with similar interests and/or illnesses. Other SBW2 features include computer-based creative expression, games and arts and crafts. Children have restricted access to pre-approved sites on the World Wide Web, although SBW2's Internet connections remain secure from public access, thereby protecting children's privacy. Further information regarding SBW2 is available at: [*www.starbright.org*].

Computer-based self-help/mutual aid groups are seen as providing benefits such as:

- linking individuals who have special concerns
- encouraging the participation of reluctant individuals
- lowering barriers stemming from sex, race and status
- promoting and improving communication
- diffusing the dependency needs of some participants (Finn, 1996)

SBW2 is seen as providing these benefits as well. It allows for both text based and video-conferencing interactions among children. While text based service delivery and self-help via computer networks have received more attention in the literature, we expect a shift in this situation as video-conferencing applications become more prevalent. Dropping prices and the emergence of Internet 2 will undoubtedly play a role in this shift (http://www.internet2.edu/). SBW2 is distinct from current Internet based video-conferencing applications in that it is a private fiber-optic, broadband network based on Sprint's ATM backbone with T-1 connection speeds to each hospital routed through 3 DS-3 hub sites around the country.

Previous STARBRIGHT World Research

SBW/SBW2 was designed to enhance the quality of life of children in the hospital, with specific goals that include reducing pain and anxiety. According to the Agency for Health Care Policy and Research (AHCPR, 1992) a variety of non-pharmacological interventions (e.g., jaw relaxation, progressive muscle relaxation, imagery, music, bio-feedback, education, and instruction) have been found to be effective in reducing pain. However, there are limited findings regarding the impact of SBW and no previous research on the impact of SBW2 on pain and related variables. SBW2's distraction, communication and social support components are seen as the most relevant in reducing pain and anxiety (cf. Christenfeld, 1997; Cleary & Edgman-Levitan, 1997; Eimer & Freeman, 1998; Hart & Alden, 1994). Past SBW users reported that they appreciated the ability to communicate with other children who had the same illness as they did (Bearison, Holden, Rode, Rosenberg & Fishman, 1999).

The rationale for using a single system design/meta-analytic approach to assess the effects of SBW is well summarized by White, Rusch, Kazdin and Hartmann (1989):

> Meta-analysis represents a potentially important adjunct to $N = 1$ methodology. The intensive examination of one subject is essential to establish functional relations between a person's behavior and environmental changes, such as the introduction of a behavioral treatment. Nevertheless, a larger number of sampling units (e.g., other persons exhibiting different behavior disorders) is generally necessary to evaluate the external validity of such individual-case demonstrations. Meta analysis of single subject experiments represents a powerful means of aggregating findings

about individuals and evaluating their generality on the basis of quantitative techniques. (p. 294-5)

Our initial study (Holden, Bearison, Rode, Rosenberg & Fishman, 1999) provided support for the utility of this analytic approach in testing the effectiveness of interventions such as SBW. The effects of the system were assessed in that study using a single subject design with nine children (a total of 702 observations). The effects of SBW were compared to the General Pediatric Milieu (GPM–definition to follow) on three outcome measures. When in the SBW condition children reported significantly less pain intensity and pain aversiveness. They also reported less anxiety in the SBW condition, but the that result was not statistically significant.

Why replicate and extend the initial outcome study of SBW? How do we know that relationships observed in a single study will be observed in different individuals, in different settings, or at different points in time? Replication begins to provide answers to these questions (Bornstein, 1990; Rosenthal, 1990). Because SBW2 was a more comprehensive system with enhanced hardware and more complex interactive activities and because more children were online at any given time, we expected to observe larger intervention effects than had been observed in the initial study. The present study replicated the main features of the initial study. It extended it by employing a more recent version of the system network (SBW2) and increasing statistical power by using a larger sample.

METHOD

SBW2 was in use in 25 pediatric departments in major medical centers across the United States at the time of the present study, although data were only collected from children hospitalized at the Mount Sinai Medical Center in New York City.

Participants

Inclusion criteria were children who were English speaking pediatric patients, between the ages of 7 and 18 years, and who were hospitalized on one of the following pediatric services: gastroenterology, hematology/oncology, nephrology, cardiology, or pulmonary. These patients may have been admitted to a general pediatric medical/surgical unit, a pediatric intensive care unit, or the bone marrow transplant unit. In addition, participants had to have a projected length of stay covering a minimum of 24 observation points. The final sample were females (59.1%) and males between the ages of 7 and 17 years (mean: 10.9 years).

Contrast Condition

As described previously, this was a within-subject design, where each individual served as her or his own control. The child's responses in the experimental condition (SBW2) were compared to their responses in the contrast condition. The contrast condition is described as the General Pediatric Milieu (GPM). In this condition, participants were engaged in one or more of the following activities: playroom group activity, individual therapeutic play activity, family interaction, visits from family or friends, eating, watching TV or video, reading, telephone, or an art activity. The GPM condition consisted of typical milieu activities for hospitalized children on pediatric medical/surgical units. Participants in intensive care units may have had more restrictions on milieu activities due to the acuity of their illnesses. For example, patients in an intensive care unit or a bone marrow transplant unit would not have had access to playroom groups or equivalent opportunities for visits.

Measurement

Self-report, visual analog scales (VAS) were used to assess outcomes. Self-report measures provide reliable and valid assessments of pain and can be used with children older than four (AHCPR, 1992). In general, VAS have demonstrated reasonable psychometric properties and are potentially sensitive to weak intervention effects (Eggebrecht, Bautz, Brenig, Pfingsten & Franz, 1989; Eimer & Freeman, 1998; Varni, Blount, Waldron & Smith, 1995).

VAS have been constructed in a variety of ways, but all ask the participant to rate their current state on the variable of interest by marking a spot between two opposing end points of a line (e.g., 'No pain' 'Most pain'). VAS can be used with children older than seven or eight who understand ordering and numbering (AHCPR, 1992). The VAS in the present study assessed: (1) pain intensity; (2) pain aversiveness; and (3) anxiety. Pain intensity and aversiveness were assessed with the Colored Analogue Scale (CAS) and the Facial Affect Scale (FAS), respectively (McGrath, 1990; McGrath et al., 1996). These scales contained graphics on one side which children used to rate both pain intensity and aversiveness. That rating corresponded to a numerical value on the other side of the scale, which was the recorded value. The CAS had a long triangle shaped area, which was marked 'no pain' at the point and 'most pain' at the base. The child slid a marker to the point on the scale that represented her or his current level of pain intensity and the research assistant then turned the scale over and recorded the corresponding value (0-10). The FAS consisted of a series of nine faces from one that appeared very happy to one that appeared very distressed (.04-.97). The FAS measures the aversive component of pain–that is how much distress a child is experiencing. An additional visual analog scale (created for the initial study) was used to assess anxiety (0-10; cf. Tuckman, 1988). In addition, the particular activity in which a participant was engaged either during the SBW2 or GPM condition was recorded at each assessment time.

Hypotheses

There were three hypotheses :

1. Children will experience less pain intensity when in the SBW2 condition compared to the GPM condition.
2. Children will experience less pain aversiveness when in the SBW2 condition compared to the GPM condition.
3. Children will experience less anxiety when in the SBW2 condition compared to the GPM condition.

Procedure

Single system designs (a.k.a. single subject designs, n-of-1 randomized trials) provide researchers with a structure to study a single case (e.g., Bloom, Fischer & Orme, 1999; Cook et al., 1993; Guyatt et al., 1988, 1990a, 1990b; McQuay et al., 1994, White, Christensen & Singer, 1992). We used a restricted alternating treatment design [e.g., BAAABBABBBBAB . . .] to determine if, compared to the GPM contrast condition [A phase–described below], the SBW2 condition

[B phase] had greater effects (Onghena & Edgington, 1994). This is a within-subjects design, where each individual serves as her or his own control.

In addition to this idiographic focus, we incorporated the '*ecological momentary assessment*' approach into the design.

> The most common way to study real-world behavior is to rely on retrospective self-report. . . . There is, however, growing evidence that such self-reports are prone to serious errors and biases arising from the characteristics of autobiographical memory. . . . Even if they were accurate, retrospective summaries would be unable to address many research questions in health psychology, because the questions being asked do not concern summary relationships. Rather they are concerned with dynamic moment-to-moment interactions. . . . To address these concerns, researchers have adopted a variety of methods, which have been labeled ecological momentary assessment (EMA) . . . or the experience sampling method . . . for collecting moment-by-moment data in real-world settings. The hallmark of EMA is the collection of repeated momentary assessments from participants in their natural environments. Its focus on momentary phenomena and immediate reporting minimizes reliance on recall and attendant biases. (Shiffman & Stone, 1998, p. 3; cf. Affleck et al., 1998; Litt, Cooney & Morse, 1998)

Data collection was confined to two, two hour segments (2:00-4:00 p.m. and 5:30-7:30 p.m.) on Mondays through Thursdays and only the earlier segment on Fridays. These segments were divided into 30-minute periods in which participants were randomly assigned to the GPM or SBW2 condition, with six consecutive 30-minute periods in either segment as the upper limit (the 'restricted' element in the restricted alternating treatment design). Figure 1 illustrates a schedule for a given participant. As can be seen, the children moved between the experimental (B) and contrast conditions (A) at random points throughout their hospital stay. The randomization sequence was different for each participant in the study.

The random assignment of treatment conditions to time segments was done prior to patient enrollment. Randomized schedules covering two-week periods were created and numbered successively. Once an eligible child was enrolled, and informed consent was obtained, that

FIGURE 1

M O N

Design Phase	A	B	A	B	A	B	A	B
Times [p.m.]	2-2:30	2:30-3	3-3:30	3:30-4	5:30-6	6-6:30	6:30-7	7-7:30
Observation	2:15	2:45	3:15	3:45	5:45	6:15	6:45	7:15

T U E

Design Phase	B	A	A	A	B	B	A	A
Times [p.m.]	2-2:30	2:30-3	3-3:30	3:30-4	5:30-6	6-6:30	6:30-7	7-7:30
Observation	2:15	2:45	3:15	3:45	5:45	6:15	6:45	7:15

W E D

Design Phase	A	A	A	B	B	A	A	A
Times [p.m.]	2-2:30	2:30-3	3-3:30	3:30-4	5:30-6	6-6:30	6:30-7	7-7:30
Observation	2:15	2:45	3:15	3:45	5:45	6:15	6:45	7:15

T H U

Design Phase	B	A	A	B	A	B	A	A
Times [p.m.]	2-2:30	2:30-3	3-3:30	3:30-4	5:30-6	6-6:30	6:30-7	7-7:30
Observation	2:15	2:45	3:15	3:45	5:45	6:15	6:45	7:15

F R I

Design Phase	A	B	B	B
Times [p.m.]	2-2:30	2:30-3	3-3:30	3:30-4
Observation	2:15	2:45	3:15	3:45

M O N

Design Phase	B	A	A	A	B	A	A	B
Times [p.m.]	2-2:30	2:30-3	3-3:30	3:30-4	5:30-6	6-6:30	6:30-7	7-7:30
Observation	2:15	2:45	3:15	3:45	5:45	6:15	6:45	7:15

T U E

Design Phase	B	A	B	B	A	A	B	B
Times [p.m.]	2-2:30	2:30-3	3-3:30	3:30-4	5:30-6	6-6:30	6:30-7	7-7:30
Observation	2:15	2:45	3:15	3:45	5:45	6:15	6:45	7:15

W E D

Design Phase	B	A	B	B	A	A	B	A
Times [p.m.]	2-2:30	2:30-3	3-3:30	3:30-4	5:30-6	6-6:30	6:30-7	7-7:30
Observation	2:15	2:45	3:15	3:45	5:45	6:15	6:45	7:15

T H U

Design Phase	B	A	A	A	B	A	A	B
Times [p.m.]	2-2:30	2:30-3	3-3:30	3:30-4	5:30-6	6-6:30	6:30-7	7-7:30
Observation	2:15	2:45	3:15	3:45	5:45	6:15	6:45	7:15

F R I

Design Phase	B	B	B	B
Times [p.m.]	2-2:30	2:30-3	3-3:30	3:30-4
Observation	2:15	2:45	3:15	3:45

35

child began the study immediately in whatever phase came next on that day on the schedule. The child was told what the timing of the GPM and SBW2 phases would be like as part of the informed consent explanation. Regardless of which condition the child was in, the research assistant approached him or her in the middle of each 30-minute period. On each occasion, the child was asked to rate her or his pain intensity, pain aversiveness and anxiety. On each measurement occasion when the child was using SBW2, the research assistant coded the following factors: whether the SBW2 system was fully or partially functioning, the particular SBW2 environment in which the child was participating, the type of communication that was occurring, and whether or not the communication was illness related. In the GPM condition, the research assistant recorded the kind of activity in which the child was engaged. Participants who completed less than 20 observations during their initial admission but who were readmitted, were retained in the study based on the previously determined, randomized schedule.

RESULTS

The hypotheses were tested via randomization tests of the mean difference between the experimental and contrast conditions for each of the three outcome variables (Onghena 1992; 1994; Onghena & Edgington, 1994). Meta-analyses were used to combine the results derived from the single system designs. Meta-analysis allows one to combine the results from individual studies into an estimate of the amount of effect across studies (in the present case, across participants). This procedure has been proposed as a method to increase the external validity of conclusions based on single system designs (e.g., Allison & Gorman, 1993; Corcoran, 1985, 1986; Gingerich, 1984; Salzberg, Strain & Baer, 1987; Scruggs, Mastropieri & Casto, 1987a; 1987b; 1987c; Videka-Sherman, 1986; White, 1987; White, Rusch, Kazdin & Hartmann, 1989; Zucker et al., 1997). The SPSS 8.0 and the Single Case Randomization Test software packages (Van Damme & Onghena, 1995) were used in the analyses.

Table 1 provides details regarding the how well the SBW2 system functioned during the study. During our initial study we expected and observed technical problems associated with the early development of the system. In the present study, there were considerably fewer techni-

TABLE 1. SBW2 Performance and Children's Usage Patterns

Area	Category	Proportion of measurement occasions
System functioning	System down	.01
	Local system operational– telecommunications down	.00
SBW2 area used by participants	Home base	.04
	Connect	.25
	Explore/Activities	.68
	Find A Friend	.02
	Not applicable	.01
Communication	Using system–no communication with others online or in room	.10
	Text conferencing	.01
	Video conferencing	.20
	Communicating with only the person in room	.01
	Communicating with person in room and with person on system	.04
	Engaged with system and talking with person in room	.65
Discourse topic	No discourse/No topic discernible	.03
	Illness related	.13
	Non-illness related	.84

cal problems. Across the entire sample, either the local SBW2 computer or some aspect of telecommunications was not fully functioning, on only 1% of measurement occasions. This table also provides data describing how participants used the system. For instance, participants were using text conferencing on 1% of the measurement occasions, whereas they were using video conferencing on 20% of measurement occasions.

Two children who enrolled in the study dropped out prior to participating. Another child was dropped from the analysis because after enrolling and starting the study her mother forbade her to use the video-conferencing aspects of the system (due to religious strictures). We set a minimum of 8 observations and a reversal pattern (child would have to have passed through ABA or a BAB pattern) as analysis inclusion criteria. Because we required each child to undergo a reversal of condition at a minimum (e.g., ABA or BAB), four additional participants were dropped from the analysis. This yielded in a final sample of 44 participants. Interspersed among the 809 completed intervention periods, were a number (n = 164) of intervention periods when children did not participate. The mean number of missing observation points was 2.1 in the SBW2 condition and 1.6 in the GPM condition. The observations were missed primarily because: (1) a child refused because they were not feeling well enough (27%); (2) a child was undergoing a procedure (24%); or (3) a child was asleep (23%).

Table 2 summarizes the effects of SBW2 for each participant on each of the three outcome measures. There were a total of 809 observation points and 2,421 observations. The order of participants in the table reflects their order of participation. Even though our a priori hypotheses were about the overall results, we report contrasts at the individual level for descriptive purposes. Given the possibility of accumulating Type 1 error, we chose a Bonferroni approach to set the analysis-wise alpha level at .05. Therefore one should reconsider these individual level contrasts at a reduced alpha level of .000378 (Cliff, 1987). At the level of the individual participants, the obtained p value was less than .000378 for 8 of the 132 possible contrasts. A different view of outcome is provided by the meta-analyses which were used to test the three a priori hypotheses. Summarizing the results across all participants the combined p value was less than the Bonferroni adjusted analysis-wise alpha level of .01666 for pain intensity, pain aversiveness, and anxiety.

As can be seen in the columns headed LR in Table 2, there was a reduction in variation across measurement occasions because participants on average (unweighted mean percentages) reported the lowest possible scale rating (i.e., establishing floor effects) for pain intensity on 47% of the measurement occasions, for pain aversiveness on 26% of the occasions, and for anxiety on 69% of the occasions (an average across participants and outcomes of 47%).

As can be seen in Table 3, the effects for all three outcomes were positively correlated. The relationship of demographic factors to effects was also assessed. The effects for all three outcomes were not statistically significantly different for female and male participants. In addition, as the positive correlation between age and anxiety indicated,

TABLE 2. Individual and Meta-Analytic Effects (N = 44 Replicated SSDs, 2,421 Observations)

Participant	n	Age	Sex	Pain Intensity	LR^2	Pain Aversive-ness	LR	Anxiety	LR
1	22	10	m	--^{3}	100	− .01 [.77]	0	.09 [.48]	95
2	26	12	m	.46 [.18]	58	.04 [.28]	73	1.08 [.09]	73
3	20	13	f	.28 [.26]	0	.08 [.01]	0	--^{3}	100
4	20	12	f	.18 [.23]	0	--^{3}	0	--^{3}	100
5	13	9	f	--^{3}	100	--^{3}	100	--^{3}	100
6	20	10	m	--^{3}	100	--^{3}	100	--^{3}	100
7	20	9	f	.05 [.47]	0	−.05 [.65]	0	− .60 [.99]	0
8	21	8	m	.20 [.35]	29	.01 [.46]	5	− .56 [.52]	43
9	21	12	m	− .05 [.56]	0	− .01 [.55]	14	.45 [.02]	62
10	21	9	f	--^{3}	100	− .00 [.76]	90	--^{3}	100
11	24	12	m	− .32 [.75]	0	− .00 [.72]	0	− .28 [.71]	4
12	24	7	m	1.43 [.18]	13	.04 [.23]	4	--^{3}	100
13	22	14	f	.52 [.14]	0	− .05 [.86]	14	--^{3}	100
14	22	13	f	− .21 [.57]	41	− .01 [.56]	0	.45 [.15]	59
15	8	11	m	--^{3}	100	− .11 [1.0]	88	--^{3}	100
16	16	16	m	−.35 [.63]	50	.11 [.20]	31	2.55 [.0001]	38
17	20	14	f	.09 [.50]	75	--^{3}	0	1.06 [.09]	30
18	24	11	f	--^{3}	100	.02 [.37]	50	.42 [.23]	92
19	16	7	f	.22 [.35]	13	− .06 [.78]	69	.22 [.43]	50
20	22	10	m	0 [.53]	0	.06 [.28]	5	− 1.64 [.96]	59
21	20	13	f	.55 [.21]	65	− .02 [.58]	0	--^{3}	100
22	16	11	m	1.51 [.11]	28	.31 [.0039]	39	2.61 [.03]	56

TABLE 2 (continued)

ID	n	Age	Sex	Pain Intensity	LR[2]	Pain Aversiveness	LR	Anxiety	LR
23	8	17	f	2.36 [.03]	0	.13 [.02]	13	2.71 [.0001]	0
24	18	11	m	.35 [.16]	78	.04 [.34]	22	.08 [.49]	94
25	14	9	m	--[3]	100	.11 [.09]	36	--[3]	100
26	8	7	f	2.25 [.0001]	13	.32 [.0001]	13	.50 [.18]	13
27	15	15	f	--[3]	100	--[3]	0	--[3]	100
28	8	12	f	--[3]	100	.07 [.30]	25	.25 [.21]	75
29	12	9	f	1.0 [.10]	8	.33 [.03]	33	.69 [.14]	25
30	22	10	f	.29 [.30]	5	− .10 [.81]	32	.94 [.11]	86
31	16	12	f	.03 [.29]	75	.04 [.23]	25	.29 [.0001]	94
32	16	11	m	1.10 [.03]	25	.27 [.01]	19	2.65 [.01]	19
33	12	11	m	.43 [.35]	0	.01 [.49]	0	1.10 [.10]	8
34	20	11	f	1.16 [.05]	40	.04 [.22]	0	--[3]	100
35	23[4]	10	f	.15 [.22]	0	− .06 [.69]	13	.10 [.36]	57
36	23	11	f	1.37 [.21]	74	.01 [.49]	52	1.77 [.08]	65
37	8	9	f	--[3]	100	.10 [.24]	0	.17 [.0001]	88
38	20	11	f	.13 [.21]	85	.00 [.50]	35	.13 [.24]	82
39	24	10	m	− .66 [.70]	0	.04 [.35]	17	− .4 [.61]	79
40	21	14	f	.19 [.0001]	95	.08 [.19]	5	.06 [.23]	90
41	24	10	f	.03 [.32]	83	− .01 [.52]	83	--[3]	100
42	19	12	f	.13 [.41]	0	.02 [.22]	0	.17 [.31]	0
43	20	9	m	.28 [.32]	0	.09 [.07]	0	--[3]	100
44	20	7	m	--[3]	100	.18 [.0001]	40	.05 [.51]	95
	809 M = 18.4	M = 10.9	59.1% f		.47		.26		.69
M				.34		.047		.39	
Wt. M				.29		.036		.32	
p for meta-analysis				.0002		.0018		.0002	

Note. The cell entries for individual participants under pain intensity, pain aversiveness and anxiety are:
(a) the individual effects − mean of A phase − mean of B phase (positive entries represent positive SBW effects). (b) [p value rounded to 2 places unless it was less than .01].
The cell entries under pain intensity, pain aversiveness and anxiety in the final rows labeled M and Wt. M are the unweighted and weighted (by n) mean effect and the p value from the meta-analysis. The proportions in the final row are the weighted (by n) mean proportions of instances where the children used the lowest possible scale rating.

[1] n of observation points [n of observations]
[2] LR = This is the percentage of observations (in both conditions combined) where the participant reported the lowest possible scale rating.
[3] Reported no variation in ratings across all observations.
[4] Six PA measures were missing for this participant.

TABLE 3. Correlations Among Age and the Effects

	Age	Pain Intensity	Pain Aversiveness	Anxiety
Age	---	---		
Pain Intensity	−.093			
Pain Aversiveness	−.100	.568**	---	
Anxiety	.492**	.554**	.422*	---

Note. N's are less than 44 due to missing data (effects elirninated due to lack of variation).
* Correlation is significant at alpha = .05
** Correlation is significant at alpha = .01

older children were more likely to experience greater effects in the SBW2 condition in regard to their perception of anxiety.

DISCUSSION

The present study contrasted the effects of SBW2 with the general pediatric milieu on participant's perception of pain intensity, pain aversiveness and anxiety. At the level of the individual child, 8 of 132 possible contrasts between the two conditions favored SBW2 and were statistically significant. As revealed by the meta-analyses, all three a priori hypotheses were supported in that children reported statistically significantly less pain intensity, pain aversiveness, and anxiety in the SBW2 condition.

These findings should be interpreted with caution for a number of reasons. The present study was conducted with a single convenience sample of children, in a single medical center, by a single group of investigators, during a single time period. These are all factors that might limit the external validity of the findings. While the contrast condition here (GPM) represents the kind of care a child could expect to receive in a pediatric service of a major, tertiary care, academic medical center, this was only an experimental-contrast condition design with a particular contrast condition. The effects that we observed might have been smaller if we had tested SBW2 against another contrast condition. Furthermore the SBW2 system is still being developed and the effects it produces may change. The relationships between outcomes and between demographic factors and outcomes were not assessed based on a priori hypotheses and are presented here merely to possibly stimulate future work. Missing data and floor effects were also observed and may impact the findings in yet to be determined ways (cf. Holden et al., 1999).

There were dramatic improvements in technical performance of SBW2 compared to our original study, where either the local SBW computer or some aspect of telecommunications was not functioning properly on 24.4% of measurement occasions. In the present study, however, these functional failures were reduced to 1% of occasions.

What does it mean that only 8 out of 132 possible contrasts at the individual level reached significance? In discussing more subtle effects than those observed here, Onghena (1994) noted that even if there are no statistically significant effects at the individual level, the aggregation of results across individuals might reveal meaningful effects. This type of situation points out the utility of this design. If a researcher who contrasts treatments using a group design takes the time to examine individual level data, in a number of instances they will likely find what we found here. That is, at the level of the entire group statistically significant effects are found. Yet, by examining the data at the individual level, the researcher will find that for some contrasts the experimental condition did much better, for other contrasts the experimental condition did about the same or a little better, and in a few instances the control condition did better. In other words, the group design focuses on *the size of the effect across participants-* which is the equivalent of the last three rows of Table 2.

We assumed that SBW2 would produce small effects on these outcomes, and that assumption dictated the choice of the present design. We were able to provide a very stringent test of SBW2 by contrasting it to high quality pediatric care and yet avoid Type II errors by employing as sensitive an analysis as possible. In the initial study, we had hypothesized that because there were only six hospitals online for limited hours, in different time zones, that there was a lack of potential community within which children could interact. Schopler, Abell and Galinsky (1998) have argued that in communications via technology, both *social presence* ("the degree of salience of another person in an interaction and the consequent salience of an interpersonal relationship," p. 257) and *social impact* ("the changes in physical states, feelings, and cognition in individuals that happen as a result of the presence or actions of others" p. 257) may be less. We further reasoned that the limited potential online community in the initial study resulted in reduced social presence and social impact. We expected that as the online community grew, along with more advanced and complex modes of interacting in SBW2 and technical difficulties were resolved, both social presence and social impact would increase and we would observe more positive effects. However, while children reported statistically significantly less pain intensity, pain aversiveness, and anxiety in the SBW2 condition, the size of these differences was slightly smaller than those observed in our original study.

Some readers may ask whether a .29 difference between conditions on an 11-point scale (for pain intensity) is clinically as well as statistically significant. Rosenthal (1991) clarifies the importance of considering the meaning of effects rather than simply making a determination based on their actual size. He refers to the randomized trial that tested the ability of aspirin to prevent heart attacks where the effect (indicating better outcomes among those using aspirin) was r = .03. Rosenthal notes that the study was halted prematurely because the effect was so clinically significant that it would have been unethical to continue.

More closely related to our work is one early study of an electronic bulletin board that focused on suicide and confronted similar qualitative findings. The authors noted that:

> participants offered each other valuable resources in terms of validation of experience, sympathy, acceptance and encouragement. They also asked provocative questions and furnished broad-ranging advice. Hostile entries were rare. However, there were few communiques that parallel the change-inducing practices more frequent within many therapeutic settings. In effect, on-line dialogues seemed more sustaining than transforming. . . . our results suggest, network communication possesses *limited but significant therapeutic potential.* (Miller & Gergen, 1998, p. 189, 198, emphasis added)

Beyond acknowledging the small improvement observed in the present study, we want to emphasize the stringency of the tests of the intervention. This was not a no-treatment or placebo control group design. SBW2 was contrasted with high quality pediatric care and the small, yet statistically significant effects should be considered in light of this. It remains to be seen whether small, yet statistically significant effects are the highest potential of network interventions or whether this is a phase in the development of network interventions and we will observe increased effects in the future. This leads to the ancillary question of cost/benefit analysis. This is a complicated analysis based in part on a variety of decisions regarding input variables (Yates, 1994). For instance, how should equipment or personnel time, etc., that has been donated or allocated for the project, be valued in terms of costs? Further, at what point in the development of a new system should the analyses be performed (costs will tend to go down as the number of units deployed or the amount of use per unit increases)? While interesting, these analyses are beyond the scope of this paper.

The present replication and extension of our earlier study, provides continued support for the effectiveness of SBW2. Moreover, it provides additional evidence regarding the utility of combining single system designs and meta-analysis to assess short acting interventions that are likely to produce subtle effects.

ACKNOWLEDGEMENTS

The authors would like to acknowledge the efforts of Cristina Greeno, Lauren Mednick, Karen Marcinczyk and Dr. Fredrick Suchy which made this project possible. In addition, we would like to thank the STARBRIGHT Foundation, the Mount Sinai Children's Center Foundation and the Mount Sinai Medical Center for their support in carrying out this research. Finally, we would like to thank Dr. Patrick Onghena of the Catholic University of Leuven for his support of this work.

REFERENCES

Affleck, G., Tennen, H., Urrows, S., Higgins, P., Abeles, M., Hall, C., Karoly, P. & Newton, C. (1998). Fibromyalgia and women's pursuit of personal goals: A daily process analysis. *Health Psychology, 17*, 40-7.

AHCPR (1992). *Acute pain management: Operative or medical procedures and trauma*. Rockville, MD. U.S. Department of Health and Human Services, Public Health Service, Agency for Health Care Policy and Research. AHCPR Publication No. 92-0032.

Allison, D. B. & Gorman, B. S. (1993). Calculating effect sizes for meta-analysis: The case of the single case. *Behavior Research and Therapy, 31*, 621-31.

Bearison, D. J., Holden, G., Rode, D., Rosenberg, G. & Fishman, M. (1999). STAR-BRIGHT World: Participants' perspectives. [p. 11-18] In W. Spitzer (Ed.), *Conference Proceedings from the Virginia Conference on Social Work Practice in Healthcare.*

Bennet, R. (1998). A virtual community for sick children. *New Age*, May/June, 20.

Bloom, M., Fischer, J. & Orme, J. G. (1999). *Evaluating practice: Guidelines for the accountable professional*, 3rd Ed. Boston: Allyn & Bacon.

Bornstein, R. F. (1990). Publication politics, experimenter bias and the replication process in social science research. In J. W. Neulip (Ed.) *Handbook of Replication Research in the Behavioral and Social Sciences.* 71-82.

Christenfeld, N. (1997). Memory for pain and the delayed effects of distraction. *Health Psychology, 16,* 327-30.

Cleary, P. D. & Edgman-Levitan, S. (1997). Health care quality: Incorporating consumer perspectives. *Journal of the American Medical Association, 278,* 1608-12.

Cliff, N. (1987). *Analyzing Multivariate Data.* New York: Harcourt Brace.

Cook, D., Guyatt, G. H., Davis, C., Willan, A. & McIlroy, W. (1993). A diagnostic and therapeutic n-of-1 randomized trial. *Canadian Journal of Psychiatry, 38,* 251-4.

Corcoran, K. J. (1985). Aggregating the idiographic data of single-subject research. *Social Work Research and Abstracts, 21,* 9-12.

Corcoran, K. J. (1986). Corcoran responds. *Social Work Research and Abstracts, 22,* 23-4.

DeVellis, R. F. (1991). *Scale development: Theory and applications.* Newbury Park, CA: Sage.

Durlach, N. I. & Mavor, A. S. (1995). Evaluation of synthetic environment systems. In N. I. Durlach, & A. S. Mavor (Eds.) *Virtual reality: Scientific and technological challenges.* Washington, DC: National Academy Press.

Eimer, B. N. & Freeman, A. (1998). *Pain management psychotherapy: A practical guide.* New York: John Wiley.

Eggebrecht, D. B., Bautz, M. T., Brenig, M. I. D., Pfingsten, M. & Franz, C. (1989). Psychometric evaluation. In P. M. Camic & F. D. Brown (Eds.), *Assessing chronic pain: A multidisciplinary handbook* (pp. 71-90). New York: Springer Verlag.

Essick, K. (1999). Where chat worlds collide. [Online], Available: (http://register.cnet.com/Content/Features/Dlife/Chat/side4.html).

Finn, J. (1996). Computer-based self-help groups: Online recovery for addictions. *Computers in Human Services, 13,* 21-41.

Finn, J. (1999). Social work on the superhighway: Issues and trends in online practice. Paper presented at Council on Social Work Education/New York University Conference, *Use of Technology in Support of Clinical Social Work,* May, 7, 1999.

Galinsky, M. (1999). Expanding the horizons of social work services: Technology-based groups. Paper presented at Council on Social Work Education/New York University Conference, *Use of Technology in Support of Clinical Social Work,* May, 7, 1999.

Gingerich, W. J. (1984). Meta-analysis of applied time-series data. *Journal of Applied Behavioral Science, 20,* 71-9.

Greenman, C. (1998, May 28). Network helps children cope with serious illness. *New York Times,* G6.

Guyatt, G. H., Sackett, D., Adachi, J., Roberts, R., Chong, J. Rosenbloom, D., Keller, J. (1988). A clinician's guide for conducting randomized trials in individual patients. *CMAJ, 139,* 497-503.

Guyatt, G. H., Heyting, A., Jaeschke, R., Keller, J., Adachi, J. D., & Roberts, R. S. (1990a). N of 1 randomized trials for investigating new drugs. *Controlled Clinical Trials, 11,* 88-100.

Guyatt, G. H., Keller, J., Jaeschke, R., Rosenbloom, D., Adachi, J. D., & Newhouse,

M. T. (1990b). The n of 1 randomized controlled trial: Clinical usefulness. *Annals of Internal Medicine, 112,* 293-9.

Hart, B. B., & Alden, P. A. (1994). Hypnotic techniques in the control of pain. In H. B. Gibson (Ed.), *Psychology, pain and anaesthesia* (pp. 120-45). London: Chapman and Hall.

Hawker, F., Kavanagh, S., Yellowlees, P., & Kalucy, R. S. (1998). Telepsychiatry in South Australia. *Journal of Telemedicine and Telecare, 4,* 187-94.

Holden, G., Bearison, D., Rode, D., Rosenberg, G., & Fishman, M. (1999). The impact of a virtual environment on hospitalized children: A pilot study with aggregation of the results of replicated single system designs via meta-analysis. *Research on Social Work Practice, 9,* 365-82.

Lebow, J. (1998). Not just talk, maybe some risk: The therapeutic potentials and pitfalls of computer-mediated conversation. *Journal of Marital and Family Therapy, 24,* 203-6.

Litt, M. D., Cooney, N. L. & Morse, P. (1998). Ecological momentary assessment (EMA) with treated alcoholics: Methodological problems and potential solutions. *Health Psychology, 17,* 48-52.

Madara, E. J. (1997). The mutual-aid self-help online revolution. *Social Policy, Spring,* 20-6.

Makris, J. (1998, October 21). The human touch: STARBRIGHT World uses video-conferencing and e-mail to help sick children make vital connections. *Data Communications,* [Online Serial], Available: http://www.data.com/issue/981021/touch.html

McGrath, P. A. (1990). *Pain in children: Nature, assessment, and treatment.* New York: Guilford.

McGrath, P. A, Seifert, C. E., Speechley, K. N., Booth, J. C., Stitt, L., & Gibson, M. C. (1996). A new analogue scale for assessing children's pain: An initial validation study. *Pain, 64,* 435-43.

McQuay, H. J., Carrol, D., Jadad, A. R., Glynn, C. J., Jack, T., Moore, R. A., & Wiffen, P. J. (1994). Dextromethorphan for the treatment of neuropathic pain: A double-blind randomized controlled crossover trial with integral n-of-1 design. *Pain, 59,* 127-33

Miller, J. K., & Gergen, K. J. (1998). Life on the line: The therapeutic potentials of computer-mediated conversation. *Journal of Marital and Family Therapy, 24,* 189-202.

Onghena, P. (1992). Randomization tests for extensions and variations of ABAB single-case experimental designs: A rejoinder. *Behavioral Assessment, 14,* 153-71.

Onghena, P. (1994). *The Power of Randomization Tests for Single Case Designs.* Dissertation at the Catholic University of Leuven, Leuven, Belgium.

Onghena, P. & Edgington, E. S. (1994). Randomization tests for restricted alternating treatment designs. *Behavior Research and Therapy, 32,* 783-6.

Rosenthal, R. (1990). Replication in behavioral research. In J. W. Neulip (Ed.) *Handbook of Replication Research in the Behavioral and Social Sciences.* 1-30.

Rosenthal, R. (1991). *Meta-Analytic Procedures for Social Research, 2nd Ed.* Newbury Park, CA: Sage.

Salzberg, C. L., Strain, P. S., & Baer, D. M. (1987). Meta-analysis for single-subject research: When does it clarify, when does it obscure? *Remedial and Special Education, 8,* 43-8.

Schopler, J. H., Galinsky, M. J. & Abell, M. (1997). Creating community through telephone and computer groups: Theoretical and practice perspectives. *Social Work with Groups, 20,* 19-34.

Schopler, J. H., Abell, M. D. & Galinsky, M. J. (1998). Technology-based groups: A review and conceptual framework for practice. *Social Work, 43,* 254-67.

Scruggs, T. E., Mastropieri, M. A., & Casto, G. (1987). The quantitative synthesis of single subject research: Methodology and validation *Remedial and Special Education, 8,* 24-33.

Scruggs, T. E., Mastropieri, M. A., & Casto, G. (1987b). Reply to Owen White. *Remedial and Special Education, 8,* 40-2.

Scruggs, T. E., Mastropieri, M. A., & Casto, G. (1987c). Response to Salzberg, Strain, and Baer. *Remedial and Special Education, 8,* 49-52.

Shiffman, S. & Stone, A. (1998). Introduction to the special section: Ecological momentary assessment in health psychology. *Health Psychology, 17,* 3-5.

Tuckman, B. W. (1988). The scaling of mood. *Educational and Psychological Measurement, 48,* 419-27.

Van Damme, G., & Onghena, P. (1995). *Manual SCRT1.1: Single Case Randomization Tests.* Research Group on Quantitative Methods. Leuven, Belgium: Catholic University of Leuven.

Videka-Sherman, L. (1986). Alternative approaches to aggregating the results of single-subject designs. *Social Work Research and Abstracts, 22,* 22-3.

White, D. M., Rusch, F. R., Kazdin, A. E., & Hartmann, D. P. (1989). Applications of meta analysis in individual-subject research. *Behavioral Assessment, 11,* 218-96.

White, J. C., Christensen, J. F., & Singer, C. M. (1992). Methylphenidate as a treatment for depression in acquired immunodeficiency syndrome: An n-of-1 trial. *Journal of Clinical Psychiatry, 53,* 153-6.

White, O. R. (1987). Some comments concerning "The Quantitative Synthesis of Single-Subject Research." *Remedial and Special Education, 8,* 40-2.

Yates, B. (1994). Toward the incorporation of costs, cost-effectiveness analysis, and cost benefit analysis into clinical research. *Journal of Consulting & Clinical Psychology, 62,* 729-36.

Zaylor, C. (1999). Clinical outcomes in telepsychiatry. *Journal of Telemedicine and Telecare, 5,* S1:59–S1:60.

Zucker, D. R., Schmid, C. H., McIntosh, M. W., D'Agostino, R. B., Selker, H. P., & Lau, J. (1997). Combining single patient (N-of-1) trials to estimate population treatment effects and to evaluate individual patient responses to treatment. *Journal of Clinical Epidemiology, 50,* 401-10.

Changing Practices with Children and Families in North Carolina: Using Technology to Facilitate Collaboration and Training

Irene Nathan Zipper
Andrew Broughton
Lenore Behar

SUMMARY. A new approach to services for children with serious emotional disturbance and their families calls for the development of systems of care. Family members participate in all aspects of service delivery, including designing, developing, and delivering services. Training and technical assistance are essential, as service providers need new skills in working with children, family members, service providers, and others in the community; and a new understanding of integrated, community-based services. Technology offers new possibilities for delivering such training. In North Carolina, the Internet is used to share information, plan training events, provide training, and exchange materials among training coordinators located around the state. *[Article copies available for a fee from The Haworth Document Delivery Service:*

Irene Nathan Zipper and Andrew Broughton are affiliated with the School of Social Work, University of North Carolina at Chapel Hill.

Lenore Behar is affiliated with the Division of Mental Health, Developmental Disabilities, and Substance Abuse Services, North Carolina Department of Health and Human Services.

Address correspondence to: Irene Nathan Zipper, School of Social Work, 301 Pittsboro St., CB #3550, University of North Carolina, Chapel Hill, NC 27599-3550 (E-mail: izipper@unc.edu).

[Haworth co-indexing entry note]: "Changing Practices with Children and Families in North Carolina: Using Technology to Facilitate Collaboration and Training." Zipper, Irene Nathan, Andrew Broughton, and Lenore Behar. Co-published simultaneously in *Journal of Technology in Human Services* (The Haworth Press, Inc.) Vol. 17, No. 1, 2000, pp. 49-67; and: *Human Services Online: A New Arena for Service Delivery* (ed: Jerry Finn, and Gary Holden) The Haworth Press, Inc., 2000, pp. 49-67. Single or multiple copies of this article are available for a fee from The Haworth Document Delivery Service [1-800-342-9678, 9:00 a.m. - 5:00 p.m. (EST). E-mail address: getinfo@haworthpressinc.com].

49

1-800-342-9678. E-mail address: <getinfo@haworthpressinc.com> Website:
<http://www.haworthpressinc.com>]

KEYWORDS. Distance learning, videoconference, training, children's
mental health, system of care

Family members and service providers are working together in new
and different ways to serve children with serious emotional disturbances. Their interactions are based on the recognition that effective
services build on strengths, address family priorities and concerns, and
rely on the combined talents of local community resources and services whenever possible. To implement these approaches, new skills
in working with children, family members, service providers, and
others in the community are needed. Training is needed for both
service providers and family members to ensure that they have the
skills needed in this context. Historically, a comprehensive training
effort in a large, rural state like North Carolina has required considerable travel and expense. This paper describes an innovative project
that uses information technology to provide an efficient alternative to
traditional training approaches and to promote quality and consistency
in training content.

The project described is an aspect of the North Carolina System of
Care Initiative of the state's child mental health office, whose purpose
is to engage service providers, family members, and administrators,
together with the academic community, in developing and defining a
new approach to service provision for children with serious emotional
disturbance and their families. The approach is grounded in values and
principles for a system of care for children and adolescents with serious emotional disturbance and their families that were first articulated
by Stroul and Friedman (1986). In this system of care, resources and
services are organized so that flexible responses to the needs of children and their families are possible (England & Cole, 1998). Service
planning and service delivery are guided by the family, services are
responsive to the culture and ethnic background of the family, informal community resources are emphasized, and interventions build on
family strengths. Service providers collaborate with each other and
with families to ensure that services are integrated and coordinated.

While technology is increasingly utilized for distance education
(e.g., Beller & Or, 1998; Reid, 1999) and for medical and psychiatric

intervention (e.g., Brown, 1998), it is new to the provision of in-service training in the mental health arena. The North Carolina System of Care Initiative uses the Internet for communication among individuals who are responsible for providing and coordinating training in local communities. These training coordinators are located across the state, frequently at considerable distance from each other. They use the Internet to share information, plan training events, provide training, and exchange materials.

The North Carolina System of Care Initiative is funded through two federal grants from the Center for Mental Health Services (CMHS) of the Substance Abuse and Mental Health Services Administration of the Department of Health and Human Services, the first beginning in 1993 and the second in 1997. This federal grant program has, as a national agenda, the development of systems of care for children with serious emotional disturbances and their families. The North Carolina child mental health office has had significant experience in the development of such systems. The most recent experience has been with the Child Mental Health Demonstration Project funded by the Robert Wood Johnson Foundation (1989-1995) and the Child and Adolescent Mental Health Demonstration Project at Fort Bragg (1989-1996). In each project, the service system approach has been refined, building upon the previous experiences.

The findings of an independent evaluation of the Fort Bragg Project have led to the current focus on changing clinical practice. The evaluation provided evidence that the reorganization of service systems alone, that is changing the structure through which services are delivered, is not sufficient to bring about improved clinical outcomes in children. Rather, the implication of the Fort Bragg findings is that clinical practice also needs to be changed to effect the desired improvements in outcome (Bickman, 1997; Salzar & Bickman, 1997). Thus, the North Carolina System of Care Initiative emphasizes a family-centered, strengths-based approach to practice, in the context of coordinated, integrated, community-based service systems.

The development of these systems of care involves changes at multiple levels. Practice in this context requires new skills of service providers and supervisors. On-going training and technical assistance are needed to encourage and support the change process and the development of new skills. The goals of in-service training are to refine or acquire skills that are generalized to the workplace, to refine those skills over time, and to teach them to others (Meyers, Kaufman, & Goldman, 1999). Internet technology offers a mechanism for delivering the training needed for this broad initiative. Using technology, it is possible to engage participants at multiple sites in interactive training activities. Learning opportunities that take place at a central site can be offered to service providers around the state. In North Carolina, the infrastructure for an elaborate statewide training program has been established with this Initiative.

THE PRACTICE CONCEPTS

Effective services are grounded in supportive relationships between families and service providers (Solnit, Adnopoz, Saxe, Gardner, & Fallon, 1997). The services emphasize strengths, recognizing that positive change builds on the assets, resources, wisdom, and knowledge that individuals bring (Saleeby, 1997). Family members participate actively in all aspects of service delivery, including designing, developing, and delivering services. This family-centered perspective is basic to the System of Care Initiative. It involves a dramatic shift in the way families and service providers work together, requiring new attitudes on the part of service providers toward the families they serve, and new skills in working with families as consumers (England & Cole, 1998; Roberts, Rule, & Innocenti, 1998). Service providers need to hold the values that support family-centered practice, and they need the knowledge and skills to relate to families in a different way. For their part, family members need to engage service providers with the expectation that they will be full partners in the service process. Strong family advocacy organizations can support this effort by working with family members in preparation for their meaningful participation in the service process, by being involved in service planning and evaluation, and by assuring that service providers understand family priorities (Osher, 1994).

Services are provided in the context of a comprehensive, integrated, community-based system of care. Everyone who participates needs a strong commitment to collaboration, as the process is carried out with the full participation of family members, local service providers, and other community resources (Simpson, Koroloff, Friesen, & Gac, 1999). However, service providers often see themselves as representatives of their respective disciplines, with differing theoretical perspectives, models, and values (Abramson & Mizrahi, 1996; Sands, Stafford, & McClelland, 1990; Uzzell, 1997). Their preparation varies in terms of their perspectives on family involvement (Bailey, Simeonsson, Yoder, & Huntington, 1990). Thus, service providers from different disciplines often find collaboration difficult. They and their supervisors need the skills for collaboration in a coordinated, integrated service system. Agency administrators and policy makers need information and skills to develop innovative strategies for funding and to provide the leadership needed for this service context. Training, involving the systematic acquisition of skills, rules, concepts, and attitudes that result in improved performance (Goldstein & Gilliam, 1990), is clearly needed in this situation.

The Context for Practice

In North Carolina, the Child and Family Services Section of the Division of Mental Health, Developmental Disabilities, and Substance Abuse Services is responsible for serving children with serious emotional disturbance and their families. Community-based mental health services are delivered through local area programs. Local communities have traditionally had the flexibility and authority to develop and design services that address community needs, with regulatory oversight and support from the Child and Family Services Section. Although all area programs must adhere to the same basic standards and guidelines, the structure allows for considerable variation in service delivery.

Model Demonstration Projects

With funding from CMHS, two model demonstration projects have been established at six sites around the state. Through these projects, local communities design and develop their local systems of care to support children with serious emotional disturbances and their families. Each of the model projects is committed to the practice priorities described above. Family members have decision-making authority about the services they use so that services reflect their concerns and priorities. Families are assigned service coordinators who maintain close ties with each child and family to assure that their concerns and priorities guide the service planning process. Families are also involved in planning and designing the child-serving system, so that services are provided in a manner consistent with local values and priorities. Since services build on strengths that exist in the family and in the community, particular attention is paid to engaging informal resources, such as local civic groups and religious organizations. Each of the six sites is establishing its own community-based governance process for services and is developing strategies for integrating local services based on these principles.

The state is committed to facilitating relationships between the academic and practice communities. To this end, the state has involved the academic community in the establishment of Public-Academic Liaisons (PALs). Through these PALs, model demonstration programs collaborate with local institutions of higher education for the benefit of both. Research, evaluation, and training are provided at the local sites by faculty members at local colleges and universities. Students are exposed to practice grounded in these concepts through field practicum placements at community agencies at the model demonstration sites, and interdisciplinary activities are encouraged at the university and practice levels (Behar, Zipper, McCammon, Spencer, McKinnon-Lewis, 1998).

The Child and Family Services Section guides the sites in the implementation of the model projects by providing guidance to the local communities, monitoring implementation, and evaluating progress. While the model demonstration projects are grounded in the basic principles outlined previously, the emphasis on local autonomy means that the projects operate in the context of widely divergent service systems. Differences include the history of interagency collaboration, the relationships among direct service providers, the strength of local family advocacy organizations, and the degree of rurality of the area, among others.

The Need for Training

Despite these differences, training needs are similar across sites. Service providers and family members need to learn what values underlie practice in a system of care, they need information about available resources, and they need specific skills in relating to families and other service providers in this context. These values, knowledge, and skills may be developed through a variety of training experiences, including interactive exercises, demonstrations of exemplary practice, case studies, lectures, and panel presentations. Participants learn from those with relevant practice experience and from each other, as they practice the needed skills and discuss issues that arise in establishing their local systems of care. These activities require both audio and video communication. Technology can be used to facilitate this process.

Both the state office and the model sites have much to gain by close communication. However, they are separated by considerable geographic distance, making regular meetings at the sites impractical. Frequent travel among the communities is time-consuming and expensive. Statewide meetings entail a major commitment of time and resources, particularly by those communities farthest from the center of the state. The state office can promote consistency across programs and ensure a measure of model fidelity by promoting connections among the model sites as they implement their systems of care.

Training Coordinators

The state office has facilitated the establishment of a group of training coordinators responsible for seeing that local needs for training are met. The training coordinators link the model programs and promote consistency in the training that is provided across the state. They are members of the local community, and are housed in local agencies involved in the System of Care Initiative.

Given the State's commitment to developing active partnerships between the public sector and academia for the benefit of both, the logical venue for this training effort was with the university community. The Children's Mental Health Project, a part of the Jordan Institute for Families in the School of Social Work at the University of North Carolina at Chapel Hill (UNC-CH), was funded by the state office to work with local communities to hire the training coordinators and provide them with ongoing support. The training coordinators are employees of the University, hired through a collaborative process involving the University, the state office, and the local site director. They were hired based on their training skills and experience, their understanding of children's mental health issues, and their enthusiasm for innovation. All the training coordinators have Bachelors degrees in human service fields; some have Masters degrees.

Technology can be used to facilitate the identification and analysis of staff training needs (Gibelman & Champagne, 1981), and the role of the training coordinators exemplifies the integration of training and technology. The training coordinators are responsible for seeing that information and opportunities for skill development are available. To this end they work with family members, service providers, supervisors, and other community members to:

- identify training needs
- identify relevant resources both locally and across the state
- arrange for training opportunities
- provide workshops around specific topics
- provide ongoing consultation around various aspects of model implementation
- evaluate training activities

The training coordinators work with service providers to review service plans and progress with the children and families they serve. When they determine that service providers need additional information or skills, the training coordinators arrange for training and/or provide it themselves. Each training coordinator maintains a record of contacts, training content, training participants, and training evaluations, for the purpose of documentation and planning. The training coordinators use technology for communication and coordination among themselves, with the State and the University, and for purposes of teaching and training.

As employees, the training coordinators have access to the resources of the University, including the library system and WWW servers. They are eligible to attend workshops and classes about new hardware and software for use in teaching and research. In addition, the training coordinators can take advantage of classes and activities that are relevant to the development of their local systems of care. For example, a graduate level social work course that was offered on a weekly basis was made available to service providers at the local sites. The course was offered using video conferencing over the Internet so that faculty members at the university were able to interact with training participants. Course materials were available on-site, so local participants would have access to the materials used at the central site. In addition to this weekly class, one-day workshops that take place at the University have been made available. A workshop for field instructors that included a presentation by the director of a national organization was recently held at the School, followed by a panel discussion among parent advocates; this workshop was made available to the sites.

TECHNOLOGY AND LOGISTICS

Technology provides the infrastructure for facilitating communication between and among the central and local sites. Initially, plans were to link four sites for both asynchronous activities (such as e-mail and pre-recorded audio and video) and synchronous activities (such as video conferencing). This has since grown to six sites and includes the state offices and UNC-CH. Plans call for four additional sites during the coming year.

Communication Among the Sites

Synchronous activities have been the primary focus of technology in this project. In the past, some linking of sites had been accomplished through video conferences using a few established video studios located at colleges and universities around the state. This method of linking was useful, but expensive and inconvenient, as it required travel to these studios. The current network makes it possible to communicate from the local agency, using a desktop computer and technology based on the H.323 standard for video conferencing. The costs of the hardware and software are minimal, if the sites already have personal computers with sufficient speed and memory to operate the system. The H.323 recommendation is an International Telecommunications Union standard for video conferencing over Local Area Networks (LANs). It is more economical and readily accessible than its main competitors, systems using the H.320 standard for video conferencing over ISDN phone lines and requiring specialized equipment.

All of the local sites already had Internet connections; none had ISDN connections, which would have been required for systems using the H.320 standard. Although not yet fully developed, the H.323 standard represents a rapidly maturing technology. Thus, using the H.323 standard lays the groundwork for future efforts as well.

The project benefits from the University's commitment to using technology for teaching and training. As this project began, UNC-CH was preparing for the H.323 standard. University technology personnel provided consultation to project personnel, and the University provided hardware and software that would allow multiple sites to engage in simultaneous video conferencing, i.e., a multi-point control unit (MCU). It also provided a gateway to allow sites with different technologies to interact. Operating in conjunction with UNC-CH's technology program assures that the effort is compatible with technology in use at the University, and with that used in other universities in the state and around the world.

Hardware and Software

There are currently several ways to accomplish video using computers and the Internet. The easiest and least expensive of these is to utilize a small video camera that is plugged into the computer's parallel port or Universal Serial Bus [USB] port. The latter is faster and less likely to interfere with peripherals plugged into the parallel port. Both of these choices rely entirely on software for video and on an existing sound card and microphone for audio. Video digitizing boards provide more options for video sources and for dealing with the video once it has been captured. With these boards it is possible to use other video cameras, input from, or output to, VCRs, etc. With appropriate software and enough disk space, it is possible to process and save the video for later use. A third option is to buy a board that handles both video and audio, an approach that can be cost-effective and efficient. These boards typically come with an inexpensive video camera, microphone, and software and they are relatively easy to set up. The latter was the option we chose.

In order to build the needed network, the following equipment and software were purchased: 400 MHz Pentium II computers, with audio cards and speakers; and Intel ProShare Video System 500 video cards and associated software. Assuming that appropriate personal computers are available, the additional cost of the video camera and software would be approximately $700. NEC MT 820 LCD projectors were purchased to project an enlarged video image, for approximately $3,900.

Because audio and video files tend to be large, the sites needed fast connections to the Internet. If, for example, the project had required only the streaming of compressed audio, a 28.8 KB modem would have been sufficient. However, interactive video and audio together generally require a T1 line (1.5MB) or its equivalent. Fortunately, each of the initial sites already had T1 connections to the Internet.

The quality of the hardware and software, and compatibility among components, are key to effective audio and video transmission. The quality of the output can only be as good as the quality of the input; when an inexpensive camera is connected to a parallel port on the computer, the quality of the video output to the Internet is likely to be inferior. High quality video requires a separate video digitizing board with the capability to connect to other video cameras. In this way a camcorder, for example, can be utilized to provide such features as zooming and panning to assure better video output. Like cameras, the microphones included with digital video cards are often not of the best quality. The quality of audio transmission is likely to be better with high-quality microphones. Our experience also indicates that some video boards are sensitive to the speed of the computer in which they are installed. ProShare's manufacturers recommend a minimum of a 400 MHz Pentium machine for this application.

Use of the Internet

Social workers and other service providers working with children and families need cost-effective distance learning opportunities (Oliver & Huxley, 1988). Such opportunities can be provided using the Internet, as service providers from all of the model sites can participate in joint training opportunities using the Internet. It offers an inexpensive mechanism for coordination, is always accessible, and is generally available as most service agencies now have Internet access.

The Internet has been evolving from a text-based repository of information to a multimedia-based vehicle for information exchange. Harasim, Hiltz, Teles, and Turoff (1995) outlined the many ways which text-based tools could be used in training and education. They focused on how these "learning networks" can expand the times, places and pace of learning for individuals. As the Internet has evolved, users can perform many more technically challenging tasks than the ones previously identified. The addition of audio and video to text in web-based applications presents a technical challenge, because the Internet Protocol's (IP) weaknesses are much more apparent when transmitting audio or video. Text is transmitted and read in packets, so that as the first pieces are read, subsequent portions are still being transmitted. Thus, the brief wait required while the pieces of text are transmitted and reassembled into a complete document or e-mail message is not problematic for the reader. The same is not true for audio or video material. Communication across telephone lines requires exchanges in "real time," whereby words are heard virtually as they are spoken and in the order in which they are spoken. In order for IP delivery to be "transparent," motion and sound must be perfectly synchronized; audio and video exchange must take place in "real time." Anything more than very slight delays in audio or video can be quite disconcerting.

Logistical Issues

A number of logistical issues had to be addressed in implementing the technology infrastructure for the training coordinators. The programs are located in different communities, with different levels of technology and support. All of the current connections are at least T1 lines, but these lines are often shared with other computers on local LANs and two are behind firewalls.

Because identical equipment is utilized at each of the sites, we were able to communicate with the systems at the local sites as soon as the computers were installed and provided with an IP address. The two exceptions have involved the use of a firewall at a local site, a problem that we hope to resolve shortly.

Use of the Technology

Training coordinators have learned how to use the computers and the ProShare software. The latter training took no more than an hour. They spent some additional time using it on their own to become comfortable with the technology. Preliminary research suggests that trainees who have been repeatedly exposed to multimedia-based training are more likely to view it as effective in achieving the objectives of training (Christoph, Schoenfeld, & Tansky, 1998). Training coordinators will make increasing use of the technology as they become more comfortable with it. They currently use video conferencing to plan for training events, problem-solve around issues in implementation, and generally coordinate project activities. It is expected that their growing ease with the technology will enhance their sense of self-efficacy and their effectiveness as trainers.

Technology personnel have had to develop additional skills and new ways of thinking to facilitate this project, and share those with the training coordinators. They have become sensitive to such issues as lighting, which is critical to the quality of the video picture, and sound, which may call for special microphone techniques for group situations, as clear audio is critical for comprehension.

EVALUATING THE EFFORT

The implementation of a training program and the attempts to evaluate it need to be treated as an intervention (Goldstein & Gessner, 1988). This initiative constitutes a complex intervention with potential impact on practice across the state. We are documenting the development of this technology-based initiative as it moves toward statewide implementation. Evaluation efforts are focusing on the effectiveness of the training provided, the use of the technology, and its value to the training coordinators. Sites using the technology will be compared with sites utilizing traditional training strategies in terms of satisfaction with training and level of skill development.

To date, the evaluation effort has been limited to process evaluation. Training coordinators have been informally polled on their reactions to the use of the technology; all are enthusiastic about its potential and see themselves as innovators. Some regularly utilize the hardware and software for purposes of communication; others have indicated that they would like further training on its use, and on technology-based pedagogical strategies.

CHALLENGES OF THE CURRENT SYSTEM

The challenges in operating the current system of communication and training are both technological and programmatic. The technological challenges are likely to lessen over time. The current equipment functions very well for desktop video conferencing; it is less effective for use with large groups of participants in classroom or auditorium settings; although acceptable, the image is far less crisp when projected to a large screen.

Another limitation has to do with the use of mixed technologies, such as gateways to communicate with systems based on the H.320 standard. Rapid changes in technology suggest that the equipment currently in place will become obsolete relatively quickly and frequently, and regular upgrades of hardware and software will be needed. Funding is available and is ongoing to ensure that the network can continue to operate with the best equipment available.

University technology personnel have made decisions about equipment, connected with related university efforts, gathered information about local sites, and established and maintained communication with local technology personnel. They have explained the potential uses of technology to the training coordinators and others at the local sites. They have installed the equipment and taught the training coordinators to use it, and they are providing ongoing training and consultation around the use of the technology. Over time, it is hoped that local technology personnel will be available to maintain this network themselves.

As technology becomes increasingly important in providing training, the requisite skills will be required of those who prepare service providers for practice. "Privileged" employees, advantaged by their technology skills, are viewed as holding more interesting jobs and experiencing a higher quality of life (Gattiker, 1990). The realities of the skills required of individuals such as training coordinators may mean that they will be among those who are "privileged," based on their technology skills. The training coordinators are enthusiastic about using a new, technology-based approach to training, which may result in greater job satisfaction, reduced employee turnover, and other benefits associated with high morale.

However, the training coordinators face considerable demands on their time and effort. This effort requires careful coordination and collaboration among multiple service agencies at multiple sites. In addition to their on-site responsibilities, the training coordinators communicate extensively with representatives of the state office, and they are closely involved with project technology and program personnel at UNC-CH. The complexity of these interrelationships, involving very different service systems and individuals working out of different settings and from different sites, can be daunting.

Because this is such a new initiative, unexpected technological and programmatic problems arise, requiring flexibility and creativity of everyone involved. As an example, when a misplaced cable connector meant that a prearranged conference did not have audio, the training coordinator had to use a speakerphone instead. In another instance, as the result of a miscommunication, the only attendee at one of the classes broadcast from the university was the training coordinator herself. Such situations present opportunities for examining the problems and improving the functioning of the network. They also require good humor and an adventurous spirit.

This developing network cannot yet function fully as conceptualized, given the realities of both the technology and the personnel involved. Compatibility of equipment, and availability and speed of connections are being addressed. Training coordinators, hired in part because of their enthusiasm for this initiative, are gradually developing the skills and the confidence they need to make full use of the technology. The first challenge is to bring the current system of four sites to an ongoing, efficient level of operation incorporating the expansions discussed below. Plans are underway to expand the system to additional sites in the coming year and, within two years, to have a statewide system of 16-20 sites in operation.

FUTURE DIRECTIONS

Although our vision is probably somewhat ahead of current reality, we are convinced that technology offers remarkable opportunities for enhancing effective practice. Local service providers and family members will be able to benefit from the expertise of presenters who are physically located elsewhere in the state and perhaps in the country. Training handouts and bibliographies will be available for download from project web sites. University-level courses utilizing technology will be offered using the Internet so that faculty at the University interact with training participants in real time. Course materials and text will be available at web sites established for that purpose.

Communication among the University, the state office, and the training coordinators already relies increasingly on technology. Information about upcoming events is currently made available to local programs on the Internet. While synchronous technologies such as video conferencing over the Internet have been effectively used, asynchronous technologies such as streaming video and simple web pages need further development for this project. The advantage of these technologies is that they are available at all times, regardless of when they originated; the disadvantage is that they require considerable preparation before being made available on the Internet. A Real Server is available to the project that will make it possible to make both live broadcasts and audio and video recordings available on the Internet. It will also make it possible to included narrated presentations on web pages.

The training coordinators have begun video conferencing for the purpose of planning training events. This method will be utilized increasingly for problem solving around issues of implementation as well as for planning. A series of university-level courses will be offered using the Internet. Such projects can benefit from additional communication among participants using such mechanisms as listservs, e-mail, chat rooms, and bulletin boards (Mesher, 1999). These will be established to support the courses as appropriate. Statewide conferences and other workshops and meetings that take place at the University will be broadcast to the local sites.

Some of the model programs have already established web sites. These will be developed for all the model sites and will include links to training materials and information about training events and workshops, both web-based and traditional. The web sites will include forms that have been developed in model programs for service planning and documentation, information about upcoming events, and other materials.

As the state office broadens implementation of this model, additional sites will join the network, increasing its complexity and its utility across the state. Four additional sites will be established during the next year; each site will be furnished with hardware and software and with a training coordinator, doubling the size of the network from four sites to eight and moving to 16-20 sites within two years. Not surprisingly, universities in geographical proximity to the model programs have become interested in using the technology, and have requested specifications for the equipment. In addition, the state office has purchased equipment so that direct access to the network is now possible from state offices as well.

SUGGESTIONS FOR REPLICATION

The benefits of using new technology to bring new messages to providers in the field are apparent. These benefits apply whether the service system is for children or adults, and whether it is a system organized by the state office or a local entity. However, for services to children, federal funding is available to state agencies for training under Title IV-E of the Social Security Act, to enhance services to vulnerable children, improve their safety and security, and to avoid the need for out-of-home placement. These training funds can be used to support the type of communication and the training network described previously.

It is important that local sites and the state office have mutually agreed-upon goals for training and have delineated the content areas for such training. As with all state-local plans, training needs assessments should be updated at agreed-upon intervals.

It is worth mentioning again the rationale for choosing an Internet-based technology, as it is our belief that this technology is easy for people to use and ultimately less expensive. Although funding is available for developing and maintaining such a training network, using existing equipment obviously minimizes the costs. Internet connections are relatively inexpensive and broadly available. Personal computers with adequate speed and capacity, as well as the additional hardware and software that are needed for this effort, are now broadly available and they have continued to decrease in price.

CONCLUSION

It is apparent that technology will be increasingly important in preparing service providers for their roles. The National Association of Social Workers (NASW) has been urged to provide on-line training for its members (Marlowe-Carr, 1997). Many issues still need to be addressed as the technology evolves. The rapid pace of development in the area of technology means that decisions about connectivity and equipment are sometimes made based on dated information. It has become apparent that the capabilities of the technology lag behind the vision for its use. Picture and sound quality, which will undoubtedly improve over time, can be quite poor without obvious explanation. The best-planned training agenda fails when connections cannot be established. Despite these difficulties, technology offers the promise of new possibilities for communicating and exchanging ideas. This project provides an exciting opportunity to participate in fulfilling that promise.

REFERENCES

Abramson, J.S. & Mizrahi, T. (1996). When social workers and physicians collaborate: Positive and negative interdisciplinary experiences. *Social Work, 41* (3), 270-281.

Bailey, D.B., Simeonsson, R.J, Yoder, D.E, & Huntington, G.S. (1990). Preparing professionals to serve infants and toddlers with handicaps and their families: An integrative analysis across eight disciplines. *Exceptional Children, 57* (1), 26-35.

Behar, L.B., Zipper, I.N., McCammon, S., Spencer, S., McKinnon-Lewis, C. (1998, June). *Partnerships with universities for human resource development.* Paper presented at Developing Local Systems of Care in a Managed Care Environment Conference. Orlando.

Beller, M. & Or, E. (1998). The crossroads between lifelong learning and information technology: A challenge facing leading universities. *Journal of Computer-Mediated Communication.* (Online), *4* (2). <*http://www.ascusc.org/jcmc/vol4/issue2/beller.html*>. (1999, July 28).

Bickman, L., (1997). Resolving issues raised by the Fort Bragg evaluation. *American Psychologist, 52* (5), 562-565.

Brown, F.W. (1998). Rural telepsychiatry. *Psychiatric Services, 49* (7), 963-964.

Christoph, R.T., Schoenfeld, G.A., & Tansky, J.W. (1998). Overcoming barriers to training utilizing technology: The influence of self-efficacy factors on multimedia-based training receptiveness. *Human Resource Development Quarterly, 9* (1), 25-38.

England, M.J. & Cole, R.F. (1998). Preparing for communities of care for child and family mental health for the twenty-first century. *Child and Adolescent Psychiatric Clinics of North America, 7* (3), 469-481.

Gattiker, U.E. (1990). Individual differences and acquiring computer literacy: Are women more efficient than men? In U.E. Gattiker, Ed. *End-User Training.* Pp. 141-180. Berlin: Walter deGruyter.

Gibelman, M. & Champagne, B. (1981). A consumer information system for staff development and training. *Journal of Continuing Social Work Education, 1* (1), 7-26.

Goldstein, I.L. & Gilliam, P. (1990). Training system issues in the Year 2000. *American Psychologist, 45* (2), 134-143.

Harasim, L., Starr, R.H., Teles, L., & Turoff, M. (1995). *Learning Networks.* Boston: Massachusetts Institute of Technology.

Marlowe-Carr, L.C. (1997). Social workers on-line: A profile. *Computers in Human Services, 14* (1), 59-70.

Mesher, D. (1999). Designing interactivities for Internet learning. *Syllabus* [Online], *12* (7), 4 pages. <http://www.syllabus.com/mar99_magfea.html> (1999, April 27).

Meyers, J., Kaufman, M.A., & Goldman, S. (1999). Promising practices: Training strategies for serving children with serious emotional disturbance and their families in a system of care. *Systems of care: Promising practice in children's mental health*, 1998 Series, Volume V. Washington, DC: Center for Effective Collaboration and Practice, American Institutes for Research.

Osher, T.W. (1994, October). *Getting me on your team: Building partnerships with families.* Paper presented at a symposium sponsored by the Westchester County Department of Community Mental Health, Westchester, NY.

Oliver, J.P.J. & Huxley, P.J. (1988). The development of computer assisted learning

(CAL) materials for teaching and testing mental health social work in Great Britain: A review of four years progress. *Journal of Teaching in Social Work, 2* (2), 21-34.

Reid, I.C. (1999). Beyond models: Developing a university strategy for on-line instruction. *Journal of Asynchronous Learning Networks*, [Online], *3* (1). <*http://www. aln.org/alnweb/journal/Vol3_issue1/JALN3_1_ma.htm*> (1999, July 26).

Roberts, R., Rule, S., & Innocenti, M. (1998). *Strengthening the Family-Professional Partnership in Services for Young Children.* Baltimore: Paul H. Brookes.

Saleeby, D. (1997). *The Strengths Perspective in Social Work Practice* (2nd ed.). New York: Longman

Salzar, M.S., & Bickman, L. (1997) Delivering effective children's services in the community: Reconsidering the benefits of system interventions. *Applied and Preventive Psychology, 6,* 1-13.

Sands, R.G., Stafford, J., & McClelland, M. (1990). I beg to differ: Conflict in the interdisciplinary team. *Social Work in Health Care, 14* (3), 55-72.

Simpson, J.S., Koroloff, N., Friesen, B.F., & Gac, J. (1999). Promising practices in family-provider collaboration. *Systems of Care: Promising Practices in Children's Mental Health*, 1998 Series, Volume II. Washington, DC: Center for Effective Collaboration and Practice, American Institutes for Research.

Solnit, A.J., Adnopoz, J., Saxe, L., Gardner, J., & Fallon, T. (1997). Evaluating systems of care for children: Utility of the clinical case conference. *American Journal of Orthopsychiatry, 67* (4), 554-567.

Stroul, B.A. & Friedman, R.M. (1986). *A system of care for children and youth with severe emotional disturbances.* (Revised edition). Washington, DC: Georgetown University Child Development Center, CASSP Technical Assistance Center.

Uzzell, D. (1997). *San Mateo: A Clinical Ethnography of a Suburban County.* Tampa: University of South Florida, Louis de la Parte Florida Mental Health Institute.

The Requirements of Community:
An Online Survey of the Social Work
Access Network (SWAN)

Michael A. Wright

SUMMARY. This study details the typical user profile of visitors to the Social Work Access Network (SWAN) website. The online survey methodology is discussed along with data that benchmarks expected response rates for this method. User preferences for additional content and interactive opportunities as well as user satisfaction with the current site are described. It is concluded that the social work professionals must seek new ways to define, organize and implement a portal on the World Wide Web by building partnerships among sites offering social work content. In support of this, SWAN must evolve to provide a platform for discussion among the social work community through online gatherings using chat and bulletin board technologies. *[Article copies available for a fee from The Haworth Document Delivery Service: 1-800-342-9678. E-mail address: <getinfo@haworthpressinc.com> Website: <http://www.haworthpressinc.com>]*

KEYWORDS. Paperless survey, community, online, web research, portal, metasite

INTRODUCTION

Mining online resources for the social work profession continues to be an important part of effective use of Internet technologies. Meta-

Michael A. Wright is a PhD candidate at the University of South Carolina Columbia and Assistant Professor at Andrews University, Berrien Springs, MI 49104-0038 (E-mail wrightm@andrews.edu).

[Haworth co-indexing entry note]: "The Requirements of Community: An Online Survey of the Social Work Access Network (SWAN)." Wright, Michael. Co-published simultaneously in *Journal of Technology in Human Services* (The Haworth Press, Inc.) Vol. 17, No. 1, 2000, pp. 69-81; and: *Human Services Online: A New Arena for Service Delivery* (ed: Jerry Finn, and Gary Holden) The Haworth Press, Inc., 2000, pp. 69-81. Single or multiple copies of this article are available for a fee from The Haworth Document Delivery Service [1-800-342-9678, 9:00 a.m. - 5:00 p.m. (EST). E-mail address: getinfo@ haworthpressinc.com].

sites, World Wide Web (WWW) sites that catalog social work online resources of varying number, have continued to proliferate (O'Shea, 1999). The age of the static website, however, is over. Interactive websites involving user input are rapidly evolving. Today, the WWW can also be used to accomplish professional development. The phrase "professional development" refers to the education and training expected of all social workers. It is a development that does not end with graduation or certification. According to the NASW Code of Ethics, ethical social workers attain and continue to develop competence in the current skills of the social work professional. Metasites are one means for social workers to continue their professional development.

This paper reports the results of an online survey to assess the satisfaction and needs of the users of the Social Work Access Network (SWAN). The assessment survey is designed to provide data for revision and continued development the SWAN website. The study assumes that users know best what they want, and seeks to answer the following questions: What are the level of satisfaction and the perceived needs of survey respondents visiting the SWAN website? The survey results offer data to support further production of online resources with the goal of professional development within the community of online social workers.

A BRIEF HISTORY OF SWAN

SWAN became the property of the College of Social Work at the University of South Carolina in 1995 when it was acquired from its creator, Peter Thomas. Since that time, the site has gone through more than a few "renovations." Throughout, the goal of connecting social workers online and providing links to other social work WWW sites has remained consistent.

The SWAN site acts as a meta-list, as do many sites, in that it lists hundreds of Internet resources related to social work. These include school Websites, listservs, and newsgroups. The hallmark of the SWAN site is the "Virtual Community" of social work professionals. In cooperation with the Social Work Café, another community-building website, SWAN maintains a database of social work professionals, students and faculty members. A data-management mechanism allows the website administrator to send electronic mail (e-mail) to all members of the SWAN site at once, as well as allowing any member to search for colleagues and e-mail them individually. Members are carried in the database until they request deletion or e-mail is returned (bounced) from the e-mail address listed for them.

Between September 22, 1997, when maintenance of the website was delegated to a PhD graduate assistant, and the Fall 1998 Social Work Educators and Practitioners Technology Conference, the number of visitors to the site doubled from about 500 to over 1,000 visitors per week. Registered members of the site increased 400%. The college was satisfied with the development of the site. Yet, at least two sessions at the September 1998 conference spoke of weaknesses in the SWAN site. The site was described as slow to be updated and as having many inoperative links. The problem was that the emphasis on increasing membership and visitors to the site was misplaced. Conference attendees who provided feedback seemed to want reliable, current information.

SWAN has taken steps to improve the slow response times and dead links. The site now has mechanisms that allow users to register and add information in real time. Yet, in the analyses by the College of Social Work Educational Technology Committee and the technology implemented by the PhD graduate assistant, it becomes apparent that one voice was missing, that of the user.

The solution, listening to the clients, is what social workers are trained from the beginning to do. Whether it be with clients facing eating disorders or general assessment interviewing, social workers are taught to listen to clients to inform service provision (Shekter-Wolfson & Woodside, 1997; Van Voorhis, 1998). This principle is applied to the development of social work resources as well. Hence, the SWAN Satisfaction Survey and Needs Assessment was initiated.

This study assesses user satisfaction with the structure of the site (i.e., content, design, navigation of the site, popular areas, etc.), and solicits input about visitor needs (e.g., news, interaction/chat, e-mail, etc.). Satisfaction (or site quality) and visitor needs are primary considerations in Website development (Lynch & Horton, 1999). In addition to quality and needs, this study investigates information about the people that access the site in terms of the capabilities of their computers.

Quality, rated by customers, is not the only concern in determining the efficacy of products and services. Loyalty must also be factored into the equation. Users may visit the site, but never share the resource with others or use the site for important needs such as their job tasks.

These four areas (quality, needs, capability, and loyalty) are used to develop a Typical User Profile (TUP). With a knowledge of the TUP, SWAN is able to assess the extent to which it is meeting current goals and determine what future directions best meet visitor's needs.

ELECTRONIC SURVEY METHODS

Though there have been extensive reviews of electronic mail (e-mail) as a method of survey research (Thach, 1995), there are fewer examinations of the online survey method via a web page interface. In comparison to traditional mail service, e-mail has lower response rates, but there seems to be no difference in the response rates of e-mail versus telephone survey methodology (Schuldt & Totten, 1994). There are challenges with this method unrelated to response rates also. Some e-mail surveys will be answered in paper form, thus reducing the perceived benefit of easier data entry.

It is not in the purview of this study to compare methods, but the promise of fewer missing values is a valuable benefit that a web or online survey has in comparison to paper-based methodology. This benefit comes with what some have found to be comparable item variability and similar internal covariance patterns to paper-based surveys (Stanton, 1998). Of course, the main benefit is coding time. This data in this study, excluding the open-ended question, was downloaded from the server and imported into SPSS for analysis in less than a half-hour.

METHOD

Participants. A total of 2,692 individual users from the SWAN member database were contacted by e-mail and invited to visit the survey online and respond. A message on the first page of the SWAN site also invited participation. A response rate of 22.2% was achieved based on 598 users responding. At the time of the survey, the SWAN database held 881 Field Professionals, 207 Faculty Members, 919 Students or Recent Grads, 26 Social Work Staff Members, 18 Information Systems Personnel, and 645 Unclassified. These categories were not tracked so the demographic characteristics of the survey respondents are unknown.

The immediate question is whether this rate of response is appropriate. Little literature exists about response rates, effectiveness and reliability related to online or paperless surveys. Basic information for producing baseline expectations is lacking (Schonland & Williams, 1996). Literature available reports response rates as low as 10% (Webster, 1995).

There are many companies conducting and consulting in online survey methodology. There is general agreement that there is a great deal of response variation depending on the respondent base and other factors. One firm, whose research division has begun to track response rates, reports a current response average of 15-20% (personal communication, T. Nelson, Perseus Development Corp., April 1, 1999). The SWAN rate was 29.2%. The creator of *Survey Assistant*, a Canadian product used in academic research, states that, of those who come to visit an online survey, about 70% become respondents (personal communication, W. C. Schmidt, March 31, 1999). The SWAN survey informed consent page was visited by 810 individuals over the course of the survey period. Of these, there was a 73.8% response rate for individuals answering the appeals to respond. In order to bolster the response rate, direct e-mail was sent a total of five times during the survey period.

Survey instrument. The survey used twenty-four forced-choice questions including a "no-response" option to gain information related to the four previously discussed areas (quality, needs, capability, and loyalty). The survey was formatted in a selection box format. All options to each question were visible to the respondent, and the "no-response" option was defaulted. To select a response, the user clicks his/her choice with the mouse. The survey was developed by the Website administrator based on questions he believed to be important in assessing the needs of the online community. The survey was piloted for one week with the faculty of the College of Social Work at the University of South Carolina. Based on the feedback from this pilot, the form was revised to include an open-ended question about the SWAN website at the end of the survey.

Quality, needs, capability, and loyalty were assessed through twenty-one closed and one open-ended questions. In addition, two general, close-ended questions provided information concerning the respondent's location in the world and whether he/she is a member of SWAN. Other demographic data was not collected because there are no plans to use data such as age, race, sex, etc., to influence the site's future development.

Procedure. A web-based mechanism was used to administer the survey. Users were contacted through e-mail five times between February 27, 1999 and March 19, 1999 and asked to visit a specified web page that housed the survey. Upon visiting the site, users were greeted with an informed consent form that asked them to read, provide their e-mail address, and click a selection box to confirm their willingness to participate and their understanding of the form. A Perl script prevented the perspective respondent from viewing the survey if they did not select the box confirming their understanding of the informed consent form. Upon clicking the "submit" button, users were transferred to the survey web-form page. In order to safeguard against duplicate responses, e-mail addresses were kept in a separate file from the survey responses. Once a user entered their e-mail address and answered the survey, they could not enter the survey again with the same e-mail address.

RESULTS

Quality. Respondents were asked to rate the quality of the SWAN Website for content, design and navigation on a six-point scale (with 6 being the highest satisfaction) so as not to allow for a midpoint. As can be seen in Table 1, over half of the respondents (51.3%) rated the site either a 4 or 5 for content. Design was rated 4 or 5 by 47.8% of the respondents. Navigation of the site was rated 4 or 5 by 42.8% of

TABLE 1. Satisfaction Rating Percentages by Response

Scale Options 1-6	Areas Rated		
	Content	Design	Navigation
(1) Most Every Site Is Better	2.7%	2.7%	3.0%
(2) Needs Work but has Potential	11.2	8.7	8.0
(3) Just Like Many Others	13.2	19.6	25.3
(4) Better than Average	36.1	34.3	28.9
(5) Few Sites Are Better	15.2	13.5	13.9
(6) SWAN Is the Best	5.9	5.4	4.2
No Response	15.7	15.9	16.7

respondents. The mean scores for content, design and navigation were 3.8, 3.75, and 3.66 respectively while the median and mode held constant at 4 ("Better Than Average") for each ranking.

In response to the question of the favorite SWAN resource, 33.8% of respondents chose the Topics/Links section of the website. It is important to note that 31.1% of the respondents chose "It's All So Good, I Can't Choose." The next highest resource chosen was the Publications Section with 9.5%. The Chat section was rated most frequently as the least favorite swan resource (19.9%). Those selecting the Chat section as least favorite used the open-ended response area to state that the chat offerings should be more targeted and purposefully scheduled with experts in various areas. Most respondents (59.9%) did not choose a least favorite section.

Needs. Users were overwhelmingly positive (90.3%) when asked if they were interested in a search engine specific to social work content. Over half of the respondents (51.2%) would like to receive e-mail messages concerning technology grants, education and social work practice on a weekly basis. Another 38.8% would welcome news messages via e-mail on a monthly basis.

Respondents welcomed the idea of viewing an online simulcast of a social work technology conference. Only 18.6% of respondents said they would not like to see the simulcast at all. Of those wishing to view a simulcast, 42.3% want to see plenary speakers and selected sessions, while 17.4% would like to view speakers, sessions and off-program meetings.

By a measure of 61%, respondents are opposed to paying for access to SWAN simulcast of a technology conference. Those who would pay are willing to compensate SWAN at a median rate of $25. Responses ranged from $5 to $150.

A majority of respondents approved the use of an online survey method. Most respondents (69.2%) said they would be interested in participating is an online survey concerning another topic.

Capability. Profiling the capabilities of the respondents included their computer hardware and software as well as their primary access point and their Internet service provider. Over 80% of respondents report Internet access speeds above 28.8kbps, 68.7% between 28.8 and 56kbps and 12.4% T1/LAN or faster. The vast majority, 82.7%, of respondents uses either Microsoft Internet Explorer or a Netscape product to browse the Web.

Respondents report accessing SWAN most from home (69.1%) and less frequently from the office (20.4%) or a school setting (5.9%). Respondents use some method other than the major Internet providers to connect from their locations. Concerning Internet service providers (ISPs), the highest percentage responded "Other" (65.9%), followed by America Online (17.6%).

Loyalty. Most of the respondents (58.4%) have told fewer than five people about the SWAN website; 25.3% have shared the site with more than five persons. Most of the respondents (71.4%) visit SWAN once a month or less. Respondents report visiting mostly on weekdays (49.3%) with numbers trailing off for the weekends (28.6%). Just over half of respondents (56.7%) selected "Just Browsing" in response to the question concerning why they use the SWAN website. The remaining respondents were divided between using SWAN for school, 15.9%, and work assignments, 20.1%.

Brief Demographics

Survey respondents were reported living mostly in the Eastern United States (52.8%). The next most reported area of the world was the Western United States with 21.6% of respondents. Approximately one-fifth of respondents originated in foreign countries. The vast majority, 88%, of survey respondents indicated that they are members listed within the SWAN database.

Open Ended Responses

Needs assessed through an open-ended question were mainly related to content. Suggestions included attention to Canadian and international content, more human services-related issues and news, more information targeted to students completing papers, practical tips and resources (including software) for practitioners, discussion or chat with leading theorists and senior practitioners, informal chat between special interest groups, information on job vacancies, full-text journal article availability for a low price, and information on scholarships and loans. A new method of listing members, by geographic region, was suggested repeatedly. Also, more than one respondent suggested that SWAN advertise more.

DISCUSSION

Typical user profile. The typical user of the SWAN website is in the U.S., probably East of the Mississippi, browsing from home on a standard (28.8-56k) modem. Their greatest frustration is not being able to find what they want easily. When they do find what they want, be it a link or a chat group, they are disappointed to find that it doesn't fit their need. The link may be dead or the chat group may have disbanded. If improvements are made to the site, the typical user may not hear about them until he/she visits the site the following month.

Satisfaction with the SWAN website is tied closely to the resources that it presents. Analysis of the results support a focus on topics and links. Though the typical user supports having an increase in the number of resources, navigation of the site must be addressed to provide more logical access to the resources. The key for the development of SWAN is that it continues to offer the most comprehensive and verified content. The perception of SWAN as an online community is crippled because it doesn't moderate any of its listed content. For example, respondents were disappointed with chat rooms listed by SWAN, yet SWAN has no chat room that it moderates. In the future, SWAN will have to take proactive steps toward being a provider of community tools rather than just a meta-list of providers. The membership list is a definite asset in that it offers searchability by keywords and interests, but users want the ability to find colleagues with various interests by variables such as state. This function is not yet implemented on SWAN. The typical user is certainly able technologically to handle the implementation of these suggestions. The speed of access to the Internet and their choice of browser provide the minimum for many advanced WWW features.

Supported future directions. The needs of the SWAN audience are more advanced than the site currently presents. In addition to a demonstration of their desire for the content suggested in the survey, open-ended suggestions spanned a wide range of logical offerings of a world-reaching professional development publication.

To meet the needs of users, SWAN could conceivably become a portal to social work on the Web. Mining the content for such an offering and keeping it up to date may be too much for one institution to accomplish with part-time staff. It is a continual process that requires identification, review, and rechecking online offerings to make sure they haven't been discontinued.

An organizing mechanism is also needed to make sense and logical connections within such mass amounts of data. This system of organizing social work online content has not been advanced yet. There has been work in the area of information retrieval within professional fields (Malet, Munoz, Appleyard & Hersh, 1999). There are also directories of services, the most well known of which are sponsored in cooperation with the Alliance of Information & Retrieval Systems (AIRS). But, the content of the profession of social work has not been mapped hierarchically. This process requires a defined set of document content description tags, a standard professional vocabulary and content descriptions (Wright, 1999).

Future online surveys need to address usage patterns in SWAN as a real measure of "loyalty." Though many enjoy what the site offers, users desire more. They desire the type of site that enables them to come together as a profession and build their careers and the social work community. One way to make this happen is to build the infrastructure for a network of social work websites. The objectives would be to centralize key portions of the maintenance workload and demonstrate social work cohesion in response to technology through the provision of web space and consistent maintenance assistance. In theory, the reduction of duplication among social work websites would enable the current social work web maintenance workforce to develop specialized content within the same time and budget constraints.

Weaknesses of the study. Some limitations of this study exist. First, given the limited response rate and the lack of demographic information collected, it is not clear who responded to the survey. It is not known whether the respondent members from the SWAN database are students, faculty members, retirees, or field professionals. It is not clear who responded to the survey. Thus, the needs assessment may be based on an unrepresentative sample of SWAN members.

After reviewing the question, "What suggestions do you have for SWAN?", the ability to organize suggestions by groups would be helpful in developing grouped areas of the website. That is, if the group represented by the respondents was known, analysis of the clustering of suggestions according to group could be used to develop new sections of the site that are tailored to specific groups.

Another limitation may be the assumption of asking users about needs. It stands to reason that, when asked, users will suggest having more content and services with little thought to the cost. Indeed, 64.4% of respondents want online simulcasts of social work conferences, but only 19.2% want to pay for them. Said another way, 54% of those who want some form of web simulcast want it free of charge. Future surveys of social work meta-sites will need to address the extent to which participants are willing to pay for additional web-based services.

A third concern is based on the lack of scholarly literature about developing websites and online community. Many reports are found in popular journals or manuscripts written for popular audiences. Few methodologically sound studies with clear scientific agendas have been published. The merit of paperless survey methodology and evaluation of online community face challenges such as inadequately tested mechanisms, untested reliability and validity of instruments when used online, and unclear sampling methods. Notwithstanding, the conclusions drawn from this study are an impetus for further exploration of online community development generally and online social work portals specifically.

Suggestions for online research. Based on this experience, there are a few guidelines for future online survey research. One of the most important steps in the development of the online survey, besides the traditional review of the literature, is the sampling. For this survey, the sample was the group whose e-mail addresses were on file with SWAN. Any prescreening that can be done with the sample should be done. For example, the large number of "unclassified" addresses in the SWAN database could have been classified. This would have made tracking of the respondent sub-groups more meaningful. Without this critical step accomplished, the data could not be classified according to respondent sub-groups. Other research procedures followed in this study are suggested for future surveys.

- Pretest the survey. Knowing in advance how persons interpret the questions is important to getting the data of interest.
- Provide a response at the conclusion of the survey thanking the participants.
- Send e-mail messages requesting respondents. Some respondents indicated that they finally completed the survey because they felt guilty.

- With an identified sample such as the one used in this study, only send reminders to those who have not responded. A few users indicated that they were tired of receiving the requests to complete the survey because they had already done so.

FUTURE DIRECTIONS

It is conceivable that many of the difficulties highlighted in this study are issues for other social work online offerings. Under the goal of developing professionals, it is important that the profession seek ways to define, organize and implement a portal to social work on the World Wide Web. Studies such as this one provide definition and direction. Initiatives such as the development of a hierarchy of Social Work Topics will provide organization (Wright, 1999).

Implementation of a network of sites can be accomplished as partnerships are built between institutions producing social work specific information online. Currently, this coalescence has been demonstrated among select individuals (http://www.geocities.com/Heartland/4862/cswhome.html). Metasites can become partners in producing content that does not duplicate the efforts of other websites. Such partnerships may be able to offset the cost of maintenance while providing low-cost platform for education, training and informing social work professionals.

SWAN may take its commitment to online community building further by moderating chat events, bulletin-board services and its own mailing list. The user survey did give some suggestions of discussion topics. Respondents seemed interested in hearing from and chatting with noted therapists and practitioners in social work. Software and server space is needed to accomplish this. In addition, the user survey respondents recommend that advertising be a top priority in order to help fund the system.

Throughout the process of developing content partnerships and online community building, the paperless survey method may prove invaluable. With further testing and exploration in scholarly literature, this method will mature into a respected method of inquiry. With its potential for quick analysis through instant porting into a computerized statistical package, the paperless survey may support more "ask the client" approaches to social work by reducing costs and difficulty of survey administration.

REFERENCES

Lynch, P. J. & Horton, S. (1999). *Web style guide: basic design principles for creating Websites.* New Haven, CT : Yale University Press.

Malet, G., Munoz, F., Appleyard, R & Hersh, W. A. (1999). Model for enhancing Internet medical document retrieval with "Medical Core Metadata." *Journal of the American Medical Informatics Association, 6(2).* 163-72.

O'Shea, D. (1998). *Social work programs and associated resources.* [Web Page]. http://socwork.uindy.edu/links/meta1.htm [July 29, 1999].

Schonland, A. M. & Williams, P. W. (1996). Using the Internet for travel and tourism survey research: Experiences from the net traveler survey. *Journal of Travel Research, 35(2).* 7(2).

Schuldt, B. A. & Totten, J. W. (1994). Electronic mail vs. mail survey response rates. *Marketing Research, 6(1).* 36(4).

Shekter-Wolfson, L. F. & Woodside, D. B. (1997). Social work treatment of anorexia and bulimia: Guidelines for practice. *Research on Social Work Practice, 7(1).* 5(27).

Stanton, J. M. (1998). An empirical assessment of data collection using the Internet. *Personnel Psychology, 51(3).* 709(17).

Thach, L. (1995). Using electronic mail to conduct survey research. *Educational Technology, 35(2).* 27-31.

Van Voorhis, R. M. (1998). Culturally relevant practice: A framework for teaching the psychosocial dynamics of oppression. *Journal of Social Work Education, 34(1).* 121(13).

Webster, K. G. (1995). The use of IT in library evaluation: Electronic surveying at the University of Newcastle. Paper presented at the Northumbria International Conference on Performance Measurement in Libraries and Information Services Northumberland, England.

Wright, M. (1999). *Taxonomy of social work topics: Organizing online content.* Manuscript in preparation. Andrews University.

A Survey
of Domestic Violence Organizations
on the World Wide Web

Jerry Finn

SUMMARY. This paper presents the results of an exploratory study of one hundred sixty-six domestic violence organizations that use the World Wide Web. Domestic violence agencies primarily used the Web to promote agency visibility and provide community education, and to a lesser extent for advocacy, direct services, and securing resources. Agency satisfaction with their Website is generally high, although more than one-third of agencies reported problems. Related issues discussed include Web-based sources of client victimization, agency legal liability, agency vulnerability to online disruption, the need to create access for low-income clients, and evaluation of Web services. *[Article copies available for a fee from The Haworth Document Delivery Service: 1-800-342-9678. E-mail address: <getinfo@haworthpressinc.com> Website: <http://www.haworthpressinc.com>]*

KEYWORDS. Domestic violence, Internet, World Wide Web, non-profit, online therapy

INTRODUCTION

There has been increasing discussion in the literature about the use of the Internet by providers and consumers of human services (Grob-

Jerry Finn, PhD, is Professor, Department of Social Work, University of New Hampshire, Durham, NH.

[Haworth co-indexing entry note]: "A Survey of Domestic Violence Organizations on the World Wide Web." Finn, Jerry. Co-published simultaneously in *Journal of Technology in Human Services* (The Haworth Press, Inc.) Vol. 17, No. 1, 2000, pp. 83-102; and: *Human Services Online: A New Arena for Service Delivery* (ed: Jerry Finn, and Gary Holden) The Haworth Press, Inc., 2000, pp. 83-102. Single or multiple copies of this article are available for a fee from The Haworth Document Delivery Service [1-800-342-9678, 9:00 a.m. - 5:00 p.m. (EST). E-mail address: getinfo@haworthpressinc.com].

man & Grant, 1998; Miller & DiGiuseppe, 1998; McNutt, 1998; Finn & Lavitt, 1994). The literature suggests that agency use of the Internet can be viewed as accomplishing five primary functions: agency visibility, direct services, community education, advocacy, and securing resources. Much of the literature has focused either on theoretical discussions of the potential of the Internet to deliver services or on descriptions of specific Internet-based Websites or services. While there are a variety of Websites that focus on issues related to nonprofit and human service organizations (Grobman & Grant, 1998; Ferguson, 1996; McNutt, 1996; Zeff, 1996), there has been little empirical study of the types of services offered online or the benefits and problems encountered by human service organizations in providing these services. This paper focuses on a survey of domestic violence agencies that provide a Website on the Internet. Domestic violence agencies were chosen for study because they often have multiple goals, serve clients who may be reluctant to seek traditional services, and engage in a variety of the functions that might be delivered or supplemented on the Internet. An examination of domestic violence organizations may therefore provide information related to the larger body of non-profit social service agencies.

Domestic Violence Services Online

The five primary functions noted above, *agency visibility, direct services, community education, advocacy, and securing resources,* are used as an organizing framework for discussion of domestic violence services on the Internet.

Agency Visibility. Domestic violence agencies are beginning to use the Internet to meet some of their needs for publicity. The Internet allows agencies to publicize their mission, services, policies, and successes to a broad audience. A Website may be seen by the agency as one sign that they are a "progressive" agency. Agency visibility is especially important since domestic violence has long been considered a "hidden crime," and the promotion of agency services is seen as one method of increasing community awareness in this area (Gelles & Straus, 1988; Walker, 1984). One indicator of the extent to which domestic organizations have a Web presence is the number of Web pages with the words "domestic violence," "spouse abuse" or "family violence." In February 1999, 24,880 Web pages were indexed by the *Hotbot* (*http://www.hotbot.com/*) search engine within the *.org* (nonprofit organization) domain. This represents a thirty-seven percent increase over a similar search six months earlier. The number of all Web pages, including *.com,* with the same words indexed by the *Altavista (http://www.digital.altavista.com/)* search engine (February, 1999) was 113,353. While these figures show that there is much activity on the Internet related to domestic violence, they are only a very rough estimate since some organizations may not be found using these search engines and others might be listed several times.

Direct Services. Finn (2000) described a variety of domestic violence organizations on the Internet that provided one or more of the following services: online assessment of violent relationships, outreach to victims and survivors, information and referral, direct services through e-mail, providing links to monitored chat rooms and online support groups, and posting stories and art of domestic violence survivors. There are several reasons that domestic violence agencies are beginning to offer their services on the Internet. Domestic violence services are seeing increased service demands in a time of limited resources. (Bachman & Saltzman, 1995; Gelles & Conte, 1990). The Internet may be used to supplement agency services or provide services to those who would not otherwise seek them. In addition, persons may not seek services or information due to other constraint factors such as care-giving responsibilities, lack of transportation, physical or social isolation, and physical or psychological disabilities. The Internet also provides consumers with a means to obtain help that is otherwise unavailable in a local community. For example, it can offer culturally relevant information on domestic violence and present service options not locally obtainable.

Concerns have also been raised about the provision of online services to clients. These include issues regarding the as yet unproven effectiveness of online treatment, the lack of visual cues, lack of availability to intervene in an emergency, difficulties inherent in synchronous communication, and potential communication failures due to technical breakdowns (Lebow, 1998). In addition, ethical concerns have been raised about the privacy, security, confidentiality, and uncertainty of online transactions (Bloom, 1998). Legal concerns about the establishment of a treatment relationship, licensing, and liability in working with clients online have also been raised (Pergament, 1998; Appleman, 1995; Lewis, 1997; Huang & Alessi, 1996; Johnson and

Post, 1996). The extent to which domestic violence organizations offer direct services or have concerns about their use is unknown.

Community Education. Many domestic violence organizations seek to increase public awareness about the nature and extent of domestic violence. Domestic violence agency Websites can present statistics on types of abuse, characteristics of abusers and victims, theories and models of the causes of domestic violence (in lay terms), descriptions of intervention services, explanations of laws and legal processes relating to domestic violence, and links to people or organizations that provide educational information. In addition, the Web's multimedia features allow educational material to include graphics, photographs, animations, art, stories, audio recordings, and video clips to enhance the presentation of materials. Finally, the information on the Internet can be routinely and easily updated so that it will remain current and relevant.

Advocacy. The advantages and potential of the Internet to organize and coordinate change efforts has been described as the most powerful tool for political organizing developed in the last fifty years (Schwartz, 1996). It allows organizations to access and provide information at relatively low cost. In addition, they can communicate and coordinate more quickly and effectively with supporters, partners, the press, the public, and policy makers (Kraus, Stein, & Clark, 1998; Young, 1997). Since their inception, domestic violence organizations have actively sought to bring about social and legal changes concerning the plight of battered women (McNutt & Boland, 1998; Mann, 1995; Mizrahi et al., 1991). Websites on domestic violence can provide an inexpensive method to inform the public about laws, policies and issues of import to a particular agency or community, to publicize national awareness campaigns, and to promote advocacy for social change.

Secure Resources. There are a number of reports of human service agency Websites being used to solicit funds, goods, services, and volunteers (Brandt, 1998; Bailey, Green, 1998; 1997; Hawthorne, 1997; Ensman, 1997; Allen, Stein, & Warwick, 1996; Moore, 1995). The proportion of funds and volunteers received has thus far generally been quite low. Recently, in a survey of human service agencies on the Internet, Finn (1999) found that approximately one-third of agencies engaged in fundraising and volunteer recruitment from their Website. There is yet no information about the extent to which domestic violence organizations utilize the Internet to secure resources or how successful they are in procuring them.

The use of the Web as a tool for assisting victims of violence and for promoting social justice is in its infancy. There is yet no empirical study of the services, costs, and benefits of using the Web by domestic violence organizations. This is an exploratory study of domestic violence agency goals and functions in using the Web. In addition, agency satisfaction and concerns with their Website are examined.

METHOD

Procedure. In order to examine use of the Internet by domestic violence agencies, three hundred agencies were selected from a pool of agencies on the Internet that were found using the *Altavista* and *Hotbot* Internet search engines. The search was conducted in June 1998. The phrases "domestic violence," "spouse abuse," and "family violence" were used to locate potential agencies. The author and an MSW research assistant selected Websites if they appeared to have a social service or education function and were a nonprofit organization with a *.org* URL address. For example, organizations such as shelters, domestic violence coalitions, and advocacy organizations were included. Once an agency was selected, its address or phone number was taken from the Website. Surveys were mailed to the agency director. A total of three mailings were used to solicit a suitable response rate.

Survey Instrument. A survey instrument using a combination of closed and open-ended questions was developed to obtain information about agency demographics (size, location, funding, length of time on the Internet, # of "hits"); goals for using the Internet; current functions of the Website; Website development issues; experiences and satisfaction with the Website; ability to secure funds, volunteers and in-kind contributions; and general comments about the agency's use of the Internet.

RESULTS

Participants: One hundred sixty-six (a response rate of 55.3%) agencies responded to the survey. The agencies represent thirty-nine different states in every region of the country as well as two agencies in Canada and one agency in Australia. Table 1 describes the demographic characteristics of the agencies. The majority of agencies had budgets under one million dollars, and had been on the Internet fewer than two years. Most agencies paid nothing or small amounts for the development and maintenance of their Website, instead relying on donations, volunteers and in-house staff.

Goals. Agencies were asked to rate the importance of the goals of *agency visibility, community education, advocacy, direct services,* and *securing resources* on a five-point scale, from 1 (Not at All) to 5 (Highly Important). Table 2 lists the mean, standard deviation, and percent of agencies that view each goal as important (4 or 5). It should be noted that the vast majority of agencies rate agency visibility (86.1%) and community education (75.6%) as Important in contrast with only about ten percent that view secure resources (12.8%), advocacy (11.4%) and direct services (9.4%) as important for their Website. As will be reported later, agency goals are related to agency Overall Satisfaction and to Problems.

Functions of the Website. Agencies were asked to check from a list of functions those that were provided on their Website. Table 3 describes the percent of agencies indicating each function. Most agency sites served multiple functions for being on the Internet. It can be seen that functions that are related to agency visibility such as describing services, mission and goals are provided by almost every agency. With regard to community education, 80.7% of agencies provide educational materials about domestic violence, although only about one-fourth of agencies provide advocacy-related legal or legislative information. With regard to direct services, the vast majority of agencies (81.4%) indicated that they provided emergency and crisis phone numbers, but only a few agencies (18.7%) indicate that they offer online counseling. Websites are beginning to be used to directly secure resources: 41.6% of agencies request volunteers, 37.3% make fundraising requests, and 23.5% solicit goods or services.

Resources: Money, Goods, or Services. Agencies were asked if they ever received donations of money, goods or services as a result of their Website. Only 63.9% of agencies responded to this question. Assuming that non-responding agencies did not receive donations (a conservative position), almost half of all agencies (46.4% [72.6% of responding agencies]) indicated that they did receive donations as a

TABLE 1. Agency Demographic Information

Agency Responses	Percent
Budget	
< $100,000	14.6
$100,000-500,000	37.8
$500,001-1,000,000	20.7
> $1,000,000	26.8
First year on the Internet	
< 1 year	18.6
1-2 years	43.9
2-3 years	24.4
3-5 years	13.1
Who originated the idea to have a Website?	
Administration	39.8
Staff	28.8
Volunteer	12.8
Combination admin. and staff	10.5
Board	5.8
Other	1.2
Who developed the Website?	
Volunteer	35.5
In-house staff	32.5
Combination of staff, volunteer, consultant	21.7
Other	10.2
*Development costs, excluding staff time and salary**	
$0	70.4
$1-1,000	13.8
$1,001-5,000	13.1
$ > 5,000	2.7
*Ongoing monthly costs***	
$0	55.5
$1-100	37.7
> $100	6.8
*Number of hits per week****	
< 100	47.5
101-1,000	42.5
> 1,000	10.0
Who manages the Website?	
In-house staff	47.0
Volunteer	27.1
Combination staff and volunteer	19.3
Consultant	6.6
How often is the Website updated?	
Never	7.5
Few times a year	54.4
Monthly	20.6
Few times a month	11.9
Weekly	3.6
Daily	3.8

*   It is not clear what is included in development costs. It may have included the costs of a Web designer, graphic design, consultant, information development, software, and data entry.

**   It is not clear what is included in monthly costs. It may have included the costs of a Web service provider, telephone charges, graphic design, and data entry.

***   Note: only 80 agencies (47.7%) answered this question.

TABLE 2. Agency Goals for Their Website

GOAL	Mean	Standard Deviation	Percent "Quite" or "Very" Important (4 or 5)
Visibility	4.52	.91	86.1
Education	4.06	1.26	75.6
Resources	2.48	1.24	12.8
Advocacy	2.07	1.19	11.6
Direct Service	1.70	1.11	9.4

TABLE 3. Website Functions

Function of Website	Percent "Yes"	Function of Website	Percent "Yes"
Description of Agency Services	97.6	Legal Information About Domestic violence	26.5
Agency Mission and Goals	96.4	Request for Goods and Services	23.5
Agency Address and Phone Number	96.4	Request for Feedback About Agency Services	22.9
Emergency and Crisis Phone Number	81.4	Forms That Can Be Submitted Online	21.7
Educational Material About Domestic violence	80.7	Stories or Art by Clients/ Survivors	21.7
Email Link to Agency Staff	59.0	Legislative Information About Domestic violence	20.9
Links to Other Domestic Violence Organizations	59.0	Offering Items for Sale As Fundraiser	18.7
Links to Educational Material	56.0	Online Counseling	18.7
Request for Volunteers	41.6	Names of Board Members	13.3
Fundraising Requests	37.3	Agency Annual Report	9.6
Name and Phone Number of Agency Staff	32.5	Search Engine for the Website	5.4
Provide Direct Services	32.5	Secure Web Server for Financial Transactions	3.6
Links to Online Support Groups	27.1	Chat room for Domestic Violence Discussion	1.2

result of their Website. The proportion of all agency contributions coming from the Website, however, was very small, ranging from < 1% to 5%, with 80% of agencies reporting that they receive 2% or less of their total donations through the Website. Agencies reported receiving a variety of donations through their Website, including monetary donations, cleaning supplies, cosmetics, soaps and lotions, raffle ticket sales, and sale of agency items such as pins and coffee mugs.

Pearson Correlation was used to test whether the goals of the agency Website were related to receiving volunteers or receiving resources. As seen in Table 4, there is a significant relationship between the agency goal to *secure resources* and actually receiving resources. In addition, the goal of *agency visibility* is related to a lesser extent to Receiving Volunteers, and is also positively related, but not significantly, to Receiving Resources. There is no significant relationship, between Receiving Resources and other agency goals or agency demographic variables.

Volunteers. Again assuming that non-responding agencies did not receive volunteers, almost half of all agencies (43.4% [61% of responding agencies]) indicated that they did receive volunteers as a result of their Website. It should also be noted that 62.2% of agencies that received volunteers also received donations of money, goods, or services.

A number of agencies provided comments related to volunteers they recruited from the Internet. Others wrote about finding a Board

TABLE 4. Pearson Correlation: Goals, Resources, Satisfaction and Problems

		Received Volunteers	Received Resources	Overall Satisfaction	Problems	Advocacy	Visibility	Education	Obtain Resources
Received Resources	r	.612							
	p	.000**							
Overall Satisfaction	r	.171	.200						
	p	.066	.043*						
Problems	r	.222	.208	−.083					
	p	.017*	.036*	.307					
Advocacy	r	.147	.000	−.006	−.053				
	p	.112	.999	.936	.514				
Visibility	r	.227	.181	.238	.292	.455			
	p	.013*	.064	.003**	.000**	.000**			
Education	r	.338	.144	.102	.081	.790	.626		
	p	.000**	.141	.205	.316	.000**	.000**		
Obtain Resources	r	.490	.547	.082	.123	.409	.541	.539	
	p	.000**	.000**	.307	.127	.000**	.000**	.000*	
Direct Services	r	.067	.126	.266	−.001	.476	.492	.579	.378
	p	.474	.198	.001**	.989	.000**	.000**	.000**	.000**

* Correlation is significant at the 0.05 level (2-tailed).
** Correlation is significant at the 0.01 level (2-tailed).

Member, a VISTA volunteer, a CPA, and Walk-a-thon volunteers. Several agencies reported receiving volunteers who provided services online including Website development, writing and editing projects, graphics design, newsletter production, and brochure development. Two agencies wrote that they received offers of help even though their Website does not request volunteers. Finally, several agencies reported that students at local colleges volunteered to do internships through the Website. One agency that received many volunteers from local colleges stated that they use their Internet site as part of volunteer orientation.

Overall Satisfaction. Agencies were asked to rate their overall satisfaction with their Internet site on a five point scale from 1 (Not at All) to 5 (Very Much). Overall, agencies were satisfied with their Internet site. The mean satisfaction was 3.57 (SD. = .97), and 55.6% rated their satisfaction as high (4 or 5). Only 13.6% of agencies rated their satisfaction as "Not at All" (1) or "A Little" (2). In addition, many agencies made positive comments about their Website experience in the "Comments" section.

Pearson Correlation was used to examine the relationship between *overall satisfaction* and agency goals. As can be seen in Table 4, there is a weak correlation between *overall satisfaction* and the agency goals of *visibility* and *direct services*. Pearson Correlation also examined the relationship between *overall satisfaction* and *receiving resources,* and found a weak association. The relationship was positive but not significant between *overall satisfaction* and *receiving volunteers.*

Evaluation of the Agency Website. Agencies were asked an open-ended question about how they evaluate their Website. The most common response, 46.5%, was that the agency does not evaluate the Website. Among agencies that do evaluate their site, the majority use a counter to obtain the number of "hits" and/or receive informal feedback via guestbook or e-mail. In addition, a variety of other evaluation outcome measures were described by a small number of agencies, including:

- number of requests for information or newsletters,
- number of items sold,
- feedback from other agencies accessing the Website,
- number of donations received,
- number of online requests for speaking engagements,
- number of contacts by the media,
- and placement and ranking of pages by search engines.

Agency Open-Ended Responses. Agencies were asked for open-ended comments about their Website experiences. One theme discussed by several agencies related to the planning and administration of the site. Agencies commented on the importance of strategic planning for the Website, including the vision, goals, target audience, cost, and functions of the Website. Care was urged in the choice of a Web designer and Internet service provider. Agencies had mixed reactions related to the use of volunteers and pro bono services. Finally, several agencies suggested that Website design should not exclude those with text-based browsers or slow modems.

Another theme related to publicizing the Website. Respondents suggested that agencies register their site with major search engines and that agencies put their Web address on all agency materials, including business cards, stationary, newsletters, advertisements, and brochures. It was also suggested that the agencies exchange links with other related Websites and post their Web address on listservs and Usenet groups that focus on the agency mission.

Agency Concerns. Agencies were asked if they experienced any problems or frustrations as a result of their Website. The majority of agencies (65.1%) responded that they did not have problems or frustrations.

Pearson Correlation was used to examine the relationship between problems and agency goals. As can be seen in Table 4, there is a weak correlation between the goal of *visibility* and *agency problems*. In addition, Chi Square was used to test the relationship between *obtaining resources* and *problems*. Agencies that receive volunteers are more likely to report problems (Chi Square 5.69 df1, p < .017). Similarly, agencies that receive resources are also more likely to report problems (Chi Square 4.41 df1, p < .036).

Agencies were also asked to comment on areas that were problematic. Lack of resources for the Website was stated most frequently as problematic. This included limited staff time to create and update web pages or to work with volunteers to do it. In addition, limited time to deal with an unexpected volume of e-mail requests was problematic. Related to these issues was frustration stemming from being dependent on volunteers to create and update the Website. This was problematic when volunteers did not follow through on their commitments or when the agency became dependent for computer services on a volunteer who later left the agency on short notice. Several agencies, however, commented on the usefulness of volunteers in creating and maintaining the Website.

Another issue that agencies reported was the need to develop new policies and procedures for dealing with online requests. This included consultation with lawyers regarding liability issues, decisions about who would respond to requests, insuring confidentiality and security of e-mail messages, and deciding what kinds of services were inappropriate for online activities.

Two agencies reported serious problems related to "attacks" through the Website. One agency described a campaign of ". . . hate e-mails, e-mail bombs, and obsessive attention by the disturbed [individual]. . . . " These included threats and abuse toward staff. The agency advised that staff names should never be put on the Website for their own protection. Another agency reported that their Website had been "tampered with," including changing all pronouns from "she" to "he" and posting "hate messages." One agency advised that all threats should be reported to the sender's Internet Service Provider and a copy of the message should be kept by the agency as documentation.

DISCUSSION

The use of the Internet is expanding at an exponential rate (GUU Center, 1998). As business interests seek to use the Internet to promote commerce of all kinds, it is likely that increased publicity, easier access, and decreased costs will make the Internet available to increasing numbers of people. The potential of serving a vast audience at relatively little cost has brought domestic violence agencies to the Internet as well.

Agency Services on the Internet. This survey suggests that domestic violence agencies have begun to use the Internet primarily to promote agency visibility and to provide community education. To a far lesser extent, they also engage in advocacy activities, provide direct services, and secure resources with their Website. Many agencies are, in fact, reaching a large audience. The impact of reaching such a large audience is yet unknown. It is not clear who the audience is or what people's goals are for visiting the site. Are people seeking help with domestic violence issues? If so, the information and referral and the community education functions of agency Websites may lead to a great increase in service demand, and agencies may not have the resources to cope with the increased requests. If, however, people are primarily seeking information or are simply curious, agency Websites may meet these information needs, thus saving the agency time to deal with more urgent service issues. Research is needed to learn more about the goals of visitors to domestic violence agency Websites. Encouraging visitors to sign a "guest book" or fill out an online form describing their reasons for visiting and their satisfaction with Website might, in part, accomplish this.

The majority of domestic violence agencies in this study view their primary agency function as direct services. Most, however, do not provide direct services online. Agencies view their Website primarily as a means of outreach and information and referral with the goal of helping women (and sometimes men) connect with in-person services. Fewer than one-fifth of agencies provide some form of online counseling. It may be that many agencies are reluctant to provide online direct services due to the ethical and legal issues that have been raised in the literature about online therapy. Domestic violence organizations involved in providing direct services on the Web should review with legal counsel the need for a disclaimer on their Website, and will have to be cognizant of liability issues that may impact their online activities.

This study did not examine the nature of "online counseling" provided by domestic violence agencies. It is not known to what extent this might involve an ongoing therapeutic relationship as opposed to a one-time request for help. In addition, services might be a supplement or follow-up to in-person services, or may serve as an alternate form of services. Further research is needed to examine the nature, extent, and effectiveness of online services.

Agencies that encourage the use of the Web to obtain domestic violence services must understand that the use of the Internet itself may create new forms of victimization for users. These include "cyberstalking" (Jenson, 1996), loss of privacy (Banks, 1998), and increased risk of violence if an abusive partner discovers online activity related to domestic violence services. Internet users, especially those who have been victims of violence, need information about password protection, encryption software, blocking and filtering software, anonymous remailers, alternate e-mail receiving sites, chat room and newsgroup safety, the potential for misinformation, and how to deal with online harassment. Further research is needed to document the extent to which Internet safety issues are being addressed by domestic violence organizations.

Community Education. Community education is seen as an important goal of over three-fourths of agencies and the vast majority has educational material about domestic violence on their Website. Only about half of agencies, however, link their sites to other educational material or other domestic violence organizations. The reasons for this are unclear. Agencies may not know about other domestic violence resources on the Web or may not wish to take the time to find and monitor links. It is also possible that some may be "territorial" and do not wish to send visitors to alternate services. Whatever the reason, the result is that there may be considerable duplication of effort in agency community education projects. The hypertext environment of the Web is an ideal medium to avoid duplication of efforts in providing domestic violence information. To facilitate community education, agencies might consider concerted efforts to establish and publicize a network of domestic violence information sites, each with a unique focus. For example, one site may focus on domestic violence statistics, another on legislation, and another on training materials, etc. These sites can be linked in a domestic violence "Web ring" in which all of the sites link to each other. The sites can undergo review by experts in the field before they are allowed to participate in the Web ring. This would conserve energies and also help provide a source of accurate information. The vast majority of agencies would then link to the Web ring. A coordinating effort might be made by an organization such as *Minnesota Center Against Violence & Abuse* (MINICAVA: *http://www.minicava. umn.edu*) that does not have a political agenda, has considerable online experience and resources, and has demonstrated a commitment to domestic violence information sharing.

Advocacy. Only one-tenth of agencies listed advocacy as an important goal of their Website, and about one-fourth of agencies provided legal and legislative information or were involved in lobbying about domestic violence issues. While the potential to reach large numbers of people has been demonstrated, there is little research that documents the effectiveness or impact of online advocacy efforts (McNutt & Boland, 1998). This study did not provide an in-depth examination of online advocacy by domestic violence organizations, and further research is needed to document unique aspects of online advocacy, online organizational techniques, and the changes made by online advocacy organizations.

Securing Resources. The Internet is increasingly being used by human service agencies for fundraising and volunteer recruitment. In this study, approximately forty percent of agencies received donations or volunteers from their Website although the percent of resources received was quite small, generally less than five percent of donations or volunteers. Fundraising and volunteer recruitment are primarily done through online written appeals. More sophisticated methods such as secure servers for credit card donations, web-based solicitations on commercial sites, or online forms for volunteer recruitment are being used by only a few agencies. Agencies will need to understand and examine the full range of new online solicitation possibilities, and research is needed to determine if these new methods result in higher rates of return for agencies.

This study suggests that using the Internet to obtain donations and volunteers, however, is a mixed blessing. Agencies that received donations and volunteers were more likely to have higher satisfaction with their Website and also more likely to report problems. This may be a result of the greater complexity of their Website and increased disruption to staff rather than problems with the donations or volunteers per se. Many agencies did not anticipate the amount of extra staff time involved in maintaining and updating the Website or in monitoring and responding to the sheer volume of e-mail inquiries. Staff time and agency funds have always been in short supply for domestic violence organizations. Agencies must consider the total costs in establishing a Web presence.

Agency Concerns. The majority of agencies reported no problems with their Website; however, a substantial minority, about thirty-five percent, indicated that they did encounter problems. Domestic violence agencies have only recently entered the online world, and many problems related to start-up issues, development, policies and procedures, and allocation of staff time will likely disappear with continued online experience. Other problems pose a continued threat for agencies. A few agencies reported "spam" and disruption of their Website. "Spam" generally refers to unsolicited commercial e-mail. It may be relatively benign in the form of e-mail business solicitations or advertising. Spam may also involve conscious attempts to disrupt the agency Website by flooding it with thousands of messages and faxes, overwhelming the server and the agency's ability to use e-mail. In addition, there have been reports of e-mail threats to staff and "e-vandalism" to disrupt the Website. Given the hostility that domestic violence agencies face from some segments of society, domestic violence agencies must be prepared to encounter attempts to disrupt their Website through spam, viruses, provocative messages, and false e-mail requests for help. Domestic violence organizations will need to provide training to staff and volunteers about the range of messages that they may receive, and contact police when receiving threatening messages. They should also consider the use of e-mail filters and virus protection software.

Domestic violence agencies also face new legal challenges in developing and maintaining their Websites. Since many agencies publish domestic violence materials that they did not create, it is important to reduce risk of liability by confirming that content on the site does not infringe on copyrights or trademark. Another issue relates to ownership of the material on the Website, especially if a volunteer has created the page. Unless there is an employee relationship or an agreement to the contrary, the creation of the Website is not a "work for hire" under copyright laws, and the creator is likely to be the author and copyright holder (Blaustein, 1997). Legally, a volunteer who worked independently to create the agency Website could simply move or delete the site because the agency may have no legal ownership of the site. In many ways the Internet has developed faster than the laws that regulate it (Hafner, 1989). In most cases, legal and liability issues are only beginning to be addressed, and domestic violence agencies, especially those engaging in direct services, should seek legal consultation.

Access to Technology. Domestic violence organizations must be able to use the technology themselves in service of their clients. Given the extensive domestic violence resources available online, the author believes that all domestic violence services should consider having Internet access and computer literate staff at their agency to better serve their clients. In addition, creating access for clients should be seen as part of a domestic violence agency's Internet strategy. Concern has been raised that development of online resources is targeted to those with access and computer skills, leaving out the poor, undereducated, elderly, and other marginalized groups who are traditionally underserved by helping agencies (Michaelson, 1996; Glastonbury &

LaMendola, 1992, Metzendorf, 1988). Domestic violence agencies have begun to meet the needs of some minority populations through providing Websites specifically for under-served groups such as Hispanic, Native American, Asian, Jewish, and Lesbian populations (Finn, 2000). They will also need to join with other community groups to promote Internet access in public places such libraries and community centers, and encourage these organizations to bookmark domestic violence resources.

Evaluation. Given limited staff time and resources, evaluation of services has often been neglected in favor of service provision. More recently, in order to improve services, satisfy funders and other constituencies, and promote accountability, many agencies have given a higher priority to program evaluation (Chambers, Wedel, & Rodwell, 1992). The majority of agencies, however, indicated that they did not evaluate their Website or that they only used a "counter" to assess the number of "hits" received. Domestic violence agencies must view their Website as a "program component" and evaluate the success, benefits, and costs of this service. Agencies can routinely ask clients and callers how they learned about their services as one way to track those coming from the Internet. When asked to do community presentations, they can ask how many people know about or have visited their Website. Another approach is to request online e-mail feedback about the site or to provide an online response form. Agencies that request volunteers, goods and services can track their source to assess the percent of responses that are a result of their Website. Use of an online form facilitates this kind of evaluation. Finally, agencies can evaluate their site using focus groups of community members and clients who are asked to visit the site and provide feedback. Evaluation of agency Websites is essential for continued improvement of services and cost justifications.

CONCLUSION

Domestic violence agencies with a variety of missions, structures, and programs are bringing their services to the Internet. Social workers, health professionals, and others involved in domestic violence intervention will need to be aware of the full range of available supportive resources, including those that reside online. In addition, they must encourage communities to provide broad access to information technology, and to use this access as an avenue for domestic violence education and intervention.

The Internet will likely play an increasing role in the organizational strategies of domestic violence agencies as more people and organizations come online. In the near future, increased bandwidth and near universal access will reshape the nature of the online environment to include two-way video and the merger of television and the Internet. This will promote a number of changes and challenges:

- agencies will use interactive two-way audio and video for online assessment, counseling, and support as an adjunct to in-person services;
- advocacy, virtual protests, and demonstrations will take place on-line;
- employers will directly link workers to health and social services through their Intranets;
- communities will be better informed about the local incidence, prevalence, and rate of prosecution of problems such as domestic violence through geographic maps linked to databases;
- and those concerned about social issues will have increasingly greater access to each other (Schoech, 1999; Cref, 1997; Valee, 1982).

Domestic violence organizations will need to become influential in the development and shaping of the ethics, targets, applications and evaluation of these new services.

REFERENCES

Allen, N., M. Stein, & M. Warwick, eds. (1996). *Fundraising on the Internet: Recruiting and renewing donors online*. Berkeley: Strathmoor Press.

Appleman, D. L. (1995). "The Law and the Internet." [Online], Available July 21, 1998: http://inet.nttam.

Bachman, R., & L. E. Saltzman 1995 *Violence against women: Estimates from the redesigned survey*. Washington, D.C.: Bureau of Justice Statistics, U.S. Department of Justice.

Bailey, Sean (1997). " Yahoo! fundraiser provides lessons for nonprofits." *Philanthropy Journal*, July, 28. [Online], Available: http://www.philanthropy-journal. org/tech/yahoofollow797.htm.

Banks, M. A. (1998). "Web psychos, stalkers, and pranksters: How to protect yourself in cyberspace" [Online], Available: http://w3.one.net/~banks/psycho.htm.

Blaustein, S. (1997). "Internet Law" [Online], Available: July 21, 1998, http://www.patentplus.com/Webaudit.html

Bloom, J. (1998). The ethical practice of webcounseling. *British Journal of Guidance and Counseling, 26*(1), 53-60.

Brandt, M. G. (1998). "Local Nonprofit Organizations at Work: A composite vision of a community presence on the World Wide Web." [Online], Available: http://www.uwm.edu/People/mbrandt/toc.htm.

Chambers, D. E., K. R. Wedel, & M. K. Rodwell. *Evaluating Social Programs.* Boston:Allyn and Bacon.

Cref, V.G. (1997). "When They're Everywhere." In P. J. Denning & R. M. Metcalfe, *Beyond Calculation: The next fifty years of computing.* Springer-Verlag: New York. p. 33-42.

Ensman, R. G. (1997). "Turn small shops into big shops via the Internet." *Fund Raising Management, 28* (June) 18-19.

Ferguson, T. (1996). *Health Online.* Reading, MA: Addison-Wesley.

Finn, J. (2000). " Domestic violence organizations on the Web: A new arena for domestic violence services." *Violence Against Women,* in press, June 2000.

Finn, J. (1999). "Seeking Volunteers and Contributions: An exploratory study of nonprofit agencies on the Internet." *Journal of Technology in Human Services, 15*(4), 24-38.

Finn, J. & M. Lavitt. (1994). "Computer-based self-help groups for sexual abuse survivors." *Social Work with Groups.* 17 (1/2), p. 21-45.

Gelles, R. J. & J.R. Conte. 1990. "Domestic violence and sexual abuse of children: A review of research in the eighties." *Journal of Marriage and the Family, 52*:1045-58.

Gelles, R. & M. Straus. (1988). *Intimate violence: The definitive study of the causes and consequences of abuse in the American family.* New York: Simon and Schuster.

Glastonbury, B. & W. LaMendola. (1992) *The Integrity of Intelligence.* St.Martin's Press, New York.

Green, M. (1998). "Fundraising in Cyberspace". The Grantsmanship Center. [Online], Available: July 9. http://www.tgci.com/publications/fall95mag/cyberled.htm.

Grobman, G. M. & Grant, G. B. (1998). *The non-profit Internet handbook.* Harrisburg: White Hat Communications.

GVU Center (1998). "GVU's 9th WWW User Survey Web and Internet Use Summary." Georgia Institute of Technology, [Online], Available: July 21, 1998, http://www.gvu.gatech.edu/user_surveys/survey-1998-04/reports/1998-04-Use.html

Hafner, A. W. (1989). "Computers and the Legal Standard of Care." *Archives of Ophthalmology,* 107(7), 966.

Hawthorne, N. (1997). "The history and development of Internet resources for volunteer programs." *Journal of Volunteer Administration* 16 (Fall), 28-33.

Huang, M. & Alessi, N. (1996). The Internet and the future of psychiatry. *American Journal of Psychiatry, 153*(7), 861-869.

Impact Online (1998). "Virtual Volunteering." [Online], Available July 15, 1998: http://www.impactonline.org/vv.

Jenson, B. (1996). "Cyberstalking: Crime, enforcement and personal responsibility in the on-line world." [Online], Available: http://www.law.ucla.edu/classes/archiv/s96/340/cyberlaw.htm.

Johnson, D. & Post, D. (1996). Law and borders: The rise of law in cyberspace. 48 *Stanford Law Review, 1367.*

Kraus, A., Stein, M., & Clark, J. (1998). "The virtual activist: A training course on netaction." [Online], at http://www.netaction.org/training.

Lebow, J. (1998). Not just talk, maybe some risk: The therapeutic potentials and pitfalls of computer-mediated conversation. *Journal of Marriage and Family Therapy,* 24(2), 203-206.

Lewis, K. (1997). Tapping technology: Legal and Liability risks on the Internet. *Magazine of Physical Therapy,* 5(3), 21-24.

McNutt, J. G. (1996). "Computer networks and the nonprofit social services delivery system." Paper presented at the 25th Annual Meeting of the Association of Nonprofit and Voluntary Actions Scholars, New York, NY.

McNutt, J. G. & Boland, D. M. (1998). "Electronic Advocacy by Nonprofit Organizations in Social Welfare Policy Formulation: A framework and results of a study." Paper presented at the 27th Annual meeting of the Association of Voluntary Action Scholars, Seattle, WA, November.

Mann, W. (1995). *Politics on the net: Surfing the world of Internet politics.* Indianapolis, IN: Que Books.

Metzendorf, D. S. (1988). "An urgent need: equal access to computers among the poor." In B. Glastonbury, W. LaMendola, & S. Toole (Ed.), *Information Technology and the Human Services,* pp. 347-349. Chichester: John Wiley & Sons.

Michaelson, K. L. (1996). "Information, community, and access." *Social Science Computer Review,* 14(1), 57-59.

Miller, D. B. & DiGiuseppe, D. (1998). "Fighting social problems with information: The development of a community database-The Violence Information Network. *Computers in Human Services.* 15 (1), 21-34.

Mizrahi, T., Downing, J., Fasano, R., Friedl &, P., McCullough, M., & Shapiro, J. (1991). *Computers for Social Change and Community Organizing.* Binghamton, New York: The Haworth Press, Inc.

Moore, J. (1995). "Fundraising by computer: the next frontier?" *Chronicle of Philanthropy.* 7 (Jan. 12) 1, 22-24.

Pergament, D. (1998). "Internet psychotherapy: Current status and future regulations." *Journal of Law Medicine,* 8, (2), 233-280.

Schoech, D. (1999). *Human Services Technology: Understanding, Designing, and Implementing Computer and Internet Applications in the Social Services.* New York: The Haworth Press, Inc.

Schwartz, E. (1996). *NetActivism: How citizens use the Internet.* Sebastopol, CA: Songline Studios, Inc.

Walker, L. (1984). *The Battered Woman Syndrome.* New York: Springer.

Young, J.E. (1997). "Building organizational capacity with technology: A strategy for assisting grass-roots environmental groups with computers and telecommunications online. Environmental Support Center, [Online], Available: July 21, 1998, http://www.rffund.org/camp/escpub.html.

Zeff, R. (1996). *The nonprofit guide to the Internet.* New York: Wiley.

Computer Technology Utilization and Community-Based AIDS Organizations

P. J. Cameron
J. R. Graham
J. D. Sieppert

SUMMARY. This study explores the computer utilization patterns of 107 community-based AIDS organizations in Canada. A questionnaire examined the current hardware/software capacities of agencies, knowledge and use of the Internet and its capabilities as a tool for psychosocial support, and barriers to computerized service provision. It also explored consumers' utilization and knowledge of computer-mediated technologies, and barriers to service. Results suggest agencies have resource-related dilemmas, relating to limited finances, time and personnel capacities. Consumers are challenged by a lack of access to computers, limited awareness of computer-mediated technologies, and other inhibiting factors. Future directions for community-based AIDS organizations are considered. *[Article copies available for a fee from The Haworth Document Delivery Service: 1-800-342-9678. E-mail address: <getinfo@haworthpressinc.com> Website: <http://www.haworthpressinc.com>]*

KEYWORDS. HIV/AIDS, Internet, information technology, computer, World Wide Web

---

P. J. Cameron, J. R. Graham, and J. D. Sieppert are all affiliated with the Faculty of Social Work, University of Calgary, Calgary, Alberta, Canada.

[Haworth co-indexing entry note]: "Computer Technology Utilization and Community-Based AIDS Organizations." Cameron, P. J., J. R. Graham, and J. D. Sieppert. Co-published simultaneously in *Journal of Technology in Human Services* (The Haworth Press, Inc.) Vol. 17, No. 2/3, 2000, pp. 103-118; and: *Human Services Online: A New Arena for Service Delivery* (ed: Jerry Finn, and Gary Holden) The Haworth Press, Inc., 2000, pp. 103-118. Single or multiple copies of this article are available for a fee from The Haworth Document Delivery Service [1-800-342-9678, 9:00 a.m. - 5:00 p.m. (EST). E-mail address: getinfo@haworthpressinc.com].

103

INTRODUCTION

A number of studies explore the significance of computer-based AIDS/HIV health promotion and awareness programs as public education tools. Bosworth (1994) notes how computer games and simulations may promote health awareness among adolescents, and Cahill (1994) stresses the particular efficacy of computer-simulated games in adolescent awareness of AIDS. Schinke et al. (1989) analyze the uses of computer-based interventions as a method of AIDS prevention, especially via interactive microcomputer use among high-risk adolescents. Growing research suggests that the use of computers and computer-mediated technologies by people living with AIDS and people who are HIV positive (PWA/PHIV) is beneficial (Vincke, Mak, Bolton, & Jurica, 1993; Boberg et al., 1995). What, however, is the norm of computer usage in AIDS community organizations? What are the prospects for future use? Are there particular technological uses that have found wide currency among community organizations and their consumers? These and other questions remain unanswered, in part because of the paucity of aggregate data on AIDS community organizations and computer use. This absence of such research is striking in three additional respects. The first is the considerable presence of web sites and discussion groups involving AIDS and HIV positive issues (Fogel, 1998), and their potentially wide utilization by PWA/PHIV. The second is the reputation of AIDS community organizations as being on the cutting edge of knowledge production, dissemination and trial use of new medicinal treatments, and of web- and e-mail-based public advocacy media (Indyk & Rier, 1991). The third is the current barriers to service access, including the limited ambulatory scope of some PWA, barriers involving geographic proximity, especially within rural or remote regions, and stigma-related barriers that inhibit many PWA/PHIV from physically entering an AIDS social service agency (Graham, Brownlee & Ritchie, 1996; Graham, Ritchie & Brownlee, 1997).

For purposes of this article, technology refers to the skills, tools, and machines that enable the storage, manipulation, and transmission of electronically-based information, and arise from a social worker, social agency, or social welfare institution. Technologies of particular significance to this study include computer hardware, computer software, other forms of technological databases, computer-based discussion groups and chat rooms, e-mail, and the Internet. The computer provides opportunities for consumers to increase mastery and self-esteem and receive feedback and achievement (Mahler & Meier, 1993), and allows consumers to participate in an interactive manner (Schinke & Orlandi, 1990). Interventions via the computer can provide assistance with problem solving, coping and communication skills (Schinke et al., 1989). Computer-mediated support has other potential advantages over non-technological social service delivery. These include ongoing support and flexibility to consumers. In an enclosed space, or if it is used at home, it may provide anonymity or comfort (Weinberg, Schmale, Uken & Wessel, 1995). In addition, computer programs can be adapted to age and culturally specific contexts (Schinke & Orlandi, 1990).

Information Technology provides consumers with many advantages over traditional methods of support. These include elimination of barriers related to transportation, travel, and scheduling. The computer serves as a method of "collectively linking geographically dispersed people" (Giffords, 1998, p. 244). For consumers in rural or remote locations, this is especially relevant. Computerized psychosocial support may be the most logical and efficient method of serving consumers in rural or remote areas.

Other advantages exist for consumers of AIDS organizations. Computers can serve consumers in their own homes, giving consumers 24-hour service, and allowing symptomatic PWA/PHIV who may be too ill to travel to an agency the opportunity to secure continued supportive services. Online support groups provide participants with what may be their only opportunity to speak with others who share similar symptoms and life experiences (Giffords, 1998).

The stigma and isolation associated with the AIDS epidemic is well documented (Poindexter, 1997; Turner, Catania & Gagnon, 1994; Britton, Zarski & Hobfoll, 1993). Any efforts to improve the psychosocial support of people living with HIV/AIDS must be made in this context. Schinke and Orlandi (1990) report that instructional software seldom considers the life experience and everyday realities of individuals from ethno-racial minority, lower-income, and disadvantaged communities. Computers have the ability to be responsive to individual contexts, and the advantage of providing relatively anonymous support to consumers. Indeed, "computer-mediated groups provide an option for people who are uncomfortable in formal groups" (Weinberg et al. 1995, p. 45).

This present exploratory study surveys the 107 community-based AIDS organizations that constitute the Canadian AIDS Society

(CAS), the major umbrella organization for the country's locally-based AIDS community organizations. While no precise numbers are available, the CAS estimates that there are approximately 200 locally-based AIDS community organizations across the country (E-mail correspondence, July 12, 1999). This study therefore has a comprehensive national scope.

METHODS

Research began in November 1998, with a semi-structured, open-ended, two-hour telephone interview of a small sample (N = 6) of executive directors and in-house computer experts of community-based AIDS agencies. The six agencies were selected from a membership list, using a non-random procedure to ensure broad representation of agency size and region. These agencies represented a mix of urban and rural communities from Eastern, Central and Western Canada. Questions explored perceptions of current computer utilization patterns of organizations, knowledge of computer-mediated technologies, and perceptions of consumer knowledge of, and access to, computers.

The next stage of research was the development of a pilot questionnaire. That instrument was derived from two principal sources, the first being qualitative information provided by telephone informants, and the second, previously utilized computer questionnaires of social service agencies (Canadian AIDS Society & Health Network of Canadian Policy Research Networks, 1997; Senner, Young, Gunn & Schwartz, 1988; Mutschler & Hoefer, 1990). The pilot questionnaire was distributed to 6 CAS member organization respondents, who completed the pilot and provided written and verbal advice regarding further revisions. A questionnaire comprised of 39 questions was the final result. It was distributed in December 1998 to the 107 member organizations of the CAS, and responses were returned in the following two months.

The questionnaire examined basic computer utilization patterns of agencies and consumers, Internet use and psychosocial support, and barriers to effective computer utilization. Items explored the current hardware and software capacities of agencies, knowledge and use of the Internet and its capabilities as a tool for psychosocial support, internal computer expertise, current computer utilization patterns, satisfaction with current technological capabilities, and barriers to computerized service provision. The questionnaire also explored agency perception of consumers' utilization patterns and knowledge of computer-mediated technologies, as well as agency perceptions of barriers to service for consumers.

The Sample

The CAS is a national coalition facilitating the development of programs, services and resources of locally based member organizations across the country. CAS member organizations that responded to the survey represent a diverse spectrum of Canadian HIV/AIDS services. All (107) member organizations of the CAS were initially surveyed, with 66 (61.7%) questionnaires returned for analysis. The characteristics of those agencies that did not respond are not known. It might be assumed, however, that agencies more involved with information technology were more likely to respond to the survey. This would lead the results to over-represent the actual computer involvement of CAS agencies. Slightly over half of the respondents (53%) self-identified as having an urban consumer focus/being in an urban area, leaving 45% of respondents who self-identified as rural or remote in geography or focus.

Respondents also varied considerably in size of agency, ranging from the two organizations that had no full-time employees, to three large HIV/AIDS agencies that employed 20, 26, and 31 full-time employees respectively. On average, respondent organizations employed 5.69 (S.D. = 5.7) full-time employees. Most also make routine use of part-time employees as well, averaging 2.9 (S.D. = 2.4) part-time workers per agency.

RESULTS

Basic Computer Use

The CAS organizations that responded to the survey show extensive use of computer technology. Sixty-five of the 66 organizations reported using computers as part of their daily functioning. Their computers were a diverse mixture of machines that appear to be aging rapidly. One HIV/AIDS organization still uses a 286 computer, 21% have 386 machines, 56% use 486 computers, and only 65% have obtained Pentium computers. Approximately one-fourth of agencies (24%) indicated that they had some form of Macintosh computer. Regardless of the type of computer used in the organization, 55% of these organizations had five or fewer computers available. The majority of these agency computers (77%) still use the Windows 95 operating system, with the remainder based primarily upon Windows 98 or Windows 3.x. Surprisingly, 18% of organizations are still using personal computers based on the DOS operating systems.

Not as surprising, however, is that funding appears to be an ongoing issue that contributes to difficulties in updating the available computer technology. Only 33% indicated that they purchased computers solely through agency funding, while almost half (49%) relied on a combination of purchased and donated computers. Twenty-three percent had acquired computers through external donations alone.

Use of Information Technology

Even though the HIV/AIDS organizations make extensive use of computers, this use is focused on the traditional purposes of word processing and administrative support. The survey asked respondents a series of questions about their development and use of innovations such as using computers for client assessments, providing information to clients electronically, and fostering the use of electronic chat rooms or discussion groups. It also included questions about the factors that might inhibit clients from making effective use of innovative computer based services.

Despite limitations in basic computer availability and funding levels, CAS member organizations appear to be interested in improving their services through more innovative computer technology. As can be seen in Table 1, the majority of the respondents (77%) indicated that they now have Internet access. An additional 14% are in the process of establishing such access for the near future. Of those with Internet access, 32% offer the majority of staff direct access to the Internet. The remainder rely on dial-up services to provide Internet access to staff. More than half (65%) of these HIV/AIDS organizations have, in fact, developed their own web page.

Staff in these organizations does make use of the Internet. Of the respondents who have Internet access for their staff, only 14% reported that staff fails to use the Internet to facilitate their work. Conversely, 68% of these same organizations report that the average staff

TABLE 1. Computer Utilization Patterns (N = 66)

Percentage of AIDS Organizations Using Computers For:

Basic Computer Uses	*Percent*
Word Processing as Percentage of All Computing	66
Accounting and Budgeting as Percentage of All Computing	22

Internet Use

Internet Access at Agency	77
Agency has a Web Page	65

Psychosocial Support

Aware of Psychosocial Applications via Computer	46
Offering Psychosocial Applications via Computer	36
Intentions to Implement Further Services	47

member spends from 1-5 hours per week using the Internet and in 21% of organizations the staff spends up to 10 hours per week on the Internet. During these hours on the Internet, respondents indicated that staff were communicating via e-mail (74% of organizations), accessing treatment information related to HIV/AIDS (60%), or accessing HIV/AIDS program information (59%). Some respondents also reported that the Internet was a useful tool for staff members to access funding information (50% of organizations) or to interface with government agencies and/or personnel (31%).

It is also clear, however, that Internet expertise seems to be concentrated in a select few staff members in most HIV/AIDS organizations. Fewer than half of all respondents (45%) said that staff members have sufficient expertise to use e-mail attachments. Even in those services where staff can use such attachments, over one-third (32%) said that fewer than 1 staff member in 4 has such expertise. In fact, 29% indicated that they had a single staff member who acted as a person with computer expertise on behalf of the organization. Despite these limitations in in-house computer skills, only 11% of organizations said that off-site computer assistance was available to them. Together these findings suggest that a minority of HIV/AIDS staff members with computer technology expertise will be called upon frequently to resolve computer difficulties for the whole agency.

It can be argued that the most innovative of human service organizations will use technology for more than administrative and staff support. Rather, they will expand this use to direct provision of services to consumers. The survey asked respondents whether they used computers to provide psychosocial supports to persons with HIV or AIDS. Respondents were split in their awareness of computer-based provision of psychosocial supports for persons with HIV/AIDS. Almost half (46%) reported that they knew about such computer uses. Thirty-six percent of these reported that they are now offering these kinds of computer-based supports. These supports were almost exclusively Internet-based, and included the use of e-mail to support clients' (36%) access to existing chat rooms on the Internet (10%), or starting their own agency-based support chat room (6%). An additional 9% of organizations reported that they were involved in ongoing, on-line support groups for persons with HIV/AIDS.

Results also indicate that a large number of these HIV/AIDS organizations intend to develop much stronger computer-based psychosocial supports for consumers. Only 21% said they had no intention to implement further computer-related services, while 47% indicated that they had definite plans to do so. These plans were varied: 27% reported that they had plans to implement e-mail services for consumers, 27% want to develop support-related web sites, 21% will implement online support groups, and 15% who are planning to implement chat rooms for persons with HIV/AIDS.

Finally, the survey asked respondents whether they were satisfied with the agency's overall computer-utilization patterns and the agency's ability to serve consumers through the use of computers. A minority of the agencies (42%) reported that they are satisfied with their current computer utilization. Similarly, 30% of organizations are content with their computer-related services at this time.

Barriers to Effective Computer Utilization

Canadian HIV/AIDS organizations appear to be equipped with limited amounts of basic computer equipment. At the same time these organizations are quickly taking advantage of the Internet, albeit in restricted ways. Accordingly, many such organizations are dissatisfied with their computer-based services. An important question therefore arises. What barriers might prevent these organizations from becoming more proactive, creative, and consistent in applying computers to service provision?

According to respondents, the major barriers center on issues of consumer access, consumer awareness, and agency funding. In terms of consumer access to computers, respondents expressed concerns about both consumers' basic access to computers and to the Internet. Sixty-two percent of the HIV/AIDS organizations estimated that fewer than 1 in 4 of their consumers currently have access to a computer in their home.

Consumer awareness about technology-mediated psychosocial supports also appears to be limited. Organizations agreed that HIV/AIDS consumers are likely aware of the use of web sites for treatment information (60% of organizations), the use of chat rooms for support (31%), electronic discussion groups as a support mechanism (18%), and e-mail as a vehicle for providing supports (12%). These results are also grounded in the experiences relayed by the organizations. Eleven percent of organizations indicated that consumers have never asked about the availability of an organizational website. The majority (77%) reports that fewer than 1 in 4 consumers asks about such web sites. The majority (68%) also note that consumers have never requested access to HIV/AIDS related chat rooms through the agency's web site or through an on-site agency computer.

The survey asked organizations to cite factors that might inhibit consumers' use of computer technology for psychosocial support or a source of treatment information. As shown in Table 2, the single most

TABLE 2. Barriers to Effective Computer Utilization (N = 66)

Percent of AIDS Organizations Ranking Barrier as Most Significant:

Consumer Barriers to Consumer Use of Computers	Percent
Poverty	60
Basic Access to Computer Technology	25
Lack of Knowledge of Computer Utilization	15
Organizational Barriers to Effective Computer Utilization	
Limitations to Annual Agency Budgets	28
Size of the Agency	23
High Costs of Hardware/Software	15
Lack of Consumer Interest	15

frequently cited barrier to consumer use of technology was identified as poverty. Sixty percent of the organizations ranked poverty as the key inhibitor of such use. Along with poverty, however, were the accompanying issues of basic access to computer technology and lack of knowledge about how computers can be used in accessing psychosocial supports.

Finally, survey respondents were asked to rank order a number of organizational factors that acted as barriers to implementing effective computer-based psychosocial support to persons with HIV/AIDS. Possible barriers included the size of the agency, limitations in annual budgets, current hardware/software capabilities, the cost of hardware/software, numbers of available computers, ability to ensure consumer confidentiality, levels of agency awareness, limited in-house expertise, literacy issues, and lack of consumer interest. Those barriers ranked first were varied. They included, however, limitations to annual agency budgets, the size of the agency, the high costs of hardware/software and lack of consumer interest in accessing computer-based support services. Together these results indicate practical issues in implementing computer-based psychosocial supports in HIV/AIDS organizations.

DISCUSSION

Clearly there are a variety of issues related to the utilization of computers by AIDS organizations. While many AIDS organizations in this survey have acquired computers and Internet access, the pervading theme of this survey is the limited availability of resources. Agencies have a variety of resource-related dilemmas that include limitations of finances, training time, and personnel. Consumers are seen by providers as challenged by a lack of access to computers in their homes, lack of awareness of various computer-related technologies, and inhibiting personal factors, such as poverty, health issues and concerns about confidentiality. Despite the barriers with which agencies and consumers must contend, a number of agencies have secured resources and are beginning to utilize information technology to supplement their services.

Agency

The survey revealed that many AIDS organizations use a mixture of rapidly aging machines, frequently rely on donated computers, and use the Internet in a limited way. Innovative service provision, such as access to chat rooms or discussion groups, is the exception rather than the rule for member organizations. This tendency appears to be consistent with social service uses in general. Previously, Pardeck, Collier Umfress and Murphy (1987) reported social service agencies did not use computer technology to its fullest potential. Over a decade later this remains true for AIDS organizations in Canada.

Communicating information about prevention and treatment of HIV/AIDS can be effectively accomplished by using the Internet as a dissemination tool (Ohles & Pierce, 1998). According to Ohles and Pierce (1998), it is critical for AIDS organizations to develop and maintain Internet sites in order to provide information rapidly to people living with HIV/AIDS. In this survey, three-fourths of AIDS organizations are equipped with Internet access, although only 32% are able to offer the majority of staff direct access to the Internet. More than half of the CAS agencies have a web page. Evaluation studies of agencies currently using the Internet are needed to determine whether these services positively impact the lives of consumers. Cost-benefit studies are especially needed to justify the funds and staff resources necessary to provide online services.

Clearly the financial capacity of AIDS organizations is a factor in their ability to implement and expand effective technological support to people living with HIV/AIDS. There are methods of reducing the financial burdens of technology provision. Agencies need to begin to plan for funds for computer resources and training in their annual agency budgets. Some community-based AIDS organizations have pursued avenues to secure free onsite access to technology for staff and consumers through donated equipment and services. Soliciting funds from corporate sponsors is one method of securing resources. Arranging an exchange of services with other agencies or with corporations is another way to acquire technologies. Innovative fundraising campaigns through mail, canvassing, and other grassroots campaigns serve to educate the community and attract funds. In addition, agencies seek grants and funds specifically for computer-related purchases. Agencies need to document and share successful solicitation strategies through their professional networks, including those that are on the Internet.

Some agencies have been successful in obtaining the services of information technology consultants on a volunteer or low-cost basis.

Agencies with limited budgets should consider actively pursuing such consultants for staff training, Website development and applications development. Greater utilization of volunteers holds much potential for the alleviation of the staff-related resource deficit apparent for agencies.

Few agencies are involved in advanced applications with computers, and fewer than half of agencies surveyed were aware of computer-based provision of psychosocial supports for persons with HIV/AIDS. Innovative computer uses, such as chat room or discussion groups, are significantly underutilized, and in many cases the potential benefits of various computer applications are simply not known. It is likely that awareness of online support will increase among AIDS organizations as these topics are discussed in the professional literature and at professional conferences. Providing such support services can be accomplished for very little cost for many smaller organizations. Since online support groups are not confined by geography, agencies can easily link consumers to online support by providing the addresses of existing Usenet and listserv groups through their regular information and referral procedures.

A number of research articles indicate staff training and attitudes toward technology are essential facilitators to improved computer applications in the workplace (Mutschler & Hoefer, 1990; Roosenboom, 1995; Finnegan, 1996; Doelker and Lynette, 1988). Indeed, the degree of staff training is one of the main correlates of computer use (Mutschler & Hoefer, 1990). Yet the survey suggests a lack of expertise available within Canadian AIDS organizations. There are several reasons this may occur. One may be the additional time required to learn specialized computer applications (Mahler & Meier, 1993). Another may be the limited priority computer use may have with respect to employee recruitment, training, and educational upgrading. In addition, financial costs associated with computer training may hinder the implementation of technological education within smaller agencies.

Nineteen organizations in the survey indicated they had a single staff member who acted as a person with computer expertise on behalf of the organization, and only seven had off-site computer assistance available to them. Matheson (1993) would define these personnel as "computer champions" and notes that the significance of champions to agency direction should not be underestimated. Agencies need to seek out champions and expand on the skills these individuals bring. Interested staff should be actively encouraged to become computer champions.

Consumers

According to respondent agencies, few consumers have access to computers in their homes, and consumer knowledge of psychosocial supports available via the computer is limited. Without access to such basic tools of technology, developing and implementing computer-mediated technologies is futile. Agencies can pursue a variety of methods to provide such access. Offering workshops, free of charge, for consumers about computer-mediated technologies can diminish barriers to use. Available onsite assistance from staff and volunteers could also help consumers who are not familiar with various technological applications. Agencies should encourage consumers interested in expanding the technological capabilities of the agency, and support their efforts to create a technologically advanced environment.

Agency respondents ranked consumer poverty as the single most important barrier to consumer use of technology. Low levels of computer access have been correlated with economic barriers (Schinke & Orlandi, 1990), and results of this survey support that conclusion. An interesting result of the survey was the relatively low level of awareness of consumers, particularly given evidence of sophisticated computer use in the AIDS social service community (Cahill, 1994; Schinke et al., 1989). AIDS organizations reported that few consumers requested information about computer related services, and that many consumers lack knowledge about how computers can be used in accessing psychosocial supports. However, considering the limited access consumers have to computers, these findings are more than plausible. Agencies should consider incorporating on site computers for clients. Another strategy to increase information technology resources for consumers is to promote linkages with other community-based organizations. For example, agencies might provide access to computers through a computer share arrangement. Donated computers could be set up in strategic public settings such as community centers, housing projects, or public libraries to provide access to consumers.

CONCLUSION

Consumers of HIV/AIDS services will increasingly seek to utilize information technology as awareness of the Internet grows in the general population. The dilemmas for service providers and the recipients of their services persists because Canadian AIDS organizations lack the financial and staff resources to expand their services, and consumers require additional resources to improve their access to, and knowledge of, computer-related technologies. Without addressing the basic issues that inhibit the advancement of technology-based supportive services for people living with HIV/AIDS, barriers may continue to block the progression of support via the computer.

This is not to suggest that technology is a panacea to successful AIDS social service delivery. But with effective utilization by social service personnel and consumers, computer technology may enhance the lives of persons with HIV/AIDS and the supplement the social services they receive. Given the recency of technological innovations and the changing face of AIDS social service delivery, there is no single model that provides answers to the complex strategic planning and leadership strategies relevant to fund raising and technology access. Nor, given diversity of agency size, urban versus rural location, and other particularities, were there any single agencies in the current study that offer a single applicable framework that might be transferable to AIDS social service technology implementation in a generic sense. AIDS organizations, however, have a strong history of grassroots service development, innovative fund raising, and mutual support. These strengths must now be applied to the development of information technology resources.

REFERENCES

Boberg, E.W., Gustafson, D.H., Hawkins, R.P., Chan, C.L., Bricker, E., Pingree, S. & Berhe, H. (1995). Development, acceptance, and use patterns of a computer-based education and social support system for people living with AIDS/HIV infection. *Computers in Human Services, 11(2)*, 289-311.

Bosworth, K. (1994). Computer games and simulations as tools to reach and engage adolescents in health promotion activities. *Computers in Human Services, 11(1-2)*, 109-119.

Britton, P.J., Zarski, J.J. & Hobfoll, S.E. (1993). Psychological distress and the role of significant others in a population of gay/bisexual men in the era of HIV. *AIDS Care, 5(1)*, 43-54.

Cahill, J.M. (1994). Health Works: Interactive AIDS education videogames. *Computers in Human Services, 11(1-2)*, 159-176.

Canadian AIDS Society & Health Network of Canadian Policy Research Networks, Inc. (1997). *Management Information System Project (Phase One) Survey*. Ottawa: Canadian AIDS Society.

Doelker, R.E. & Lynette, P.A. (1988). The impact of learner attitudes on computer-based training in the human services. *Journal of Continuing Social Work Education, 4(3)*, 2-7.

Finnegan, D.J. (1996). Unraveling social workers' ambivalence toward computer technology: an analysis of the attitudes of social work students towards computers and social work practice. *Computers in Human Services, 13(2)*, 33-49.

Fogel, S.C. (1998). HIV-related internet news and discussion groups as professional and social support tools. *Health Care on the Internet, 2(2/3)*, 79-90.

Giffords, E.D. (1998). Social work on the Internet: an introduction. *Social Work, 43(3)*, 243-251.

Graham, J.R., Brownlee, K. & Ritchie, I. (1996). AIDS, social work, and the coming home phenomenon. *The Social Worker, 64(4)*, 74-84.

Graham, J.R., Ritchie, I. & Brownlee, K. (1997). AIDS social service in Canada's north. In R. Delaney, K. Brownlee, & J. Graham (Eds.), *Strategies in northern social work practice* (217-228). Thunder Bay: Center for Northern Studies.

Indyk, D. & Rier, D.A. (1991). Grassroots AIDS groups: Marginal innovators? *American Sociological Association (ASA) Papers*.

Mahler, C.R. & Meier, S.T. (1993). The microcomputer as a psychotherapeutic aid. *Computers in Human Services, 10(1)*, 35-40.

Matheson, A.D. (1993). Innovative use of computers for planning in human service organizations. *Computers in Human Services, 9(3-4)*, 383-395.

Mutschler, E. & Hoefer, R. (1990). Factors affecting the use of computer technology in human service organizations. *Administration in Social Work, 14(1)*, 87-101.

Ohles, J.A. & Pierce, J. (1998). AIDS service organizations and their presence on the Internet. *Health Care on the Internet, 2(2/3)*, 11-23.

Pardeck, J.T., Collier Umfress, K. & Murphy, J.W. (1987). The use and perception of computers by professional social workers. *Family Therapy, 14(1)*, 1-8.

Poindexter, C.C. (1997). In the aftermath: serial crisis intervention for people with HIV. *Health and Social Work, 22(2)*, 125-132.

Roosenboom, P.G.M. (1995). Solving the problems of computer use in social work. *Computers in Human Services, 12(3-4)*, 391-401.

Schinke, S.P. & Orlandi, M.A. (1990). Skills-based, interactive computer interventions to prevent HIV infection among African-American and Hispanic Adolescents. *Computers in Human Services, 6*, 235-246.

Schinke, S.P., Orlandi, M.A., Gordon, A.N., Weston, R.E., Moncher, M.S. & Parms, C.A. (1989). AIDS prevention via computer-based intervention. *Computers in Human Services, 5(3/4)*, 147-156.

Senner, L., Young, B.G., Gunn, S.R. & Schwartz, C.L. (1988). Computer use in the Human Services. *Computers in Human Services, 3(3/4)*, 101-110.

Turner, H.A., Catania, J.A. & Gagnon, J. (1994). The prevalence of informal caregiving to persons with AIDS in the United States: caregiver characteristics and their implications. *Social Science and Medicine, 38(11)*, 1543-1552.

Vincke, J., Mak, R., Bolton, R. & Jurica, P. (1993). Factors affecting AIDS-related sexual behavior change among Flemish gay men. *Human Organization, 52(3)*, 260-268.

Weinberg, N., Schmale, J.D., Uken, J. & Wessel, K. (1995). Computer-mediated support groups. *Social Work with Groups, 17(4)*, 43-54.

Virtual Volunteering:
Online Volunteers Providing Assistance
to Human Service Agencies

Jayne Cravens

SUMMARY. A growing number of agencies involve volunteers via home or work computers and the Internet. The Virtual Volunteering Project [http://www.serviceleader.org/vv/] has researched and worked with more than 100 organizations involving online volunteers to document the benefits of online service for agencies, volunteers and audiences served, and to disseminate ways agencies can incorporate virtual volunteering into their organizations. This paper describes the Virtual Volunteering Project and summarizes data from a variety of sources that highlight the activities of agencies and volunteers engaged in virtual volunteering and the factors associated with success in virtual volunteering programs. *[Article copies available for a fee from The Haworth Document Delivery Service: 1-800-342-9678. E-mail address: <getinfo@haworthpressinc. com> Website: <http://www.haworthpressinc.com>]*

KEYWORDS. Virtual volunteering, volunteer management, cyber culture, World Wide Web, volunteer

---

Jayne Cravens has managed the Virtual Volunteering Project since its inception in December 1996. She has presented numerous national conferences regarding online service delivery and online culture. A professional in nonprofit management for more than 10 years, she resides in Austin, Texas.

Address correspondence to: Jayne Cravens, Charles A. Dana Center, UT-Austin, Natural Sciences Annex 2.208, 2613 Speedway, Austin, TX 78712.

[Haworth co-indexing entry note]: "Virtual Volunteering: Online Volunteers Providing Assistance to Human Service Agencies." Cravens, Jayne. Co-published simultaneously in *Journal of Technology in Human Services* (The Haworth Press, Inc.) Vol. 17, No. 2/3, 2000, pp. 119-136; and: *Human Services Online: A New Arena for Service Delivery* (ed: Jerry Finn, and Gary Holden) The Haworth Press, Inc., 2000, pp. 119-136. Single or multiple copies of this article are available for a fee from The Haworth Document Delivery Service [1-800-342-9678, 9:00 a.m. - 5:00 p.m. (EST). E-mail address: getinfo@ haworthpressinc.com].

INTRODUCTION

The Internet is a revolutionary means of communication that promises to transcend geographic boundaries: where one works, receives social support, engages in recreation or serves one's "community" need no longer be tied to where one lives. As a result, new forms of health and human service programs are being delivered on the Internet (Brandt, 1998; Virtual Volunteering Project, 1999; Ensman, 1997; Ferguson, 1996; Schwartz, 1996; Moore, 1995; Maciuszko, 1993; Johnson, 1987). These include online information and referral, advocacy activities and even offering direct services. In addition, agencies have begun to use the Internet to secure resources and to recruit and involve volunteers (Finn, 1999).

As a result of funding cuts during the 1980s, increased caseloads in social problem areas such as AIDS, drug use, teen pregnancy and medical indigence, and increasing pressure from political and corporate sectors to give community members a first-hand look at the public and nonprofit sector agencies serving them, many health and human service organizations have had to increase the number of volunteers involved in the agencies activities (Menefee, 1997; Dundjerski et al., 1997). Various national campaigns, such as America's Promise, have created an enhanced awareness of the benefits of volunteering, which in turn has lead to more people than ever before looking for community service opportunities. While the ranks of potential volunteers increase and more agency staff are required to involve volunteers, however, few have received training in the effective management of volunteers, nor in how to create meaningful opportunities for them (Ellis 1997, Billitteri, 1997, Brudney, 1993). Also, work and lifestyle changes have changed the commonly-held view of potential volunteers–the traditional image of the middle-aged suburban mother volunteering a few hours a week is giving way to loaned executives, one-time-one-day volunteers, workers looking for opportunities to train in new skills and youth looking for experiences to apply in the workplace.

The Internet has begun to be seen as a vehicle for effective volunteer recruitment that targets a variety of audiences (Finn, 1999; Landesman, 1998; Cravens, 1997; Hawthorne, 1997). In addition to posting information about volunteering on individual Web sites, many agencies are utilizing high-traffic third-party "meta-sites," offering searchable databases of volunteering opportunities to as many as 15,000 people a day (e.g., Impact Online [http://www.impactonline.org/]; Action Without Borders [http://www.idealist.org/]; Project America [http://www.project.org/]). It is likely that as use of the Internet continues to grow, it will be seen as an increasingly important tool to support volunteer recruitment and management.

This paper examines another way to use the Internet in volunteer management: *"Virtual Volunteering,"* in which volunteers conduct their activities for agencies and clients over the Internet, in whole or in part. The paper describes the Virtual Volunteering Project (The Project), an online resource and set of services that provides guidance to agencies and volunteers interested in virtual volunteering programs. Based on the data and the experience of the Virtual Volunteering Project staff, issues related to successful virtual volunteering programs are considered. In addition, it summarizes data from a variety of sources that highlight the number and types of agencies and volunteers engaged in virtual volunteering.

VIRTUAL VOLUNTEERING

Why Virtual Volunteering?

Many people search for volunteer opportunities they can complete via home or work computers because of time constraints, personal preference, a disability, or a home-based obligation that prevents them from volunteering on-site. In addition, in our increasingly mobile society, volunteers may still have ties to a previous geographic community and wish to contribute to its welfare even though they no longer live there. Virtual volunteering allows anyone to contribute time and expertise to not-for-profit organizations, schools, government offices and other agencies that utilize volunteer services without leaving his or her home or office.

Virtual volunteering also allows agencies to expand the benefits of their volunteering programs by allowing more volunteers to participate and by involving volunteers in new areas. This type of volunteering may help agencies further cultivate community support and further augment staff resources and existing volunteer program.

What Is Virtual Volunteering?

The *Virtual Volunteering Project [http://www.serviceleader.org/vv/]*, based at the Charles A. Dana Center at the University of Texas at Austin, defines virtual volunteering as people providing volunteer service via the Internet and their home or work computers, and agencies using the Internet to involve volunteers. The Project has documented a variety of ways volunteers are using the Internet to support an organization, including:

- conducting online research: finding information for a grant proposal or newsletter, gathering details on legislation that could affect an agency's clients, searching for news articles on a particular topic, etc.;
- electronically visiting someone who is homebound, in a hospital, in a rest home or in a remote location;
- providing online mentoring and instruction (telementoring or teletutoring);
- staffing an e-mail or chat room support line, where people send questions or concerns and trained volunteers answer them;
- working with other volunteers or clients to create a project, such as gathering news for a neighborhood Web site, or gathering historical information on a particular time or region to post on a Web site or use in printed material;
- providing professional expertise: answering an agency's questions regarding human resources, accounting, management or legal issues; writing a speech; developing a strategic plan for a particular department; designing a newsletter, brochure, logo, database or Web site, etc.;
- conducting online outreach and advocacy: preparing legislative alerts to be sent via e-mail, keeping track of legislation that could affect an agency's clients, etc.;
- translating a document into another language;
- making a Web site accessible for people with disabilities; and
- surveying volunteers via e-mail about experiences with an agency or program, keeping track of volunteer hours, inputting volunteer opportunities into third party volunteer recruitment data banks, etc.

Online volunteers provide a variety of services for human service agencies by supporting staff and other volunteers or working directly with clients and audiences. Assignments can also have different levels of "virtuality." For instance, a volunteer may talk with a client via e-mail in addition to regular face-to-face visits. Some agencies use the Internet as a way for all volunteers to report progress, regardless of where or how service is performed, or use the Internet as a vehicle for volunteers to exchange ideas with each other [see: http://www.serviceleader. org/vv/orgs/].

Online volunteering has been going on since the Internet first started networking remote computers–people offering advice and services to others outside of the scope of what they are paid to do. USENET newsgroups are an excellent example of this. The Virtual Volunteering Project narrowed its focus, however, to online volunteering affiliated, formally or informally, with a human service agency or charitable cause.

The Virtual Volunteering Project was launched in December 1996 because Impact Online (IOL) [http://www.impactonline.com/], a not-for-profit organization that maintains an online database of volunteering opportunities all over the U.S., had been inundated with requests from people who wanted to provide support via their home or work computer. These volunteers were interested in performing a variety of tasks such as helping agencies build Web sites and tutoring young people online. Impact Online involved some of these volunteers in its own activities [http://www.serviceleader.org/vv/vols96.html], but tried to send the majority to other agencies with missions more in line with the volunteers' objectives. Few of these volunteers were placed in online assignments, however, because most agencies did not understand how to involve them. To address this gap, Impact Online envisioned the Virtual Volunteering Project to encourage and assist in the development of online volunteering opportunities. The focus of the Project they envisioned would be to create and promote resources for agencies and to profile agencies already engaged in virtual volunteering. Initial support for this project was secured from the James Irvine Foundation, the David and Lucile Packard Foundation and the Morino Institute.

The Project delivers its resources via the Web [http://www.serviceleader. org/vv/], providing information and examples related to screening, monitoring, tracking and evaluating online volunteers. Available materials include sample online orientations, applications and assignments. In addition, information is provided to help agencies involve people with disabilities in virtual volunteering programs, including resources to make a Web site accessible for people with disabilities and those using assistive technologies. The project also provides information on how to get staff involved in such a project and how to evaluate an organization's readiness for such a program.

The majority of the Project's materials are geared towards nonprofit organizations and public sector organizations, including human service agencies: to help them introduce the concept to their agency, to prepare staff for the involvement of online volunteers, to create online assignments, and to screen, evaluate, assign and recruit online volunteers. Some materials are focused on volunteers themselves, however, to help them find and create online opportunities and to help them work effectively in online assignments.

Foundation for Successful Virtual Volunteering Programs

The Virtual Volunteering Project defines a successful virtual volunteering program as one in which:

- all volunteer activities are in support of the agency's mission,
- online volunteer service is actively encouraged, valued, and supported by all staff members, and,
- online volunteers are recognized for their contributions to the same degree as onsite volunteers and other agency supporters (such as donors).

A successful virtual volunteering program quickly matches potential online volunteers with assignments, keeps track of volunteer activities, and provides support for these activities. Virtual volunteering involves technology, of course, but what makes a virtual volunteering program successful is what makes any service program worthwhile: good systems for training, placing, managing, and tracking volunteers; meaningful evaluation of the volunteer program and its impact on an agency's mission-based activities; and ongoing commitment and support from the staff.

When the Project was officially launched in 1996, one of its advisors, Susan Ellis, an internationally-recognized expert in volunteer management and volunteerism, predicted that the key to involving volunteers virtually would be the organization's success at involving volunteers in traditional, face-to-face situations. Per her comments, as well as the initial feedback from agencies and volunteers, one of the first tools developed by the Project was an assessment instrument for agencies: *"How do I know if my organization is ready for virtual volunteering?"* [http://www.serviceleader.org/vv/ready.html]. The focus of this instrument is not on the organization's technological capabilities, but rather, its overall volunteer management. Any successful volunteer project, whether it be virtual or otherwise, must be related to the mission of the agency, provide staff training and time for management of the project, incorporate meaningful and useful tasks, assess volunteer motivation and skills, provide ongoing communication with volunteers, and assess the success of the volunteer program from the agency and the volunteer's perspective (Campbell & Ellis, 1995; Ellis, 1996b).These criteria were incorporated into the Project's virtual volunteering assessment guide.

Virtual volunteering is similar to telecommuting, which involves paid staff supporting a company via a home computer and the Internet. Issues include management and work styles, commitment to supervision and involvement, and other human factors, rather than technology. Therefore, the Project referenced several online telecommuting to help organizations create online assignments and supervise online volunteers (Moskowitz, 1996; Kelley and McGraw, 1995; *Pacific Bell Network Telecommuting Guide,* 1997).

Methodology in Creating Virtual Volunteering Project Materials

Available literature on volunteer management is based on traditional volunteer programs. At the time of this Project's launch, little was known about the ways that programs could adapt onsite volunteer management practices to the online environment. The Virtual Volunteering Project sought to obtain feedback and first hand experience from agencies and volunteers to determine the ways online volunteers were engaging in service, the factors for success in online volunteer service programs, and the extent to which the Project's materials were useful in facilitating virtual volunteering development. To achieve this, the Project pursued four strategies:

- Informal online surveys of agencies [http://www.serviceleader. org/vv/vvnow.html] and volunteers [http://www.serviceleader. org/vv/vquest.html] that engaged (or were attempting to engage) in virtual volunteering. These surveys were not pre-tested, nor did they have a scholarly or academic focus; their purpose was to get informal, first-hand feedback from people engaged in virtual volunteering;

- inviting feedback from both agencies and volunteers in e-mails, via the Web and at workshops involving Project representatives;
- working directly with selected agencies to help them initiate or expand involvement of online volunteers; and,
- soliciting feedback of online volunteers in activities that support the Project itself.

During 1997 and 1998, surveys were delivered via the Project's Website, e-mailed directly to organizations the Project manager knew or suspected were involving online volunteers, and were posted to online discussion groups relating to volunteers, not-for-profit, or advocacy organizations. In addition, surveys were created specifically for organizations using VolunteerMatch [http://www.volunteermatch. org] to recruit online volunteers (n = 105), and volunteers who signed up for virtual opportunities on this service (n = 245). VolunteerMatch, which is Impact Online's (IOL) centerpiece program, was chosen because of the Project's past association with IOL and because it lists the greatest number of virtual volunteering opportunities of any online recruitment database. Finally, the Project also included questions in its own application for potential online volunteers [http://www.serviceleader.org/vv/volapp.html] so staff could track demographics, past volunteer experiences (on or offline) and interests of those wanting to volunteer virtually.

The feedback generated from all of these various forms is available and summarized on the Project's Web site [http://www.serviceleader. org/vv/admin/]. It's worth noting that this information was formatted and summarized largely by online volunteers themselves, working on behalf of the Project [http://www.serviceleader.org/vv/vols98.html].

Another source of feedback was information obtained by working directly with agencies to help them set up or expand a virtual volunteering program. The original Affiliate organizations were selected based on their knowledge of basic volunteer issues; their success with volunteers in traditional, face-to-face settings; their vision for virtual volunteering at their own organization; their commitment to collaborating with the Project; their knowledge of basic Internet navigation and use; and their demonstrated commitment to timely communications via e-mail. The Project formed an Affiliates program [http://www.

serviceleader.org/vv/affiliate.html] to help staff establish collaborations that would allow them to detail first hand the realities of setting
up and maintaining such a program. The Project staff provided technical assistance to the 13 Affiliate organizations via phone, a private
e-mail discussion group, and, for more than half of the group, in a
face-to-face setting. The Affiliate agencies also asked questions and
provided assistance to each other via the discussion group.

The Project itself involved more than 100 online volunteers in
support of its activities during its first two years [http://www.serviceleader.
org/vv/vols01.html]. This allowed staff to document first hand the realities
of working with volunteers via cyberspace. Another reason to involve
volunteers was because the Project has a commitment to the involvement of the cyberspace community in its activities, just as do other
organizations that work to involve their local communities in on-site
programs. In addition to completing volunteer assignments, many of
these volunteers also offered suggestions and information for materials on the Project Web site.

Feedback Results and Implications

Using informal feedback, survey data [http://www.serviceleader.
org/vv/admin/], and profiles of agencies and volunteers featured on the
Virtual Volunteering Project Website, it is possible to create a general
profile of the people who are performing online service, the agencies
they are assisting, and the kinds of service being performed. This is
not a formal evaluation based on rigorous methodological standards,
but rather is one person's (the Virtual Volunteering Project Manager)
observations based on a combination of survey data, agency feedback,
experience in volunteer management of online volunteers, and discussions with online volunteers. Much of the data used to identify the
following results is available at: [http://www.serviceleader.org/vv/admin/].

It is not possible to determine the population of online volunteers or
the agencies that utilize them because there is no central registration of
organizations or individuals engaged in any type of volunteering, let
alone online service. In addition, many organizations that involve
online volunteers don't know the terms "virtual volunteering" or
"cyber service," and do not distinguish virtual involvement as different from on-site service.

The Project has identified almost 200 agencies involving online
volunteers, and profiled more than 100 such agencies on its Web site

[http://www.serviceleader.org/vv/orgs/]. The Project has also compiled more than 400 e-mail addresses of volunteers interested or engaged in virtually volunteering. Based on informal observations by the Project staff and advisors, however, these numbers likely greatly underestimate those who are involved in virtual volunteering activities.

Who Is Volunteering Virtually?

The Project received online feedback through surveys and its application for online volunteers from more than 100 people volunteering virtually, ranging in age from 14 to 75. Most were between the ages of 18 and 50, with no large cluster of people anywhere within this range. The median age is 31. Approximately twenty people ages 14 to 17 have contacted the Project looking for online volunteer opportunities because the agencies they wanted to help on-site had prohibitions against involving anyone under 18, or because they had no transportation to an on-site volunteer assignment. There have been fewer than half a dozen online volunteers over 70 who have contacted the Project about online volunteering experiences.

The majority, more than 60%, of online volunteers in contact with the Project identified themselves as Anglo or of European descent. The next largest group, approximately 10 percent, identified as people of Asian or East Indian descent. Fewer than 5% said they were African American or Hispanic, and none identified as American Indian. About 25% of respondents did not answer questions relating to age or ethnicity, and a few expressed anger that the questions were asked at all. The Project makes it clear on its forms and surveys that the questions are asked only for statistical purposes, but a few people have said these questions defeat the idea that everyone is "equal" on the Internet. The limited ethnic diversity among online volunteers reflects the much cited technology gap in Internet access for ethnic minorities in the United States (Stevens, 1999). Gender, however, appears to be equally distributed among online volunteers, with males and females each accounting for approximately 50% of online volunteers.

More than 25% of online volunteers and more than 35% of the agencies involving online volunteers, based on survey and application responses, are in California, in or near the San Francisco or Los Angeles metropolitan areas. Other areas with relatively large numbers of online volunteers are the greater Washington, D.C./Philadelphia metropolitan areas, New York City, the Boulder/Denver Colorado metropolitan areas, Florida, North Carolina and Texas. All of these areas have a higher number of Internet users per capita than the rest of the country (ZDNet, 1998). The large numbers in California could also be because Impact Online has a well-established reputation in the state.

More than 75% of online volunteers have performed or are also performing volunteer service in on-site, face-to-face settings. Most reported very positive experiences as on-site volunteers, and looked at online volunteering as another way to "help others" or "give back." Fewer than 10% of respondents reported wanting to volunteer online as a permanent alternative to traditional, face-to-face volunteering.

Convenience and schedule flexibility were the two most common cited reasons for individuals choosing to volunteer online. A few reported an interest in online service just to see what it was like, or because they felt guilty for spending so much time online and wanted to do something more constructive while on the Internet. Many reported using virtual volunteering as a way to develop certain skills (for example, Web design). About a dozen people said they prefer online volunteering to on-site volunteering because a disability or health issue makes traditional service difficult. One person noted that, when volunteering online, *"People see me, not the* (wheel) *chair."*

What Agencies Are Involving Online Volunteers?

Agencies generally reflect the same geographic representation as online volunteers, although the Western states of Washington, Oregon and Arizona also have many agencies engaged in virtual volunteering [http://www.serviceleader.org/vv/orgs/]. Virtual volunteering seems to have taken hold with agencies in Western states in particular. In combination, online volunteers and agencies in contact with the Project represent half of all states. Canada, as a region, ranks third behind California and New York as having the most agencies and individuals who engage in virtual volunteering.

There seems to be no particular trend in staff size for agencies involving online volunteers. Based on the surveys completed by agencies for the Virtual Volunteering Project, some are all-volunteer organizations with no staff, some have as many as 50 employees, and there is a wide range of agencies in between.

Approximately 31% of agencies involving online volunteers have a specific focus on technology as part their mission: community networks and freenets being the most common. One example of a technology-related agency using online volunteers is the Digital Clubhouse Digitally Abled Producers Project [http://dap.digiclub.org], which pairs youth with disabilities and youth without disabilities to teach multimedia, universally accessible Web page production, networking and career skills. Agencies that do not focus on technology as part of their mission involved online volunteers in staff-assistance roles, primarily building Web sites or performing online research. It has been difficult to identify organizations engaged in online volunteering that already had traditional, face-to-face service opportunities that matched volunteers with clients, because there is no central registry of such agencies, and search engines and Web directories do not list such agencies under one identifiable category.

How Do Most Volunteers Connect with Online Assignments?

More than 25% of online volunteers said they performed an online assignment for an agency that they or a family member or friend were already working with offline, or with whom they had a personal connection (knew a staff member). The second most frequently cited reason for virtual volunteering was related to having volunteer opportunities with an agency that had a mission they personally supported. When potential volunteers did not already have a personal connection with an organization, they looked for opportunities using Web search engines and directories, Yahoo! [http://www.yahoo.com] being the most frequently used. They searched using the word "volunteer," or looked for agencies based on mission and program types (improving the environment, working with the elderly, etc.) in which they were interested.

What Are the Most Common Tasks of Online Volunteers?

Approximately 45% of online volunteers who answered the Project survey created or maintained Web sites for an organization. More than 40% of volunteers have performed online research, provided technical assistance to staff and clients, and helped with online marketing and activism, such as posting alerts to appropriate online discussion groups.

The Project staff has identified more than 20 organizations that match online volunteers with clients, such as students in mentoring or tutoring, but none of these organizations have been willing to allow the Project to survey their volunteers, and none have provided feedback, even in summary, about the experiences of these volunteers. These organizations, on the rare occasion that they have responded to this request, have said they do not have the resources or time to comply. Information about 18 of these organizations is available online, indexed at [http://www.serviceleader.org/vv/orgs/mentor.html].

What Do Agencies and Volunteers Dislike About Virtual Volunteering?

Both volunteers and agencies cited the lack of face-to-face contact as the biggest drawback of online service. Volunteers also frequently cited a lack of response from agencies, particularly in letting the volunteers know how their work made a difference at an agency. The number one complaint of volunteers who tried to use Volunteer Match to sign up for online opportunities was lack of follow up by the agency. Approximately 30% never heard from the agencies that used this service to say they needed online volunteers, and more than 70% were never actually placed in an online assignment.

Although the Project is set up specifically to assist agencies, the feedback from volunteers, such as what they disliked most about online volunteering, suggested a need for resources to assist individuals as well. While the majority of materials on the Project site are focused on agencies, a significant number are for volunteers. An example is *"Tips on Volunteering Virtually"* [http://www.serviceleader. org/vv/vvtips.html], which encourages volunteers to take the lead in initiating and maintaining communications with an agency. These and other materials for volunteers promote the idea that volunteers can encourage good volunteer management on the part of agency they serve; for example, a volunteer writing his or her own written task description if the agency does not provide one, as a way to clarify expectations and boundaries.

What Factors Promote or Impede the Success of a Virtual Volunteering Program?

Almost all of the factors cited in the surveys as impeding the success of virtual volunteering related to overall organization management, which greatly affects the management and involvement of volunteers. For agencies, the most common obstacles cited in survey responses were lack of time on the part of the supervisor to manage the program and lack of a system to create assignments and match volunteers to those assignments. The Virtual Volunteering Project manager has observed that this is also a top complaint of managers working in traditional, face-to-face volunteer settings, and believes this reflects the overall need for better volunteer management training and support. Only two organizations of the more than 100 in contact with the Project cited a lack of volunteers as an impediment.

More than 50% of agencies using VolunteerMatch in January 1999 to recruit online volunteers and who responded to the Project survey stated that they did not have any system to screen, orient or supervise online volunteers. Therefore, most did not meet the requirements outlined in the Project's instrument to assess an organization's readiness to engage in online volunteering [http://www.serviceleader.org/vv/ready.html]. The Project staff feels this lack of preparation and organizational readiness are the chief reasons that the majority of volunteers who used VolunteerMatch never actually engaged in an online assignment.

Some volunteer managers said they had difficulty relating to volunteers online. For instance, one agency reported, "It's difficult to know whether someone hasn't written you back because they're no longer interested or because they're unavailable." These types of comments led to the creation of materials that deal specifically with online communications from the human perspective (as opposed to the technology perspective). The first was *"Online Culture"* [http://www.serviceleader.org/vv/culture.html], which notes the variety of communication styles of online volunteers and provides first-hand accounts and advice from the Project Affiliate agencies. This Web page cites numerous other resources providing guidelines for online communication.

Development of clearly written task descriptions and a good communication process for delivering these assignments to volunteers are cited most by agencies as the key to success in virtual volunteering programs. It is worth noting that most agencies that said they have a successful virtual volunteering program also have a staff person whose primary responsibility is volunteer management. All of these criteria are cited as necessary for a successful program in *"How do I know if my organization is ready for virtual volunteering?"* [http://www.serviceleader.org/vv/ready.html]. However, while the Project has this and other resources that address the issues cited by those surveyed regarding what promotes or impedes the success of a virtual volunteering program, most organizations providing feedback were unaware of these resources before they embarked on virtual volunteering. The Project hopes to secure funding in its fourth year to increase awareness of its resources to agencies that involve volunteers.

FUTURE DIRECTIONS

The Internet is not a fad. Neither is virtual volunteering. Most agencies report an onslaught of interested individuals once they announce a virtual volunteering opportunity. As more agencies involving volunteers go online, it is likely that opportunities for virtual volunteering programs will expand. Agencies will need assistance in creating successful virtual volunteering programs.

As is suggested in the data collected by this Project, the success of a virtual volunteering program is tied directly to an organization's level of expertise in volunteer management and organizational commitment to volunteering programs in general. While the government and corporate sectors increasingly promote volunteerism in their national agenda, few organizations are addressing the critical need for better training and resources for those who manage volunteers. The Virtual Volunteering Project has an established relationships with organizations such as Directors of Volunteers in Agencies (DOVIA) and the Association for Volunteer Administrators (AVA), and will continue to use these relationships to generate support for more training and resources for volunteer managers, thereby creating the groundwork necessary for successful cyber service.

In our contacts with human service agencies, it appears that more and more agencies are using the Internet to communicate with all volunteers, regardless of where their service is performed. A growing number of agencies use e-mail and Web-based systems for all volunteers to report progress. In addition, based on our research using online search engines to identify such groups, there appears to have been a great rise in the number of online discussion groups, via e-mail or real-time communications, through which volunteers can interact with staff, clients or each other. The Project is working to address the needs of supervisors of volunteers as they increasingly use technology in the management of all volunteers. For instance, the most recent materials added to the Project's Web site are to help agencies wanting to set up such online discussion groups and to help volunteers who moderate or facilitate such groups [http://www.serviceleader.org/vv/vhosts.html].

An increasing number of organizations are contacting the Project about involving online volunteers with clients, including schools wanting to match online volunteers with students. Many corporations find the idea of funding telementoring or teletutoring programs attractive because of the cutting-edge sound of such programs; however, organizations are cautious about the idea because of questions around how online volunteers will be screened and supervised in interactions with young people, and possible liability issues. The Project has a growing list of organizations with successful existing programs [http://www.serviceleader.org/vv/direct/]. In addition, it provides suggestions for ensuring safety in online volunteering programs [http://www.serviceleader.org/vv/safety/], including information on creating policies and procedures to protect both volunteers and staff online, suggestions and examples for involving online youth volunteers, and guidelines for bringing together youth and adult online volunteers. Because the Project is now under the Charles A. Dana Center, a research unit within the University of Texas with a primary focus on schools, staff will work directly with schools in both virtual volunteering and improving community involvement overall.

The cluster of online volunteers and agencies in only a few metropolitan areas indicates a lack of familiarity with virtual volunteering and its potential benefits in many of the sectors that involve volunteers. The Project has never engaged in an offline, printed dissemination of its materials. Outreach has been done only via the Project's Web site, other organizations' Web sites, various online discussion groups, e-mail, stories in major metropolitan newspapers, articles in trade publications, and via workshops in conjunction with other organizations. If funding permits, the Project hopes to address this situation in the Fall 1999 with a direct mail campaign to more than 2,000 key organizations and networks throughout the United States.

Most agencies that involve volunteers do not have a technology focus. To reach more of these organizations, there is a need for professional associations of not-for-profit organizations, schools, government agencies and other organizations that involve volunteers to provide information and resources via their existing channels about virtual volunteering. The Project hopes to partner with such groups to produce materials to achieve this goal.

While addressing technology gaps, such as the gap in minority representation on the Internet, is not part of the Project's mission, helping agencies reach diverse audiences through virtual volunteering programs is very much part of the Project's focus. In its next phase, Project staff will seek to collaborate with agencies addressing gaps in technology access and training, and will create and link to resources that can help agencies reach and involve a variety of populations as volunteers.

The future of virtual volunteering will be driven by real-life needs, wants and concerns. Further development of Virtual Volunteering Project materials will continue to be tied directly to the ongoing feedback of agencies and individuals. This requires an ongoing commitment to program evaluation and consumer feedback. The Project hopes to expand its evaluation efforts through further development of online and e-mail-based surveys. The Project staff has its own ideas of the future of virtual volunteering, but it is the other agencies and online volunteers themselves that will ultimately decide what's next.

REFERENCES

Billitteri, Thomas J. (1997). "Research on Charities Falls Short." *Chronicle of Philanthropy*, (November 27), cover story.

Bowen, P. (1997). "Exploration of public issues in the United States, Canada, and beyond: trends in volunteerism, a Canadian perspective." *Journal of Volunteer Administration*, 15, Spring, 4-6.

Brandt, M.G. (1998). "Local Nonprofit Organizations at Work: A composite vision of a community presence on the World Wide Web." Online: *http://www.uwm.edu/People/mbrandt/toc.htm*.

Brudney, Jeffrey L. (1993). "1992 Association for Volunteer Administration Membership Survey: Summary of Results." June 1993.

Cravens, J. (1997). "What use is the Internet to a nonprofit organization (NPO)?" Online: Nonprofit Organization FAQ. http://www.eskimo.com/~pbarber/npofaq/06/05.html

Campbell and Ellis, S.J. (1995). *The (Help) I-Don't-Have-Enough-Time Guide to Volunteer Management*. Philadelphia: Energize, Inc.

Demko, P. (1996). "Do-good men prove hard to find." *Chronicle of Philanthropy*, 8, (March 21), 1, 12, 14, 17.

Dundjerski, M., Hall, H., Moore, J., and Williams, G. (1997). "Whether panned or raised, summit focused nation's attention on volunteers." *Chronicle of Philanthropy*, 9 (May 15), 33-35.

Ellis, S.J. (1996a). *The Volunteer Recruitment Book*. Philadelphia: Energize, Inc.

Ellis, S.J. (1996b), *From the Top Down: The Executive Role in Volunteer Program Success.* Philadelphia: Energize, Inc.

Ensman, R.G. (1997). "Turn small shops into big shops via the Internet." *Fund Raising Management*, 28 (June) 18-19.

Finn, J. (1999). Seeking Volunteers and Contributions: An exploratory study of nonprofit agencies on the Internet. *Journal of Technology in Human Services*, 15(4) 24–38.

Gorski, H.A., Hodgkinson, V.A., Knauft, E.B., and Noga, S.M. (1995). "Giving and volunteering in the United States: trends in giving and volunteering by type of charity." Volume II. Washington: Independent Sector.

Hawthorne, N. (1997). "The history and development of Internet resources for volunteer programs." *Journal of Volunteer Administration*, 16 (Fall), 28-33.

Johnson, S. (1987). "Nonprofit and Public Service Telecomputing," Paper presented at the First International Human Service Information Technology Applications Conference, Birmingham, England, September.

Kelley, B. and McGraw, B. (1995). *"Are You Are Ready For Telecommuting," "Successful Management in the Virtual Office."* Online, no longer available. Released May 10, 1995.

Landesman, C. (1998). "Nonprofits and the World Wide Web." Online: July 9, http://www.nonprofits.org/parlor/website.html.

Maciuszko, K.L., (1993). "A quiet revolution: community on-line systems," *Online*, 14(6), November.

Menefee, D. (1997). "Strategic administration of nonprofit human service organizations: A model for executive success in turbulent times." Administration in Social Work, 21(2), 1-19.

Moore, J. (1995). "Fundraising by computer: the next frontier?" *Chronicle of Philanthropy.* 7 (Jan. 12) 1, 22-24.

Moskowitz, R. (1996), MicroTimes magazine, Online: [http://microtimes.com/155/telecommuting.html].

Pacific Bell Network Telecommuting Guide (1996). *"Are You Ready To Telecommute? An Objective Checklist To Determine If Your Company . . .,* Online [http://www.pac-bell.com/products/business/general/telecommuting/tcguide/index.html]

National Mentoring Partnership (1997) *"Provider Diagnostic.* Online: [http://www.mentoring.org/organizations.html]

Stevens, C. (1999) "Tech gap widens based on race, income, locale." *Philanthropy Journal:* Nonprofits and Technology, Online, available: [http://www.pj.org].

Schwartz, E. (1996). NetActivism: How citizens use the Internet. Sebastopol, CA: Songline Studios, Inc.

Virtual Volunteering Project (1999). Online:, available: http://www.serviceleader.org/vv/.

ZDNet (1998) "Most Wired Cities," Online, available: http://www.zdnet.com/yil/content/mag/9803/citynumb.html].

Online Fundraising
in the Human Services

Jerry D. Marx

SUMMARY. This paper examines emerging possibilities for use of the Internet in human service fundraising. Human service managers must compete for limited funds with their counterparts in educational, religious, health, and other nonprofit organizations. There is enormous potential for raising funds over the Internet; yet, this approach to resource development may not be appropriate or effective in some instances for certain human service agencies. The selection of fundraising approach must be consistent with the organizational context in which it is used. This paper provides examples of cases where use of the Internet may prove to be an effective method for human service fundraising. It also examines cases where use of the Internet may not be a good match for the organizational context, whether in terms of ethics or dollars raised. *[Article copies available for a fee from The Haworth Document Delivery Service: 1-800-342-9678. E-mail address: <getinfo@haworthpressinc. com> Website: <http://www.haworthpressinc.com>]*

KEYWORDS. Internet, online, fundraising, human services, technology

The distinctive challenges faced by managers in private nonprofit human services are increasingly recognized. These include fundraising in a time of increased demand for services and decreased public

Jerry D. Marx, DSW, is Assistant Professor, Graduate Social Work Program, University of New Hampshire, Murkland Hall, Durham, NH 03824 (E-mail: jdmarx@hopper.unh.edu).

[Haworth co-indexing entry note]: "Online Fundraising in the Human Services." Marx, Jerry D. Co-published simultaneously in *Journal of Technology in Human Services* (The Haworth Press, Inc.) Vol. 17, No. 2/3, 2000, pp. 137-152; and: *Human Services Online: A New Arena for Service Delivery* (ed: Jerry Finn, and Gary Holden) The Haworth Press, Inc., 2000, pp. 137-152. Single or multiple copies of this article are available for a fee from The Haworth Document Delivery Service [1-800-342-9678, 9:00 a.m. - 5:00 p.m. (EST). E-mail address: getinfo@haworthpressinc.com].

support; motivating volunteer governing boards; volunteer recruitment in the era of two-income families; and measuring outcomes when the product is "a changed human life" (Kelly, 1998; Drucker, 1990). Given this complexity, there is a growing body of literature on nonprofit management. It is expected that this emerging literature will increasingly address the use of new information technology for a variety of purposes including financial management (billing, budgets), case management (client case histories and other documentation) as well as fundraising.

In terms of human service fundraising, new software can help administrators manage information regarding donor gifts and pledges, prospective donors, receipts, and related reports and letters. The new software can be used in various types of fundraising: planned giving, special events (walkathons, auctions, etc.), major gifts, direct mail, capital campaigns, telemarketing, grant proposals, and membership development. CD-ROMs can be purchased that list board affiliations and biographical information on thousands of corporate, foundation, and nonprofit board members. CD-ROMs are also available that profile thousands of corporate and foundation giving programs. Furthermore, databases in DOS, Macintosh, and Windows versions provide information on federal grant opportunities as well as private and corporate foundations (The Chronicle of Philanthropy, 1998).

Yet only a few publications in the nonprofit management literature (Allen, Warwick, and Stein, 1996; DeAngelis, 1997; Finn, 1999; Johnston, 1999; Kelly, 1998; Miller and Strauss, 1996; Zeff, 1996) explore the potential impact of using the Internet for resource development. Today, development staff can participate in online discussions of fundraising through the Internet. There are World Wide Web sites that focus on specific fundraising methods such as planned giving and grant proposals. Other Web sites offer links to hundreds of foundations, while others provide data on federal grants (The Chronicle of Philanthropy, 1998).

The purpose of this article is to assist human service professionals involved in fundraising in examining the emerging possibilities and limitations of online fundraising. Although there is enormous potential for fundraising over the Internet, this approach to resource development may not be appropriate or effective for all human service agencies. The selection of a fundraising approach must be consistent with the organizational context in which it is used. In other words, the choice of fundraising methods must be an extension of the organization's mission, long-term objectives, and program development strategies (Howe, 1991).

ORGANIZATIONAL CONTEXT

Too often in human services, professionals responsible for raising funds proceed with the "cart before the horse." That is, they pursue funding opportunities and strategies with little regard for organizational context. If they are lucky enough to obtain a large grant, for example, they then try to adjust the organization's mission and long-term objectives to coincide with the terms of the grant. Former low-income "housing" agencies become "substance abuse treatment" facilities overnight. Such an approach leads to vague organizational missions, conflicting and irrelevant long-term objectives, confused board members, high staff turnover, and poor quality (Drucker, 1990; Howe, 1991).

A more professional approach to human service fundraising starts with an organizational mission that identifies the agency's purpose (what it does for whom) and related agency values (Howe, 1991). The mission is based upon an assessment of community needs as well as organizational strengths and weaknesses. Long-term objectives are established to fulfill this mission and programs are then developed to achieve the organization's objectives. Only after this foundation of planning is completed should human service fundraisers consider various fundraising approaches-including the use of the Internet.

Emerging Online Fundraising Opportunities

Once a human service organization decides to develop a program, typical sources of funds include individuals, government agencies, corporations, private foundations, and other nonprofit service organizations like United Way of America. These potential funding sources are traditionally solicited through one or more ways: written proposals, direct mail, telephone appeals, special events (auctions, raffles, etc.), and planned giving (bequests, etc.). Human service organizations are now starting to add a new medium to their portfolio of fundraising approaches–the Internet. The Internet can be used at every stage of the development process: identification, cultivation, solicitation, follow-up, and finally, stewardship (Kelly, 1998; Semple, 1993).

Identification. First, potential funders need to be identified. This often takes much background research by fundraising professionals. The great strength of the Internet is the easy access to unlimited information throughout the world. This information includes the formal funding priorities of thousands of foundations, including private, community, and corporate foundations. In addition to foundations, many corporations make donations directly to nonprofit organizations. The funding priorities of these corporate "direct giving" programs can also be found on the Internet. Furthermore, some Web sites include news of actual grants recently awarded by foundations and corporations to various nonprofit organizations. For example:

- The Foundation Center maintains a World Wide Web site [http://www.foundationcenter.org] that provides links to over 600 grantmaker Web sites (The Foundation Center, 1999).
- The Philanthropy Journal Online [http://www.pj.org] provides news articles on a variety of philanthropy topics including recent corporate and foundation grants (The Philanthropy Journal Online, 1999).

Cultivation. The next stage of the development process is the "cultivation" stage. Once prospective donors have been identified, these prospects need to be informed about the human service organization prior to solicitation. Donors are more likely to give to groups and causes with which they are familiar. Once interested in a specific human service organization, prospective donors may choose to get further involved in the organization, perhaps through volunteering or membership. A 1996 survey of giving and volunteering in the United States, done by The Gallup Organization for the Independent Sector, indicates that those who volunteer in human service organizations are five times as likely to make a donation (Marx, in press).

The Internet can be used as one of several ways to cultivate prospective donors (Johnston, 1999; Allen, Warwick, and Stein, 1996). Nonprofit organizations are increasingly establishing Web sites on the World Wide Web. These Web sites provide much more information about the human service organization and its cause than can be provided in most direct mailings or agency brochures. An informative Web site will provide information on the organization's mission, history, facilities, board of directors, executive director and other staff, agency finances, and specific programs and services. What is more, the Web site should allow potential donors to get further involved with the organization as volunteers or advocates. For example:

- The American Red Cross Web site [http://www.redcross.org] offers detailed information on all of its many programs, including the latest news on current disaster relief services. This information is complemented by color photos of people assisted by these services. The agency also offers a virtual tour of its museum and a "this month in history" calendar with historical facts about the Red Cross. For disaster relief, there is a "How you can help link" with a "give your time and skills" option for those interested in volunteering (The American National Red Cross, 1999).
- Second Harvest [http://www.secondharvest.org], the nation's largest chain of food banks, attempts to build interest in the organization by providing an online version of its magazine and the results of its quadrennial survey on hunger in America on its Web site (Demko & Dundjerski, 1998, p. 39).
- Similarly, the Enterprise Foundation [http://www.enterprise foundation.org], which promotes neighborhood development in Maryland, publishes an online magazine that highlights people and organizations involved with various community projects (Marchetti & Wallace, 1997).
- Some organizations, particularly advocacy organizations like the Rainforest Action Network [http://www.ran.org], give their visitors a chance to get involved with the cause by providing contact information on individuals or institutions that are the target of advocacy campaigns. Better yet, some organizations enable their supporters to send an e-mail or fax a letter directly from their Web site to a politician or company on a specific issue (Johnston, 1999).
- Amnesty International [http://www.amnesty.org] uses its Web site to sign up supporters for specific campaigns, such as the 50th Anniversary of the Declaration of Human Rights. Supporters signed an online petition that was later presented to the United Nations (Johnston, 1999).
- Two advocacy groups, Third Millennium [http://www.thirdmil. org] based in New York and Economic Security 2000 Action [http://www.economicsecurity2000.org] based in Washington D.C., co-sponsored an online march on Washington in January of 1999. "The Billion Byte March," as it was called, asked supporters to

sign an e-mail letter regarding social security reform. The e-mail messages were then sent to Congress and the White House en masse to coincide with the President's State of the Union message (Economic Security 2000, 1999; Demko, 1998).

Solicitation. After the prospective donor is acquainted, preferably even involved, in the human service organization, that person may be ready to make a financial gift to the agency. Although it sounds obvious, those that are asked to give are much more likely to make a donation. "The ask," therefore, needs to take place. Most donors start out making relatively small contributions, often as part of an organization's annual giving campaign or through special events.

The Internet can be a useful solicitation vehicle for small donations from individuals (Johnston, 1999; Zeff, 1996). An effective site on the World Wide Web will provide the prospective donor with several options for giving. The first and fastest way is to donate online using a personal credit card. Although many people are still apprehensive about sharing personal credit card information on the Internet, it is expected that this fear will dissipate as ever more secure transaction methods are developed and as the practice becomes a common part of our culture. The successful online bookstore, amazon.com, has 1.5 million customers and no record of credit card security problems (Johnston, 1999).

However, for more cautious donors, the Internet can facilitate more traditional giving by telephone or mail. For those who wish to donate by phone, the Web site may provide 1-800 telephone numbers with English and Spanish (or other language) options. For those who prefer to send a check or pledge card by mail, the best Web sites provide a contribution form to printout as well as the organization's mailing address. To illustrate:

- The American Red Cross does all of the above on its World Wide Web site. In addition, since it is a national organization with many local chapters, the Red Cross gives the potential donor the option of giving directly to the national office or to a specific local chapter. In the latter case, the Red Cross helps the donor to find the address of the nearest chapter by asking the person to enter their local zip code (The American National Red Cross, 1999).

For those apprehensive about the use of credit cards online, about 150 nonprofit organizations around the nation are now allowing supporters to make pledges online that are charged to their telephone bills. The telephone company subsequently makes the donation directly to the charity. In this way, the donor's credit card number does not have to be given out online (Blum & Hall, 1998).

Memberships are also used by many human services to generate revenue to support their programs. The Internet can enhance membership recruitment also. The Web site can be used to describe the benefits that individuals receive as a result of their membership contribution. Color photos can show the attractive merchandise that members receive, including items such as magazines, t-shirts, computer screen savers, or bumper stickers. Individuals (or other organizations) simply make their membership contribution in one of the several ways described earlier-by credit card online, phone, or mail. Examples of organizations that have used the Internet to boost membership include:

- The Gay, Lesbian, and Straight Education Network [http://www.glsen.org] based in New York works to eliminate homophobia in schools all over the country. The group recently found that about five percent of its membership first found out about the organization through the Internet (Demko & Moore, 1998).
- The World Wildlife Fund USA [http://www.worldwildlife.org] averaged 70 new online memberships per month from April of 1997 to April of 1998 (Johnston, 1999).

Another way for human service organizations to solicit donations from individuals is through special events. Auctions, raffles, walkathons, road races, home and garden tours, bake sales, car washes, fashion shows are all traditionally used by human service organizations to raise funds for programming. The Internet is increasingly used as a vehicle for conducting auctions. Human service organizations can either list their items with an online auction house or create their own online auction site. An online auction house will typically charge a commission fee (ranging from 2.5% to 5.0%) and many also charge a small listing fee (Johnston, 1999). For most human service organizations, however, the auction house will generate more potential bidders and pay for the expensive cost of advertising on major search engines such as AltaVista and Yahoo. Although some online auctions may end up losing money (like any special event), some examples of successful online auctions include:

- Operation USA [http://www.opusa.org], an international relief group headquartered in Los Angeles, raised $135,000 in a combination live and online auction in 1997. Over 100 of the bids were placed online (Demko & Moore, 1997).
- Ken Margolis Associates manage the "Artrock Auction," which raised $15,000 for the Save the Earth Foundation [http://www.savetheearth.org] (Allen et al., 1996).

Follow-up. After the "solicitation" stage of the development process comes the "follow-up" stage. Follow-up is crucial to successful fundraising. Prospective donors need to be reminded of their pledges. Donors need to be thanked after sending their contribution. The entire process needs to be evaluated. The Internet can assist human service professionals in all of these areas. E-mail messages can be employed to periodically remind prospective donors about their pledges. Thank you notes and receipts can be electronically sent via e-mail or the Web to donors almost immediately after receiving a contribution.

- UNICEF [http://www.unicef.org], for example, sends a thank you note on agency letterhead via its Web site that can be printed by the donor if a temporary receipt is desired. The thank you note includes the name and the address of the donor, the dollar amount of the gift, the date of the gift, and a statement of tax deductibility (Johnston, 1999).
- Amnesty International USA [http://www.amnesty.org] sends an e-mail message confirming each gift (Johnston, 1999).

With respect to evaluation, human service organizations are able to get feedback from donors and other supporters on various organizational issues through the Internet. The Children's Defense Fund [http://www.childrensdefense.org], for instance, gives supporters the option on its Web site to e-mail suggestions for adding to its parent information and resource list. Organizations can evaluate their solicitation process by asking for feedback on various aspects of their Web site-including their contribution pages. A short questionnaire can be filled out online by organization members, other donors, and other visitors to the site. Survey participants do not have to search for a pen with which to complete the questionnaire or walk the completed questionnaire to a mailbox.

Stewardship. The "stewardship" stage of the development process refers to the need to attend to your donors all year long, not just immediately after a gift. Agency supporters want to stay connected to the cause; they want to keep abreast of agency developments and events; they want to see the tangible benefits and outcomes related to their donations. Human service agencies have historically accomplished all of this through agency newsletters, annual reports, newspaper articles and editorials, and periodic open houses.

The Internet, once again, can assist in this phase of the development process. With more and more people using the Internet, agency supporters can check in on the organization frequently without having to leave their homes. Agency newsletters, brochures, and annual reports can be displayed on the Web site. Donors can e-mail questions to agency personnel, while agency leaders can send periodic e-mail messages to loyal agency supporters. Virtual tours of new facilities can be offered. The minutes of past board meetings as well as the agendas for future agency meetings can be provided on the Web or through e-mail. Furthermore, if appropriate, photos of agency clients can add an online face to program service statistics. To illustrate:

- United Way of America [http://www.unitedway.org] provides its supporters with online annual reports and IRS 990 forms (United Way of America, 1998).
- Mothers Against Drunk Driving, better known as MADD [http://www.madd.org], regularly gives relevant articles from the Associated Press and other sources to its supporters in its Web site (Mothers Against Drunk Driving, 1999).
- Junior Achievement of New York [http://www.ja.org] uses its Web site to provide an up-to-date schedule of organizational activities in the New York area ("Junior Achievement Takes Its Cause To The Web," 1997).
- The Children's Wish Foundation [http://www.childrenswish.org], based in Atlanta, Georgia, regularly updates an online journal featuring pictures and stories of ill children and wishes that have been filled by the foundation ("Children's Wish Foundation Establishes Web Site," 1998).

Limitations to Human Service Online Fundraising

There are several instances where the use of the Internet for human service fundraising may prove to be relatively ineffective, whether in terms of ethics or practical outcomes (i.e., dollars raised). For example, organizations that regularly cultivate prospective large donors (i.e., major gifts from individuals), in an effort to fulfill their missions in their respective communities, should not depend on the Internet for such solicitation (Kelly, 1998). The cultivation of major donors needs to be as thorough and effective as possible. The relatively small number of major donors allows human service organizations to give full attention to these prospects. With major gifts, face-to-face contact between organizational leaders and the donor is considered critical to fundraising success. This might include regular visits in person to the prospective donor. The more personal the approach, the better. Face-to-face contact allows for close proximity, which promotes intimacy, trust, and caring–all prerequisites for major gifts. Usually major gifts are solicited after a person has shown substantial interest, even involvement in the organization (Dean, 1993). Dependence on the Internet in this method of fundraising would be considered superficial, perhaps resulting in the loss of sizeable donations.

This is not meant to suggest that the Internet cannot be of some use in soliciting major gifts. As previously stated, the Internet can be used to generate interest and involvement by prospective large donors, thereby building the foundation for a major gift. And as discussed earlier, the Internet can be employed in researching prospective major donors (Kelly, 1998). Such online research can provide information on an individual's stock transactions and other property holdings, the existence of a family foundation, membership on corporate and foundation boards, as well as relevant demographic information such as the age of the individual. For-fee online search services include Dialog [http://www.dialog.com], and Nexis [http://www.nexis.com].

A second instance where the Internet may prove to be less effective for fundraising is the case of small, grassroots human service organizations, which comprise the vast majority of human service organizations. As stated earlier, many prospective donors are hesitant to make online donations or buy a nonprofit's merchandise (e.g., t-shirts, caps, calendars, etc.) over the Internet using their personal credit cards; the fear of online fraud, including online impostors and fraudulent sites, is still prevalent in America and around the world. Yet, using a credit card is the fastest way to purchase organizational merchandise or to make an individual donation over the Internet. Much of the willingness by the public to use credit cards online depends upon name recognition (Johnston, 1999). In this respect, large national and international human service organizations with "brand names" like the Salvation Army, the Red Cross, United Way of America, and the Girl Scouts of America have a major advantage over local grassroots human service organizations, which are not recognized nationally. These grassroots organizations with local missions and service objectives may not find the staff expense of maintaining a high quality Web site justified by the dollar amount of online donations and purchases.

To address this limitation, small, local organizations may want to organize national networks with similar human service organizations and increase their public service announcements as a group to promote better name recognition nationally. Another strategy would be the inclusion of links by a national organization such as United Way of America to small organizations, perhaps grouped according to related causes or geographic regions. United Way of America already does this to some extent by including links to local United Way agencies, which then provide information on their local member human service organizations.

Small, local human service organizations, given their limited budgets, may also be more negatively affected than larger agencies by the cost of doing nationwide fundraising online. States and municipalities have the right to impose regulations on charitable solicitations including registration fees. These fees and the staff time needed for proper registration nationwide could conceivably cost an agency several thousand dollars–up to $10,000 or more (Mercer, 1998). Organizations that ignore these responsibilities, or employ other organizations such as an auction house that neglect regulations, could face legal liabilities (Williams, 1998). All organizations looking to do online fundraising need to stay informed of their legal responsibilities. One way to do this is by reviewing the American Association of Fund-Raising Counsel Trust for Philanthropy's publication, "Annual Survey of State Laws Regulating Charitable Solicitations" (Mercer, 1998).

Controversial human service agencies offer a third instance in which a specific organization and the Internet may not be an effective match. As previously discussed, human service organizations are beginning to use online auction houses to raise funds for their human services. However, many online auction houses avoid working with controversial organizations due to fear that they may upset other client organizations and many of their regular bidders (Johnston, 1999). In addition, controversial agencies run the risk of "civil disobedience online" (Johnston, 1999, p. 185), given the ability of hackers to disrupt Web site and e-mail operations by blocking access to certain Web sites or inundating an agency with e-mail. Organizations that might experience these difficulties include:

- The Boy Scouts of America due to its controversial stance on the participation of the gay population in the organization's activities.
- Planned Parenthood because of its connection in the minds of Pro-Life groups with the abortion issue.
- Needle Exchange Programs because of the public debate over the appropriateness of supplying drug addicts with clean needles in an effort to prevent the spread of AIDS.

Another source for online fundraising, corporations, may also prove to be problematic, and therefore, ineffective for some human service organizations. Corporations are increasingly using "strategic philanthropy" and "cause-related marketing" to further various strategic business goals and objectives (Marx, 1998, 1997, 1996). In the former, strategic philanthropy, corporations (e.g., a publishing house) make donations to nonprofit organizations (a literacy project) with the expectation that the gift will produce positive benefits to the corporation (increased sales from a more literate population) at some point in the future. In the latter case, cause-related marketing, a corporation may enter into a formal agreement to make a contribution to a selected nonprofit organization for each purchase of a company product.

The Internet is a perfect tool for promoting such partnerships between corporations and nonprofit organizations. To illustrate:

- IGive [http://www.iGive.com], a membership organization headquartered in Evanston, Illinois, offers members the opportunity to donate to their favorite charity when they buy products from participating merchants. A percentage of the purchase price goes to the buyer's favorite cause. As of March 11, 1999, 42,383 members had donated a total of $288,128, which helped support 4,236 causes (iGive.com, 1999).

- Anheuser-Busch Inc., maker of Budweiser Beer, has links on its Budweiser Web site [http://www.budweiser.com/linkinfo.html] to The Nature Conservancy [www.tnc.org] and other wildlife and conservation nonprofit organizations. Anheuser-Busch gets to associate its product with the great outdoors, much like Coors and Rolling Rock beers, while building support for these groups.
- The International Red Cross runs an online lottery in partnership with a commercial organization called the International Lottery in Liechtenstein Foundation or "InterLotto" for short (Johnston, 1999). InterLotto [http://www.interlotto.com] runs the lottery, while the Red Cross gets 25 percent of the gross revenue.

For many human service organizations, such online partnerships with corporations may not be an option for ethical reasons. It is difficult to imagine a substance abuse prevention and treatment agency doing a partnership with a beer company. Such a relationship, while good for a company claiming to promote responsible drinking, may even result in decreased support from the general public for the nonprofit organization. The corporate partnership contradicts the mission and long-term objectives of the human service organization. Therefore, use of the Internet to raise funds in such a manner would be inappropriate, and possibly ineffective. Similarly, it is hard to imagine an agency that provides service to people addicted to gambling or a program that provides financial management counseling to low-income families entering into an online partnership with a lottery company, even one promoting responsible gambling, if there is such a thing. Again, such fundraising efforts by human service organizations may, in fact, produce a public relations backlash for the nonprofit, resulting in decreased community support. In these situations or more subtle examples such as support from corporations that have poor management-labor relations, the human service agency should consider its organizational value system before deciding on the corporate support.

A final instance where the Internet may prove to be less than effective is in planned giving. Organizations that solicit a significant number of planned gifts should not rely on the Internet for such solicitation. In a "planned gift," an individual donor makes a decision to make a gift of an asset to a charitable organization, yet the charity usually does not receive the actual financial benefit of the gift until some time in the future, typically after the individual donor dies (Kelly, 1998). This is why planned giving is often referred to as "deferred giving." The benefit to the nonprofit organization is deferred until some future time. The simplest and most basic instrument for planned giving is the charitable bequest, which is a gift made through an individual's will. However, other more complex and technical instruments for planned giving are increasingly being employed, including charitable remainder trusts, charitable gift annuities, pooled income funds, and charitable lead trusts (Kelly, 1998). Dependence on the Internet to administer these planned giving instruments is not prudent, given the technical complexity of this type of philanthropy. Also, because a small percentage of donors are in a position to do planned giving and since the benefits to charitable organizations of this type of philanthropy are typically large, face-to-face communication is most effective. Web sites can be used to provide introductory information to prospective donors on planned giving, but as with any major gifts, any requests for information should be followed by more personal attention and ultimately face-to-face communication.

CONCLUSION

The number of human service and other nonprofit organizations using the Internet is growing rapidly (Demko & Moore, 1998). From 1992 to June of 1998, the number of registered Internet addresses that end in ".org," the designation most often used by nonprofit organizations, increased from 500 to about 114,000.

Similarly, the number of prospective donors using the Internet to research and contribute to various charitable organizations is increasing. Today, for example, GuideStar [http://www.guidestar.org], a Web site established by Philanthropic Research, Inc., provides prospective donors with program and financial information, including IRS Form 990 data, on over 650,000 nonprofit organizations (GuideStar, 1999; Vimuktanon, 1997).

Professionals responsible for fundraising in human service organizations need to be aware of the strengths and weaknesses of the Internet as well as the opportunities and threats presented by this new technology. Used with insight and precision, the Internet can complement other fundraising efforts of human service organizations, perhaps leading to greater support for needed human services.

REFERENCES

Anheuser-Busch, Inc. (1999). *Other Anheuser-Busch sites.* Retrieved July 20, 1999 from the World Wide Web: http://www.budweiser.com/homepage/default.html.

Allen, N., Warwick, M. & Stein, M. (Eds.).(1996). *Fundraising on the Internet.* Berkeley, CA: Strathmoor.

Blum, D.E. & Hall, H. (1998, December 17). Phone billing option offered to encourage donations. *The Chronicle Of Philanthropy*, p. 35.

Children's Wish Foundation establishes web site. (1998, January). *Fundraising Management 28* (11), 7.

Dean, J.C. (1993). The two faces of development. *Fundraising Management 9*, 26-28.

DeAngelis, J. (1997). *The grantseeker's handbook of essential Internet sites.* Alexandria, VA: Capitol Publications.

Demko, P. (1998, September 24). Advocacy groups marching for changes in social security. *The Chronicle Of Philanthropy*, p. 45

Demko, P. & Dundjerski, M. (1998, March 12). Anti-hunger group updates web site. *The Chronicle Of Philanthropy*, p. 39.

Demko & Moore. (1998, Oct. 8). Charities put the web to work. *The Chronicle Of Philanthropy*, pp. 1, 41-44.

Demko & Moore. (1997, Nov. 13). On-line charity auction nets promising results. *The Chronicle Of Philanthropy*, p. 35.

Drucker, P. (1990). *Managing the non-profit organization.* New York: HarperCollins.

Economic Security 2000. (1999). *Billion byte march.* Retrieved March 19, 1999 from the World Wide Web: http://www.economicsecurity2000.org/signup.html.

Finn, J. (1999). "Seeking Volunteers and Contributions: An exploratory study of nonprofit agencies on the Internet." *Journal of Technology in Human Services*, 15(4), 39-56.

GuideStar. (1999). *Charity search.* Retrieved March 18, 1999 from the World Wide Web: http://nonprofit.guidestar.org/ search/search.cfm.

Howe, F. (1991). *The board member's guide to fundraising.* San Francisco: Jossey-Bass.

IGive.com.(1999). Statistics retrieved March 18, 1999 from the World Wide Web: http://www.iGive.com/html/splash.cfm.

Johnston, M. (1999). *The fund raiser's guide to the Internet.* New York: Wiley.

Junior Achievement takes its cause to the web. (1997, September). *Fundraising Management 28*(7), 8.

Kelly, K.S. (1998). *Effective fund-raising management.* NJ: Lawrence Erlbaum.

Marchetti, D. & Wallace, N. (1997, December 11). New Internet magazine on community development. *The Chronicle Of Philanthropy*, p. 43.

Marx, J.D. (1998). Corporate strategic philanthropy: Implications for social work. *Social Work*, 43(1), 34-41.

Marx, J.D. (1997). Corporate philanthropy and United Way: Challenges for the year 2000. *Nonprofit Management & Leadership*, 8(1), 19-30.

Marx, J.D. (1996). Strategic philanthropy: An opportunity for partnership between corporations and health/human service agencies. *Administration in Social Work*, 20(3), 57-73.

Marx, J.D. (in press). Women and human service giving. *Social Work.*

Mercer, E. (1998).*How can we use the Internet for fundraising?* Retrieved November 24, 1998 from the World Wide Web: http://www.nonprofit-info.org/misc/981027em.html.

Miller, J.D. & Strauss, D. (1996). *Improving fundraising with technology.* San Francisco: Jossey-Bass.

Mothers Against Drunk Driving. (1999). *Hot issues.* Retrieved March 19, 1999 from the World Wide Web: http://www. madd.org/hot_issues/default.shtml.

Semple, R.F. (1993). *The development process.* Unpublished manuscript.

The Chronicle of Philanthropy. (1998). *The non-profit handbook.* Washington D.C.: The Chronicle of Higher Education.

The Foundation Center. (1999). *What is The Foundation Center?* Retrieved July 19, 1999 from the World Wide Web: http://www.foundationcenter.org/ about/whatisfc.html.

United Way of America. (1998). *United Way of America's Annual Reports and 1996 Form 990.* Retrieved March 18, 1999 from the World Wide Web: http://www.unitedway.org/usaway.html.

Vimuktanon, A. (1997, October). Non-profits and the Internet. *Fundraising Management, 28*(8), 25-28.

Williams, G. (1998, December 3). Court upholds registration of fund-raising consultants. *The Chronicle Of Philanthropy,* p. 30.

Zeff. R. (1996). *The nonprofit guide to the Internet.* Somerset, NJ: Wiley.

Zeff, R. (1996). Cyber-fundraising. In N. Allen, M. Warwick & M. Stein. (Eds.), *Fundraising on the Internet* (pp. 8.1-8.18). Berkeley, CA: Strathmoor.

Liability and the Internet:
Risks and Recommendations
for Social Work Practice

Mary Banach
Frances P. Bernat

SUMMARY. Use of the Internet for counseling and information services has increased dramatically in the last five years. Although the Internet may benefit consumers by helping them secure needed services and resources, social workers and social service agencies who provide counseling over the Internet need to be aware of the legal risks associated with its use. Among the most salient concerns that need to be addressed are client confidentiality and privacy of records, appropriateness of treatment services, and the duty to warn others of harm that a client might pose to them. This paper looks at these legal concerns in light of appropriate Social Work practice and recommends methods to abate the risks that might occur when Internet counseling and service is provided. *[Article copies available for a fee from The Haworth Document Delivery Service: 1-800-342-9678. E-mail address: <getinfo@haworthpressinc.com> Website: <http://www.haworthpressinc.com>]*

KEYWORDS. Internet, liability, counseling, malpractice, risk management

---

Mary Banach, DSW, ACSW, is Assistant Professor, Department of Social Work, University of New Hampshire.

Frances P. Bernat, JD, PhD, is Associate Professor, Administration of Justice Department, Arizona State University West.

[Haworth co-indexing entry note]: "Liability and the Internet: Risks and Recommendations for Social Work Practice." Banach, Mary, and Frances P. Bernat. Co-published simultaneously in *Journal of Technology in Human Services* (The Haworth Press, Inc.) Vol. 17, No. 2/3, 2000, pp. 153-171; and: *Human Services Online: A New Arena for Service Delivery* (ed: Jerry Finn, and Gary Holden) The Haworth Press, Inc., 2000, pp. 153-171. Single or multiple copies of this article are available for a fee from The Haworth Document Delivery Service [1-800-342-9678, 9:00 a.m. - 5:00 p.m. (EST). E-mail address: getinfo@haworthpressinc.com].

153

INTRODUCTION

The World Wide Web has been heralded as an innovative and provocative medium within which people can connect (Goodman, 1998; Lim, 1996). Within the past few years, there has been a proliferation of Internet sites that provide useful information on mental health from an array of social service providers. The benefits associated with the provision of Internet social service health care include expedient services, convenience, low cost, and time savings. Consumers with Internet access can gather information rapidly and comfortably in their own home (Gellman, & Frawley, 1996; Giffords, 1998; Hannon, 1996; Lebow, 1998; Miller & Gergen, 1998; Sampson, Kolodinsky, & Greeno, 1997; Winzelberg, 1997).

Some consumers have gone further than mere information gathering and have participated in self-help, e-mail, and chat groups, engaged in "cybertherapy," or completed computer therapy diagnostic programs. Self-help groups are Internet sites that enable persons to "talk" with other persons in the group/room about specific topics or concerns, and online groups exist for every issue that is found in face to face self-help groups (Lempert, 1995; Madara, 1997; The American Clearinghouse, 1999). Cybertherapy enables a consumer to have a counseling session with an on-line therapist. On-line therapists attempt in a short amount of time to address the concerns of their clients, generally at a reduced cost to the client. In this regard, the therapy might last for only a session or two, address a non-serious issue (i.e., they won't address alcohol or drug dependency), and cost less than if the client had an in-office session (Childress, 1998; Lebow, 1998; Miller & Gergen, 1998). Online therapy may be via e-mail, chat or audio/videoconference. Computer diagnosis programs enable consumers to answer a series of multiple choice questions in order to discern whether they have a particular problem. The program will usually then provide the consumer with potential treatment options (Selfgrowth, 1999).

The benefits associated with Internet counseling interchanges include providing persons with help, advice, empathy, and support. Consumers may also be able to reframe their problems with the on-line help (Miller & Gergen, 1998). Because on-line consumers can get information and services easily and anonymously,[1] consumers who might otherwise forego treatment and services have another outlet for receiving help. Other benefits include support for those with access barriers such as transportation, disability, agoraphobia, poor interpersonal skills, inability to communicate verbally, and care-giving responsibilities. Other benefits include the provision of a stable support for those who travel or move, and those who are geographically isolated from services (Childress, 1998; Lebow, 1998).

With its many potential benefits, Internet services also contain new potential liability risks for practitioners and social service agencies (Lebow, 1998). In order reduce liability risks, the professional should incorporate risk management principles and avoid situations in which he or she might engage, or be charged with, professional misconduct. Although provision of services by mental health practitioners via the Internet has, for the most part, yet to be challenged in courts of law, practitioners are wise to consider basic liability issues as part of sound professional practice. While these issues have not been addressed in social work practice, cases involving telehealth are beginning to be tried and provide some guidelines for considering risk and liability issues.

Internet social service providers face some of the same liability risks that face-to-face service providers have. But, Internet service providers have to consider these liability risks as they might arise within a different forum–the Web. The maintenance of confidentiality and privacy of records, appropriateness of treatment interventions, and the duty to warn are issues that have particular complications when services are generated over a computer. Additional issues related to mental health professional Codes of Ethics that need consideration include: the duty to provide emergency medical treatment; the duty to provide appropriate referrals; the duty to avoid inappropriate relationships; the duty to provide appropriate assessments; and the duty to receive appropriate supervision (American Association for Marriage and Family Counselors, 1998; American Psychiatric Association Principles of Medical Ethics, 1998; American Psychological Association Ethical Principles of Psychologists and Code of Conduct, 1992; Code of Ethics of the American Association of Pastoral Counselors, 1994; National Association of Social Workers Code of Ethics, 1998; American Association for Certified Counselors Code of Ethics, 1999; National Board for Certified Counselors Standards for the Ethical Practice of Web Counseling, 1998). At the time of this writing, only the American Psychological Association, the National Association of Social Workers, and the National Board for Certified Counselors have specifically addressed some of the issues related to provision of Internet services. Ethical codes in general have not caught up to the provision of online social services (Ainsworth, 1999).

Background

The Internet has been viewed as "communication on steroids" (Beckman & Hirsch, 1996, p. 86). The speed with which communication, albeit linear,[2] is transmitted may both facilitate and complicate dialogue. Before considering the effects of what is transmitted, a hurried click sends the message racing to the receiver or receivers. One can argue that the pauses and ability to think about what is being transmitted can occur before the click, however, transmission via the Internet is instantaneous. For the practitioner and consumer alike, the danger with this speed is that an impulse to share information may have neither been authorized nor curbed in any way. Practitioners who may be accustomed to discussing client situations with colleagues may mistakenly assume that their Internet communications will not be widely disseminated. For example, a practitioner who is working in her or his office, has the office door closed, and is alone when transmitting an Internet communication, might assume that they have acted reasonably to preserve client confidentiality. After all, a practitioner who observes these behaviors during a phone conversation or face-to-face conversation with a colleague has acted in a reasonable manner and within their professional responsibilities–even if some unknown third person has intercepted the conversation. However, if consumer information is forwarded to others, the practitioner can lose control over the ability to limit who may receive the information and a breach of professional protocol may result. With a simple click on the computer, someone outside the practitioner's intended colleagues may forward computer messages to any number of persons, groups or audiences (Huang & Alessi, 1996). E-mail messages may also be misdirected, in that a user may misdirect a message when sending correspondence.

A practitioner may, with a client's permission, share information with colleagues in order to facilitate expedient delivery of services. Such a practice is commendable. However, the practitioner should understand that information and data sent through cyberspace could leave him or her vulnerable to legal and professional malpractice risks associated with loss of confidentiality, maintenance and privacy of records (Lewis, 1997).

The risk discussed above is a matter of amount of access to confidential client information unintended parties may have to the client information. Practitioners and clients should be aware that their communication is "stored" in a medium that may be accessed and used by persons who are outside the confidential umbrella of the practitioner (the practitioner's staff and professional colleagues). Clients have the right to share their confidential therapeutic communications with others, but practitioners have a duty to preserve such communications. Practitioners should make sure that the form of their communication and the method of its delivery would protect the client from third party interceptions.

Another concern that has been raised with Internet transmissions is that they might lack the context found in face-to-face communication. In other words, the reliance on linear conversation ignores powerful messages contained and observed in non-verbal communication (Childress, 1998; Stofle, 1999). As Bloom (1998, p. 55) states, "Many critics question this practice, citing traditional counseling theories which are highly critical of counselors who cannot and do not attend to client visual cues." Shapiro and Schulman (1996) indicate that Internet therapeutic services can be compared to other media psychology, such as call-in talk shows or advice columns. Critics of on-line therapy note that practitioners do not have the opportunity to get to know their clients and discuss fully client concerns and issues. The nature of an Internet communication is different than face-to-face communications (Suler, 1999; Suler, 1997), but such communications can be as effective as more traditional forms of therapy. As more persons engage in cybertherapy and "feel comfortable" discussing personal matters online, then this intervention method can help to fill the service delivery needs of those who prefer the relative anonymity of on-line counseling. Practitioners need to be aware that they might need to modify their communication style to compensate for the lack of visual and auditory cues that they otherwise use in face-to-face and oral communications with a client (Lebow, 1998; Miller & Gergen, 1998).

Legal Parameters for Practice by Social Workers

Social work practitioners can be held legally accountable for actions committed during the course of their work in which a client has been injured. At a basic level, practitioners may risk the loss of their job or be the subject of a disciplinary action undertaken by their state licensing boards (Barker & Branson, 1993). In addition, practitioners may also be subject to civil or criminal court proceedings–such proceedings may take on a number of forms and can be based upon any number of legal principles (Saltzman & Proch, 1990). In general, however, civil proceedings can be based on the consumer's belief that the practitioner's action or inaction amounted to malpractice. The remedy for a finding of malpractice is monetary damages. If the practitioner's conduct rises to a level such that the criminal law may have been violated (e.g., fraud in the filing of insurance claims), the state may pursue a criminal prosecution against the practitioner. Criminal convictions may result in loss of the practitioner's freedom (e.g., incarceration) or the imposition of a fine by a court.[3] Our society is a very litigious one. While criminal prosecutions against practitioners are rare and highly unlikely unless sexual misconduct is alleged, malpractice claims against them are increasing. Consumers are demanding that "their rights" be protected and are seeking legal redress for their malpractice claims against social workers and other mental health practitioners (Besharov, 1985; Reamer, 1994; Reamer, 1995). Although not all claims against social workers are substantiated, social workers should take care about their potential vulnerability to such suits.

Reamer (1995) found that the most frequent claims of malpractice against individual social workers from 1969 to 1990 were for breach of confidence/privacy, failure to correctly diagnose a problem, incorrect treatment, and sexual impropriety. This paper will focus on how practitioners providing services on the Internet can minimize malpractice risks associated with issues of maintaining client confidentiality, making correct diagnoses, and providing appropriate treatments.[4] Because the other categories may affect Internet social worker practice, Internet practitioners would be wise to consider the relevance of the other malpractice categories given the unique characteristics of the Internet as a method of service delivery.

Liability Issues and the Connection to Services Offered on the Internet

Confidentiality and the Right to Privacy

Confidentiality is a cornerstone of professional practice, assuring clients of the right to reveal private concerns in an environment offering a safe and predictable place to explore difficult issues. Healthcare providers are bound to maintain the confidentiality of client records under state licensure laws and regulations (Gellman & Frawley, 1996). Confidentiality has been recognized by the courts as essential in facilitating healing and growth within the confines of therapeutic relationships (Pergament, 1998). Provision of services via the Internet raises serious confidentiality concerns as a result of the medium itself.

Two essential considerations arise when the Internet is used as the medium of communication. For practitioners offering information and advice (a.k.a. counseling), there are particular concerns about the medium of exchange. In contrast to face-to-face practice, Internet communication preserves all exchanges verbatim (Hannon, 1996; Sampson, Kolodinsky & Greeno, 1997). Although practitioners may, when counseling clients, record interviews for learning or teaching purposes, by and large exchanges are recorded in case records in summary fashion. The hazards with verbatim accounts are twofold: those accounts may risk being intercepted in transmission; and, the exchanges remain potentially recorded in perpetuity. Should a client or practitioner be involved in a malpractice action, either the client or practitioner could use verbatim transcriptions as evidence.

Insecure (e.g., agencies not using encryption programs) servers can leave a client's communications open to interception by third parties. For agencies sharing information about clients through the Internet, e-mail transmissions have not been seen as necessarily either secure or confidential by experts (Glossbrenner, 1990). Practitioners and agencies may not be able to completely guarantee confidentiality to consumers in services provided through the Internet (Rahav, 1994). Consumers unaware of this risk may hold practitioners accountable if what they thought to be confidential dialogues and information are uncovered or intercepted by third parties. One way to protect Internet conversations that are meant to be confidential from interception is to use an encryption program. While a good hacker may break encryption programs, it is generally believed that the programs will deny access to unintended parties (Ackerman, 1998). The efforts used by a practitioner to use encryption programs and to instruct their clients to properly use them will help practitioners assert that they have acted reasonably in keeping client records confidential.

A second consideration related to the issue of client confidentiality is the degree of privacy a consumer can expect when receiving services (Freeman, 1995). Client records are protected by privacy protection under licensure statutes and regulations. In general, the rules pertaining to paper records and computer-based records are the same but little uniformity exists among state licensing laws. In addition, there is confusion regarding who may access client data and how that data may be accessed (Gellman & Frawley, 1996). State rules pertaining to the protection of a client's privacy when a computer is utilized should be consulted to guide Internet counseling service practitioners to maintain their client's needs for privacy.

Internet clients' need privacy in their communications, as would face-to-face clients. Clients receiving services from social workers may enter helping relationships because of concerns about their own safety, such as with victims of domestic violence, or because of worries about someone they love, as with individuals related to alcoholic family members. In situations with clients in which safety is a consideration, Internet service practitioners need to assure their client's safety as they would in other treatment modes (e.g., face-to-face counseling settings). For example, a victim of domestic violence may be "caught" through the perpetrator's checking up on Internet connections or by observing computer "conversation." The desire to get help by securing information unfortunately could put the victim at greater risk because of the perpetrator's potential reaction. It is the responsibility of the Internet practitioner to inform their clients about the risks associated with Internet counseling. In order to avoid or minimize these risks, clients need to be encouraged to use an encryption program while on-line and to make sure that their computer does not physically store computer messages if the clients are concerned about their physical safety. As in face-to-face counseling settings, the practitioner must make reasonable efforts to ensure a client's privacy.

The practitioner should not forego using the Internet of service delivery just because the medium is new and the method of service delivery is still undergoing development. Protecting a client's rights to confidentiality and privacy may require a practitioner to continually update her or his computer system and instruct clients and staff in their usage. The practitioner should not be discouraged in using the Internet service delivery, he or she just needs to understand that their professional duties may require them to consider different methods of protecting client files, records, communications, and confidences.

Accuracy of Assessments and Duty to Intervene Appropriately

Under the best of circumstances with face-to-face contacts, accurate reporting by clients, and good skills by practitioners, assessments can be tricky (Klerman, 1990). With Internet services, practitioners are reliant on client descriptions of their situations without the ability to observe the associated behavioral cues that may tell a different story (Stofle, 1999). Practitioners are also offering advice or counseling based on abbreviated "snapshots" presented by clients in a linear narrative form. Although admittedly, much can be discerned about client situations and actions to remediate problems, assessments are curtailed at best with e-mail transmissions.[5]

A different set of concerns surfaces when considering assessments of clients when offering services through the Internet (Childress, 1998). Although professionals delivering services to consumers through face-to-face meetings may encounter constraints in their ability to accurately assess because of variety of limitations including time and what is revealed (Klerman, 1990), these constraints are multiplied considerably with Internet transactions. Shapiro and Schulman (1996) indicate that there is a high potential for misdiagnosis as a result of potential misperceptions by either the consumer or the practitioner. The practitioner may base their response to a consumer based on a few seconds of what is revealed in a short written correspondence. Misdiagnoses or inaccurate assessments have given rise to malpractice cases against practitioners (Klerman, 1990; Kutchins & Kirk, 1987).

A cybertherapy practitioner may have to rely on the limited information that he or she receives from a client (Pergament, 1998). As with other methods of service delivery, practitioners may be limited by whom they may be able to contact for information. In the delivery of Internet services, however, extended family members or other collaterals may not be able to be accessed because they may not have access to the Internet and may not reside in the same geographic area. Regardless of the client's desire or willingness for other individuals or agency involvement, these links may not be possible.

The accuracy of an online assessment may also be called into question if a client uses an online diagnostic tool or instrument. The validity and reliability of these tools when used online has generally not been determined, and their results must be used only in conjunction with other forms of assessment. In addition, some mental health related sites offer psychological assessment instruments to any user who visits the site. If a client uses an online tool, without the added benefit of a consultation, the client may mistakenly believe that they have or do not have a particular problem that needs to be addressed. Clients who are already in a counseling relationship with a therapist may question their clinician's diagnosis and treatments with an "uninformed" difference of opinion.[6] It should be stressed that online assessments can be helpful, but that a user may need to follow-up any online assessment with a professional consultation.

A final difficulty in regard to accuracy of assessments occurs as a result of cultural and regional differences (Sampson, Kolodinsky & Greeno, 1997). The fact that cyberspace transcends geographical distances creates possibilities for both new understandings of differences but also profound misunderstandings. What is communicated and what is understood are filtered through the lens of these geographical limitations. For example, the crime victimization concerns of a young male living in an inner city with a high crime rate will be different from someone living in a suburban area with a low crime rate. Online therapists must be sensitive to cultural and regional variations and to the increased chance of error in assessment that may result.

When Is a Client a Client?

Another conceivable liability concern for practitioners and agencies revolves around the question of when and whether a potential client actually becomes a client. A second related question is when will a client no longer be considered a client. The importance for agencies and practitioners of these questions is when the obligation and responsibility towards a client begins and ends. With Internet services, there may be an implicit assumption on the part of consumers that a fiduciary relationship has been established on the basis of an e-mail transmission. A fiduciary relationship is one in which a professional owes the highest duty towards a client or consumer by virtue of the trust that is conferred (Schroeder, 1995). Although an answer to an e-mail transmitted question may not be regarded as solidification of a fiduciary relationship by a practitioner, a consumer may regard it otherwise.[7]

A series of malpractice cases initiated against physicians by patients involving telephone consultations may be considered by courts as precedents in potential malpractice cases involving services provided through the Internet. In *Grondahl v. Bullock* (1982), for example, a telephone consultation with a physician was regarded as proof that a continuing physician-patient relationship existed and that the physician was attending and examining the patient. In this case, the plaintiff, June Grondahl sued Dr. Matthew Bullock for malpractice as a result of telephone consultations for medications. June Grondahl contended that her condition, based on a faulty diagnosis by Dr. Grondahl, worsened by his failure to attend to calls she made to him with symptoms he told her to ignore. The Court relied on a prior case (*Schmidt v. Esser*, 1931) to articulate three factors to determine when treatment ceases: "(1) whether there is a relationship between physician and patient with regard to the illness; (2) whether the physician is attending and examining the patient; and (3) whether there is something more to be done" (*Grondahl v. Bullock*, 1982, p. 3).

In *Shane v. Mouw* (1982), the Court held that a telephone conversation between a plaintiff and physician subsequent to treatment may constitute part of the treatment. Finally, in a case that may be most pertinent to services provided through the Internet, the ruling in *Miller v. Sullivan* (1995) found that a telephone call affirmatively advising a prospective patient as to a course of treatment can constitute professional services for the purposes of creation of a physician-patient relationship.

These cases are important to consider in light of the ambiguity existing with Internet services. As noted, although a practitioner may well view the information and/or "advice" as the end of the relationship, a client may view that information as the beginning of a relationship. Moreover, the third factor articulated in *Grondahl v. Bullock* (1982) should be seriously contemplated since in situations described by clients seeking information or advice because merely giving a response to a client when clients are seeking a response to a client may not be enough if "more needs to be done." In a self-help group, a practitioner may have difficulty in knowing the extent of services to render to the client and whether the practitioner's services are sufficient under the *Grondahl* test for malpractice. It is probably best to err on the side of providing client services and reasonable efforts for a referral should the client's problems be more extensive than can be handled through the practitioner's Internet service. In this regard, a practitioner should make sure that if they are offering online counseling services that they regularly check their e-mail and respond to clients within a reasonable time. If a practitioner is not going to be online daily and intends to respond to inquiries on a weekly or more infrequent basis, then the practitioner must make this clear to potential clients in a disclaimer so that they understand the limits of the service offered by the practitioner.

Duty to Warn–Exceptions to Confidentiality

One obligation increasingly imposed by state statutes and case law on practitioners is the duty to warn potential victims if a consumer issues threats. The duty to warn attained notoriety with the California case of *Tarasoff v. Board of Regents of the University of California* (1976). In this case, a client threatened to kill a woman who had ended a relationship with him. Despite the practitioner's actions, including reports to his supervisor and the police, he was found to be legally liable because the intended victim was not notified. Subsequent to this case, many states have included criteria for the duty to warn in statutes (Kagle & Kopels, 1994; Pergament, 1998). Practitioners can thus be held accountable if actions are not taken should a consumer issue threats.[8]

Internet services clearly present difficulties in relation to the duty to warn. One difficulty for practitioners is which state statutes apply under these circumstances. Although there is similarity between some statutes, the actions required of practitioners in order to avoid liability vary. In instances in which the practitioner and the consumer of services reside in different states, the question of the appropriate actions is called into question (Johnson & Post, 1996). A practitioner may (and should) be familiar with the criteria in their own state, but will not necessarily be familiar with another state's statutory criteria in the duty to warn. Even the savvy practitioner who quickly uncovers criteria in other states is dependent on the consumer's honesty in relating their location.

The possibility of not knowing where your client actually resides presents a profound obstacle in regard to the duty to warn. Given the potential for relative anonymity of cyberspace communication, a practitioner confronted with a potentially homicidal or suicidal client would have great difficulty in facilitating needed help. Coupled with the difficulties of accurate assessments in this arena, there are associated hazards of locating the intended victim and authorities in the geographical location in which the client resides. The inability to know or follow-up with notifying intended victims and police leaves the practitioner who has been told of an intended action by a client vulnerable to future malpractice claims by victims or family members of the client (Kagle & Kopels, 1994).

Risk Management and Guidelines for Practice when Using the Internet

Use of Disclaimers

One important way that practitioners (and agencies) can minimize liability risks in Internet use is to have a carefully worded disclaimer attached to their Web site. A disclaimer has the same properties of initial contracting in that it cautions the consumer of services about what the practitioner can and cannot offer (Beckman & Hirsch, 1996). Although a disclaimer has not been viewed by some as a panacea to risk avoidance (Lewis, 1997), a clearly worded statement has the benefit of proclaiming what the perils of receiving services or utilizing information may include. Practitioners need to be particularly clear about the limitations of communication without the benefit of face-to-face contact (Pergament, 1998). Careful discussion of billing, confidentiality, informed consent, parameters of services, and what the consumer can expect need to be stated explicitly (Shapiro & Schulman, 1996). As noted above, a practitioner should make sure that the nature and extent of the services to be provided are clearly articulated. As an example, Dr. Leonard Holmes details the parameters of what can be expected and the limitations of what is offered in a specific Website disclaimer (Holmes, 1999). In addition to detailing the limits of what can be expected, Dr. Holmes' disclaimer contains carefully worded legal language indicating that the consumer agrees to hold Dr. Holmes harmless should any damages be incurred by the consumer as a result of utilizing the information provided in the Web site. This disclaimer also indicates that any disputes would be governed by New York State, which is where Dr. Holmes is licensed.

Practitioners and agencies offering Web sites, although serving primarily a psycho-educational function, would also do well to include disclaimers. The disclaimer would serve the purpose of cautioning the consumer about the limitations of services provided through the Internet and that information provided is necessarily generalized and may not completely fit with the consumer's situation. A disclaimer ideally would also indicate that the information provided does not constitute a fiduciary relationship in that the provider or practitioner cannot assume responsibility for results of the consumer's subsequent actions. The American Counseling Association (1999) in its Web site's "Welcome" disclaimer is an excellent example of the specific language that can protect an agency. This disclaimer also contains legal language indicating that the consumer agrees by accessing the Web site to assume all responsibility for any and all potential adverse effects that may be incurred.

Disclaimers should also direct consumers to get comprehensive medical evaluations in order to rule out any underlying physical problems (Klerman, 1990). A statement detailing the limits of what can be assessed without a comprehensive medical evaluation would reduce liability risks since the practitioner is being clear about their own constraints. A suggestion to seek additional psychological services is also warranted as an adjunct to services sought on the Internet.

Knowledge of Resources

A second guideline important for providers of services through the Internet involves the need for practitioners to be sophisticated in the use of the Internet and locating local services for clients (Lebow, 1998; Pergament, 1998). This is particularly true in situations involving crisis intervention or when there is a threat of harm. Facility with locating and accessing needed services and resources beyond what can be provided in non face-to-face contacts is crucial so practitioners will not run the risk of potential malpractice claims by dissatisfied clients.

Knowledge on the part of practitioners also necessitates knowing the way geographical differences have to be taken into consideration. For assessments to be accurate, cultural factors are essential to include as variables in the way individuals function. Services that might be suggested need the same degree of cultural and geographical sensitivity on the part of the practitioner. Since consumers or clients by virtue of geographical distances may have very different values, expectations, resources, and sensibilities, the practitioner needs to be aware of this possibility so as not to provide inappropriate advice or treatment.

Confidentiality Limits and Safeguards

A third broad area in Internet services is the provision of confidentiality and safeguards. As noted, although encryption may not be completely fail safe, its use allows providers to offer consumers a semblance of privacy (Freemen, 1995). Encryption involves the scrambling of messages through software programs so that the data can only be accessed through the use of a "key" or code to unscramble it (Higgins, 1996; Mitchell, 1997). Encryption clearly mandates that providers not only be knowledgeable about the mechanisms involved and be able to educate consumers about how to use it, but also have the software available for use.

Within social service agencies and networks, security systems need to be designed so as to limit the amount of client information to what is needed by the staff member. For example, billing clerks do not need to have access to detailed clinical information on a client. A sophisticated system would require that some forms of "lockouts" be in place to restrict data (Gellman & Frawley, 1996). All personnel in agencies with computer generated and disseminated information would also need to be held to the same confidentiality requirements as professionals who are bound by licensing laws (Rahav, 1994).

Practitioners offering services through Internet exchanges would also do well to discuss confidentiality concerns with consumers at the beginning of their interactions. Along with the limits of confidentiality outlined in carefully worded disclaimers, practitioners need to help consumers consider the security and privacy in their own environment. The extent to which consumers are able safely to disclose personal information needs to be thoroughly explored.

CONCLUSION

The advent of computer generated services has produced possibilities of rapid access to needed goods and services, extensive dissemination of information and knowledge, and support systems that might otherwise be difficult to locate. The speed of transmissions and the ambiguity that may arise in solely linear communication creates situations involving potential liability risks for agencies and practitioners. Although some professional Codes of Ethics have grappled with attempting to provide guidelines for practitioners, there are many issues and situations remaining unclear (American Counseling Association, 1999; American Psychological Association, 1992; National Association of Social Workers, 1998; National Board for Certified Counselors Standards for the Ethical Practice of WebCounseling, 1999). This article has outlined some of the concerns and issues that need to be considered when providing computer-generated services. Agencies and practitioners would do well to protect themselves from being vulnerable to malpractice claims by considering some of the guidelines offered.[9]

NOTES

1. Anonymous users may be those who use particular chat rooms or use diagnostic tools that do not require the user to fully disclose their identities. Absolute anonymity may not be available if the state needs to ascertain a user's identification. For example, the police may need to identify a user because the user committed a crime over the Internet (e.g., spread a virus). A user's identification may be ascertained through their Internet service provider.

2. The term "linear" communication means that the communication that transpires over the Internet is structured in such a manner that one person transmits a written statement before the other party transmits a written response. In face-to-face communications, multiple methods of communication (oral, written, non-verbal) may engender the conversation. In addition, during a face-to-face communication, multiple parties may speak at one time.

3. Professional licensing authorities may subsequently hold a hearing and use the criminal conviction to determine whether a practitioner has violated their professional rules of conduct. Such a hearing might result in suspension or revocation of a practitioner's license.

4. Sexual impropriety by an on-line therapist could occur if the therapist engages in any number of inappropriate sexual communications with a client. It is beyond the scope of this paper, however, to distinguish between appropriate discussions about sex with a client and inappropriate sexual conduct (e.g., cybersex). The professional community will need to explore this area more fully and define what is and is not acceptable.

5. It is possible that as computer technology advances and picture Internet transmissions become commonplace, some of the particular concerns raised in this paper that stem from linear Internet communication will be eased or eliminated.

6. We do not suggest that clients should never question their therapists' opinion or method of treatment, rather we caution online users to seek additional help in determining if an online assessment is accurate.

7. A fiduciary relationship entails more than a consumer utilizing a Web site link. In essence, the provision of a Web site link by a practitioner or agency may be regarded as similar to the provision of a telephone number to an outside resource. However, if a practitioner or therapist responds to an e-mail message or has on "online chat" with a consumer, a fiduciary relationship may be established. This may be litigated in the future, but it is reasonable at this time to presume that the fiduciary relationship needs a formal establishment of a relationship and hence a unilateral contact is not enough.

8. Although the U.S. Senate (1996) has initiated a study examining the impact and potential effect of developing mutual recognition of licensing laws between states particularly in light of telehealth services, at present, a practitioner is governed by the state in which she or he resides.

9. We would like to sincerely thank the editors and reviewers for their comments and suggestions. These suggestions assisted us greatly in revising and strengthening the article.

REFERENCES

Ackerman, W. (1998). Encryption: A 21st century national security dilemma. *International Review of Law, Computers & Technology, 12*(2), 371-395.

Ainsworth, M. (1999). Ethics: Will you be properly cared for? *ABCs of "Internet Therapy."* [Online] Available: *http://www.metanoia.org/imhs/ethics.htm*

American Association for Certified Counselors. (1999). *Code of ethics and standards of practice.*

American Association for Marriage and Family Counselors. (1998). *Code of Ethics.*

American Association of Pastoral Counselors. (1994). *Code of Ethics.* [Online] Available: *http://www.aapc.org/ethics.htm*

American Psychiatric Association. (1998). *Principles of Medical Ethics with Annotations Especially Applicable to Psychiatry.* [Online] Available: *http://www.psych.org/apa_members/ethics_index.html*

American Psychological Association. (1992). *Ethical principles and code of conduct.* [Online] Available: *http://www.apa.org/ethics*

American Counseling Association. (1998). *Welcome.* [Online] Available: *http://www.counseling.org/disclaimer.htm*

American Self-help Clearinghouse. (1999). [Online] Available: *http://www.cmhc.com/selfhelp*

Barker, R. & Branson, D. (1993). *Forensic social work: Legal aspects of professional practice.* NY: The Haworth Press, Inc.

Beckman, D. & Hirsch, D. (1996). Rules of the road: Legal ethics may be speed bumps on the Internet superhighway. *American Bar Association Journal, 82,* 86.

Besharov, D. (1985). *The vulnerable social worker.* Silver Spring, MD: National Association of Social Workers.

Bloom, J. (1998). The ethical practice of webcounseling. *British Journal of Guidance and Counseling, 26*(1), 53-60.

Childress, C. (1998). Potential risks and benefits of online psychotherapeutic interventions. *International Society for Mental Health Online.* [Online] Available: *http://www.ismho.org/issues/9801.htm*

Freeman, E. (1995). When technology and privacy collide. *Information Strategy, 11*(4), 41-46.

Gellman, R. & Frawley, K. (1996). The need to know versus the right to privacy. In T. Trabin (Ed.), *The Computerization of Behavioral Health Care.* San Francisco, CA: Jossey-Bass.

Giffords, E. (1998). Social work on the Internet: An introduction. *Social Work, 43*(3), 243-252.

Glossbrenner, A. (1990). *The complete handbook of personal computer communications: The bible of online world.* NY: St. Martin's Press.

Grondahl v. Bullock, 318 N.W. 2d 240 (1982).

Goodman, P. (1998). Domestic violence resources on the Internet. *The Journal of the*

American Medical Association. [Online] Available: *http://www.ama-assn.org/sci-pubs/journals/archive/jama/vol_280/no_5/jn80003x.htm*

Hannon, K. (1996). Upset: try cybertherapy. *U.S. News & World Report, 120*(9), 81-82.

Higgins, K. (1996). The encryption prescription. *Communicationsweek, 641*, 63-67.

Holmes, L. (1999). Mental health resources. [Online]. Available: *http://mental health.about.com*

Huang, M. & Alessi, N. (1996). The Internet and the future of psychiatry. *American Journal of Psychiatry, 153*(7), 861-869.

Johnson, D. & Post, D. (1996). Law and borders: The rise of law in Cyberspace. *48 Stanford Law Review*, 1367.

Kagle, J. & Kopels, S. (1994). Confidentiality after Tarasoff. *Health & Social Work, 19*, 217-222.

Klerman, G. (1990). The psychiatric patient's right to effective treatment: Implications of *Osheroff v. Chestnut Lodge. American Journal of Psychiatry, 147*(4), 409-418.

Kutchins, H. & Kirk, S. (1987). DSM-III and social work malpractice. *Social Work, May-June*, 205-211.

Lebow, J. (1998). Not just talk, maybe some risk: the therapeutic potentials and pitfalls of computer-mediated conversation. *Journal of Marriage and Family Therapy, 24*(2), 203-206.

Lewis, K. (1997). Tapping technology: Legal and liability risks on the Internet. *Journal of Marriage and Family Therapy, 24*(2), 203-206.

Lim, R. (1996). The internet: Applications for mental health clinicians in clinical settings, training, and research. *Psychiatric Services, 47*(6), 597-599.

Miller, J. & Gergen, K. (1998). Life on the line: The therapeutic potentials of computer-mediated conversation. *Journal of Marriage and Family Therapy, 24*(2), 189-202.

Miller v. Sullivan, 625 N.Y.S. 2d 102 (1995).

Mitchell, P. (1997). Confidentiality at risk in the electronic age. *Lancet, 349*(9065), 1608.

National Association of Social Workers. (1998). *Code of ethics.* Washington, D.C.: NASW Press.

National Board for Certified Counselors, Inc. (1998). *Standards for the ethical practice of WebCounseling.* [Online] Available: *Nbcc@nbcc.org*

Pergament, D. (1998). Internet psychotherapy: Current status and future regulation. *Journal of Law Medicine, 8*(2), 233-280.

Rahav, M. (1994). Perils of computerization. *Hospital & Community Psychiatry, 45*(5). 499-500.

Reamer, F.G. (1994). *Social work malpractice and liability.* New York: Columbia University Press.

Reamer, F.G. (1995). Malpractice claims against social workers: First facts. *Social Work, 40*(5), 595-601.

Saltzman, A. & Proch, K. (1990). *Law in social work practice.* Chicago, IL: Nelson-Hall.

Sampson, J.P., Kolodinsky, R. & Greeno, B. (1997). Counseling on the Information Highway: Future possibilities and potential problems. *Journal of Counseling and Development, 75*, 203-212.

Schmidt v. Esser, 236 N.W. 622 (1931).

Schroeder, L. (1995). *The legal environment of social work.* Washington, D.C.: NASW Press.

Selfgrowth.com. (1999). [Online] Available: *http://www.selfgrowth.com*

Shane v. Mouw, 323 N.W. 2d 537 (1982).

Shapiro, D. & Schulman, C. (1996). Ethical and legal issues in e-mail therapy. *Ethics & Behavior, 6*(2), 107-124.

Stofle, G. (1999). Thoughts about online psychotherapy: Ethical and practical considerations. [Online] Available: *http://members.aol.com/stofle/onlinepsych.htm*

Suler, J. (1999). The psychology of cyberspace. *Psychology of Cyberspace–Overview and guided tour.* [Online] Available: *http://www.rider.edu/users/suler/psycyber/psycyber.html*

Suler, J. (1997). The final showdown between in-person and cyberspace relationships. *Online Psychology of Cyberspace.* Available: *http://www.rider.edu/users/suler/psycyber/showdown.html*

Tarasoff v. Board of Regents of the University of California, 551 P.2d 334 (1976).

U.S. Senate. (1996). A bill to provide reimbursement under the Medicare program for telehealth services, and for other purposes. 104th Congress. [Online] Available: *ftp://ftp.loc.gov/pub/thomas/c104/s2171.is.txt*

Winzelberg, A. (1997). The analysis of an electronic support group for individuals with eating disorders. *Computers in Human Behavior, 13*(3), 393-407.

INTERNET:
A Framework for Analyzing
Online Human Service Practices

Joanne Levine

SUMMARY. The Internet and related electronic communication technologies are used by human service professionals for many functions ranging from the storage and transmission of sensitive medical information to online counseling. Yet, there are many aspects of telecommunications law that work against privacy and thus the potential for ethical dilemmas has increased. This paper explores and discusses the complex reasons contributing to these ethical dilemmas. The article also presents a human service oriented framework, INTERNET, for analyzing and resolving these dilemmas. *[Article copies available for a fee from The Haworth Document Delivery Service: 1-800-342-9678. E-mail address: <getinfo@haworthpressinc.com> Website: <http://www.haworthpressinc.com>]*

KEYWORDS. Internet, ethical dilemmas, human services, ethics

The Internet and related technologies have exponentially expanded the opportunities for accessing and disseminating information. Through the Internet both human service providers and consumers have access to a growing supply of information on mental health, health, diseases, services and products. Healthcare Websites that focus on everything from cancer to fatigue are booming. It is estimated that the World Wide Web adds 25,000 new sites each month (Berglund, 1997).

Joanne Levine, DSW, MPH, is Assistant Professor, University of Houston, Graduate School of Social Work, Houston, TX 77204-4492. (E-mail: jlevine2@uh.edu).

[Haworth co-indexing entry note]: "INTERNET: A Framework for Analyzing Online Human Service Practices." Levine, Joanne. Co-published simultaneously in *Journal of Technology in Human Services* (The Haworth Press, Inc.) Vol. 17, No. 2/3, 2000, pp. 173-192; and: *Human Services Online: A New Arena for Service Delivery* (ed: Jerry Finn, and Gary Holden) The Haworth Press, Inc., 2000, pp. 173-192. Single or multiple copies of this article are available for a fee from The Haworth Document Delivery Service [1-800-342-9678, 9:00 a.m. - 5:00 p.m. (EST). E-mail address: getinfo@haworthpressinc.com].

The Internet may also be conceptualized as a social technology. People with common interests almost anywhere in the world can find each other and talk, listen, and sustain connections over time. Virtual meetings are flourishing. America Online has more than 350 and Prodigy has more than 400 virtual meetings ranging from organized special interest groups to informal discussion groups. It is reported that an estimated 3.4 trillion e-mail messages were delivered in the U.S. in 1998 and that 2.1 billion e-mail messages are sent daily by U.S. users (Sproull & Faraj, 1995; Karger & Levine, 1998; Grohol, 1999).

Clearly, the Internet and related information technologies are some of the major technological achievements of our time. However, they are some of the many contemporary scientific advances that have expanded our capabilities in ways far exceeding most people's wildest imagination. Fifty years ago, who would have imagined cloning animals, in vitro fertilization, machines that sustain life? Who would have imagined genetic testing, gene therapy, and fertility treatments so powerful that some women unable to conceive give birth to octuplets? We struggle to cope with and demystify the social implications of these dramatic and profound changes. The ethical issues stirred up by these scientific innovations challenge religious beliefs, cultural values, laws, and codes of ethics. When applied to ethical dilemmas that arise in the use of these technologies, normal ethical guidelines strain and sometimes buckle under the pressure.

While distressing, ethical dilemmas are a normative aspect of these technologically sophisticated times. Given this, a model will be presented which human service providers may apply when analyzing ethical conflicts in clinical cases involving the use of electronic communication technologies. A relevant case example in a health care setting will illustrate an application of this model.

AN OVERVIEW OF MAJOR ETHICAL AND LEGAL ISSUES ARISING FROM THE USE OF ELECTRONIC COMMUNICATION TECHNOLOGIES IN THE HUMAN SERVICES

Major ethical concerns arising from the use of electronic communication technologies in the human services involve privacy, confidentiality, and informed consent–all of which are essential elements of the helping relationship. They are also both legal and ethical obligations of human service professionals (Dickson, 1998).

Privacy refers to conditions of limited accessibility to various aspects of an individual's capacity for solitude and bodily inviobility (physical privacy) as well as anonymity and secrecy (informational privacy) (Cushman & Detmer, 1997; Dickson, 1998). Confidentiality is derived from the right to privacy and refers to the obligations of individuals and organizations to appropriately use information under their control (Cushman & Detmer, 1997; Welfel, 1998). Finally, informed consent means that a human service or other practitioner will not intervene in the life of a client (or release confidential information) unless the client has consented. Informed consent has two aspects. The first is disclosure by the provider of important information the client needs to decide whether or not to participate in treatment. The second aspect is free consent, which means that the decision to engage in an activity is made without coercion or undue pressure (Lowenberg & Dolgoff, 1996; Welfel, 1998).

A critical dilemma underpins modern society's concerns about privacy, confidentiality and informed consent. Namely, the need to re-examine the proper balance between the competing values of personal privacy and the free flow of information in a democracy. As well, the diffusion of electronic information technologies at the national and international levels has created ethical conflicts between the competing goals of efficiency and privacy, confidentiality and informed consent (Information Infrastructure Task Force, 1997). A range of complex factors contributes to these ethical concerns.

First, over the past decade human service providers, agencies, and hospitals have steadily increased their use of computer and other electronic technologies. Human service providers have expanded their repertoire to include e-mail, listservs, and the World Wide Web. Many of these technologies can make personal information accessible beyond the confined parameters of an individual computer or a single organization (Cwikel & Cnaan, 1991). According to a survey reported in the *New York Times*, 80 percent of hospitals now use the Internet for a range of functions including communicating patient information, sharing techniques, data sharing with other institutions and providers, advertising, and communications both within and outside the hospital. In 1996, 9% percent of hospitals reported using the Internet to provide information (including personal medical records) directly to patients;

by 1998 that number had increased to 16%. In 1996, 13% of hospitals reported using the Internet to share data; by 1998 that had increased to 27%. While using the Internet for such purposes may be cost effective, serious questions are raised about ensuring the privacy of such highly personal information. Unfortunately, safeguards to ensure the privacy of electronically transmitted information have lagged behind their widespread use (Freudenheim, 1999; Karger & Levine, 1998).

Secondly, limitations exist in current laws around privacy rights and the transmission, storage, and retrieval of electronic information. These legal deficiencies exist despite a greater emphasis on privacy resulting from the growth of telecommunications technologies in healthcare coupled with the explosion of Internet and Intranet applications. The history of regulation for health information shows that control has traditionally been at the state level. More than two thirds of states have passed legislation to regulate health information practices. However, this has lead to an inconsistent array of laws that makes it almost impossible to operate health services at the interstate level without raising issues related to jurisdiction (Cushman & Detmer, 1997).

Businesses and the U.S. government have adopted sector-specific privacy legislation, regulation, and voluntary codes to achieve the desired level of privacy protection. The differing levels of protection and different remedies have resulted in several troublesome characteristics of our approach to safeguarding privacy and the use of electronic communications technology. First, the sector-based approach protects privacy on a piecemeal basis resulting in rules that are neither consistent nor predictable from sector to sector. This makes it more difficult for consumers to anticipate how their personal information will be used in a particular setting. Secondly, no federal agency exclusively coordinates government privacy initiatives, which in turn, creates difficulties for business and governmental agencies operating in today's networked environment. This is especially problematic where there is a transfer of personal data across state lines. Thirdly, the voluntary codes of privacy adopted by the private sector are unenforceable so that noncompliance has very little consequence (Information Infrastructure Task Force, 1997).

Reviewing relevant federal legislation, all of which have significant gaps around the privacy of electronically transmitted information, further highlights the above points. The Federal Privacy Act of 1974, as amended by the Computer Matching and Privacy Act of 1988, remains the premiere model for protecting the privacy of an individual's records stored in a Federal agency. However, it does not have jurisdiction over electronic records and communications by non-federal entities including health and human service institutions, insurance companies, and employers (Dickson, 1998; Gelman, Pollack, & Weiner, 1999; Rock & Congress, 1999). The Electronic Communications Privacy Act of 1986 (ECPA) is a federal law that provides certain levels of privacy when using online systems. However, it does not provide online users the automatic right of privacy from system operators who store messages. Since a system can be easily configured to store messages that pass through it, operators have the ability to review stored messages passing through their system (Rose, 1995). The 1996 Health Insurance Portability and Accountability Act also poses major threats to personal privacy because it calls for "universal patient identifiers" to facilitate the linking of all patient files. This information sharing does not require the client to give informed consent. Clients are therefore at risk that their medical information can be used in a deleterious manner (Gelman, Pollack, & Weiner, 1999).

A third factor that contributes to the complexity of ethical concerns is the growth in managed care, which is rapidly becoming the predominant method of financing and delivering health care to the general public, including Medicare and Medicaid recipients (Perloff, 1996). Broadly defined, private managed care plans now cover more than two-thirds of all privately insured Americans. Many state and federal governments are encouraging (and in some cases requiring) that Medicare and Medicaid beneficiaries join managed care plans. For example, in 1992 there were 96 Medicare HMOs covering 1.6 million members; by 1995, that number had risen to 165 with 2.6 million members (Karger & Stoez, 1998).

There are many reasons why managed care can pose threats to confidentiality, privacy and informed consent. For one, managed care heavily relies upon utilization reviews. The increased usage of electronic data collection and storage depends on an intensive information foundation at a micro level. Each patient's health care history is used as an input to systemic analysis of the providers and institutions that constitutes the "practice plan." Extensive justifications are typically recorded at stages in the individual's course of care, particularly for referrals from the "gatekeeper" primary care practitioner to sub-specialists. Intimate medical information becomes eligible for examination by third parties (Lu, 1997; Strom-Gottfried & Corcoran, 1998).

While the majority of practitioners in managed care settings find their efforts facilitated by electronic medical records, they can rarely guarantee that a patient's health information will be limited to them. As discussed earlier, no legal safeguards exist to fully ensure the privacy and confidentiality of health information that is stored, transmitted, and retrieved in electronic form (Cushman & Detmer, 1997; Dickson, 1998; Gelman, Pollack & Weiner, 1999; Rose, 1995). While case law is continually evolving, at present there is no case law which specifically addresses confidentiality and managed care. The decision in the California *Menendez v. Superior Court* case (1992) supported a client's right to confidentiality if they believed that this disclosure would remain confidential (Dickson, 1997; Rock & Congress, 1999).

A fourth factor is the growth of Health Data Organizations (HDOs) that operate under the authority of government, private, or non-profit organizations. The mission statement of The National Association of Health Data Organizations (NAHDO) notes that their major function is "to improve health care through the collection, analysis, dissemination, public availability, and use of health data."[1]

As the above mission statement implies, HDOs have access to databases of patient identified, non-aggregated health information. Their chief mission is the public release of analyses performed on the data. Data is acquired from individual health records kept by doctors and hospitals as well as a wide range of secondary sources, e.g., financial transactions from private insurance companies. As a result, HDOs have electronic databases with highly personal, and sometimes identifiable, patient data. Human service professionals may not be aware that client data will end up with an HDO. As such, they may unwittingly act in an unethical manner by not informing their clients about the potential use of their medical, social, financial and other personal records (Dickson, 1998).

A fifth factor is electronic workplace surveillance, where employers search employee computer files, voice mail, e-mail, and other networked forms of communication. This is relevant for human service workers who may communicate with clients via e-mail regarding personal problems, appointments for mental health services, or even counseling (see section on telehealth to follow). Many corporations justify their surveillance of their employee's networked forms of communication as a way to ensure quality control, security, and efficiency. A 1997 survey conducted by the American Management Association of executives at 301 American companies revealed that 22 percent of the firms reported engaging in searches of employee computer files, voice mail, e-mail, and other forms of networked communications. For companies with one thousand or more employees, 30 percent of the firms engaged in such conduct. However, only 18 percent of the respondents reported having written policies regarding electronic privacy for employees (American Management Association, 1997).

Electronic communications accessed through employers belongs to the employer, not the employee. If the employer is a governmental agency, the human service worker may find their e-mail messages subject to public records (Dickson, 1998; Kasser, 1996). In short, employees should understand that electronic systems might be monitored without prior notice. Employee challenges around employer access to their e-mail have generally not been successful (Kasser, 1996).

The fifth factor is the growth in telehealth, the use of electronic technology to deliver health related services, including counseling and psychological services. There has been a growing trend to use telehealth for a wide range of mental health functions including assessment, diagnosis, intervention, consultation, education, research and surveys. These services use web pages, e-mail, chat rooms, videoconferencing, telephony (real-time audio over the Internet), electronic forums, and/or electronic forms (Karger & Levine, 1999; Beel, 1999).

Distance is irrelevant since telehealth transcends state and national boundaries. Issues that affect human service providers impacted by telehealth include licensing, liability, privacy, informed consent, the therapist/client relationship, and reimbursement (Beel, 1999; Karger & Levine, 1999; Parkin & Stretch, 1996; Weinberg, Schmale, Uken, & Wessel, 1996). Professional groups are responding to the growth of telehealth by preparing statements that examine its risks and benefits, and address the main ethical questions that arise from this use of the Internet. Codes of ethics and/or position statements by professional organizations for three major mental health care providers–social workers,[2] psychologists[3] and psychiatrists[4]–reveal similar themes around the use of electronic communications technology in clinical practice. These themes include requiring the practitioner to inform clients of the limitations, risks and the need to take precautions (e.g., not using identifying information, and using passwords and encryption) to maintain the confidentiality of electronically transmitted client information (National Association of Social Workers, 1997; American Psychological Association, 1996; American Psychiatric Association, 1998).

Responses by these professional associations acknowledge the widespread diffusion of electronic communication technologies into the human services and the need for providers to remain vigilant about maintaining confidentiality. Professional groups continue to struggle with the confidentiality dilemmas raised by third-party reimbursements, the computerization of client records, and the widespread access to human service providers via electronic communication technologies (Welfel, 1998).

THE LIMITS OF LAW, CODES OF ETHICS, AND THE IMPORTANCE OF FRAMEWORKS FOR ETHICAL ANALYSIS

The law may offer a mode of resolution in situations where ethical issues arise. Yet in these types of situations, legalistic interventions are frequently inadequate and may lead to more conflict (Spinello, 1997). Principles and values embodied in professional codes of ethics are important because they help to clarify expected standards of behavior in the face of ethical dilemmas. While a code of professional conduct may provide unmistakably clear guidance in only a few situations, it does embody principles and values that can guide human service providers faced with dilemmas emerging from electronic information technologies and biomedical advances (Abramson, 1983; Gant & Giddens, 1998; Linzer, 1999; Karger & Levine, 1999; Spinello, 1997; Welfel, 1998).

Frameworks for ethical analysis are useful in dealing with the complex ethical dilemmas arising from the use of electronic communication technologies in the human services. Such is the case in health care, where models for analyzing ethical dilemmas have been frequently used to deal with conflicts that arise from using biomedical technologies. Issues emerge around how vigorously medical treatment should be pursued, to what degree it is appropriate to interfere with the quality of a patient's life, and the need for dignity in death. These ethical issues persist despite the availability of legal instruments (i.e., living wills and durable powers of attorney) and the Patient Self-Determination Act of 1990 (Abramson, 1990; Abramson & Black, 1985;

Chapin, 1987; Dzieglielewsi, 1998; Freedman, 1998; Gant & Giddens, 1998; Levine, 1997; Macklin, 1984; Mailick & Ullman, 1984; McGee, 1997; Osman & Perlin, 1994; Reamer, 1986; Roberts, 1989).

FRAMEWORKS FOR THE ANALYSIS OF ETHICAL DILEMMAS IN HEALTH CARE AND THEIR RELEVANCE AND LIMITATIONS WHEN APPLIED TO DILEMMAS IN ELECTRONIC COMMUNICATION TECHNOLOGIES

Three frameworks used by human service professionals in analyzing ethical health care dilemmas have some relevancy when applied to electronic communication technologies. The first two frameworks were developed for ethical dilemmas arising from HIV/AIDS (Gant & Giddens, 1998; Linzer, 1999) while the third, PRACTICE is not disease specific (Perlin, 1992).

A unique aspect of the PRACTICE framework is the use of this term as an acronym, which in itself appears to serve an important purpose. Human service professionals frequently practice in host settings, such as health care, where it is sometimes difficult to maintain a professional role, identity, and values (Cowles & Lefcowitz, 1995; Levine, 1997; Roberts, 1989). Hence, it is important for an ethical dilemma framework to bring forth associations that reinforce the role, identity, and values of the human service professional. These associations may serve to remind human service professionals of their primary mission–service, social justice, and maintaining the dignity and worth of the individual–while they employ the ethical analyses which each letter of the acronym proscribes (National Association of Social Workers, 1997; Welfel, 1998). Remaining focused on their professional mandate may also encourage human service professionals to act in accordance with their principles when facing ethical dilemmas that arise in unsupportive work environments.

While each of these frameworks analyze ethical dilemmas differently, there are major areas of commonality that include using a process oriented approach to analyzing the ethical dilemma; justifying the selection of ethical principles to frame the dilemma; and the justification of actions based on the ethical principles at stake. All three frameworks also share the deontological approach to ethical analysis. This approach posits that human service professionals experience ethical discomfort from the need to balance competing principles and to systematically analyze the justifications for choosing one principle over another. The deontological perspective also argues that certain actions are correct regardless of our desires (Beauchamp and Childress, 1994; Linzer, 1999; Lowenberg & Dolgoff, 1996). In the deontological approach a variety of principles and rules with the potential for flexibility may be applied to an ethical dilemma (Linzer, 1999).

All three frameworks are based on five ethical principles for human service professionals (Abramson, 1983; Kitchener, 1985; Osman & Perlin, 1994; Cushman & Detmer, 1997; Welfel, 1998; Gant & Giddens, 1998):

- *Autonomy.* The right of self-rule including deliberate choices rooted in the right to privacy and the idea of individual freedom and self-governance.
- *Beneficence.* The obligation to promote the well being of others, especially those to whom care is offered. This is an important ingredient in the obligation to help those in need even when it inconveniences or limits the freedom of the helper.
- *Nonmaleficence.* The obligation to avoid inflicting physical or psychological harm on others and to protect them from danger.
- *Fidelity.* The obligations to keep promises, to tell the truth, and to be loyal.
- *Justice.* The assumption that all people should be treated equally, which presumes reciprocity, impartiality, and equality.

While aspects of the above frameworks are useful in analyzing ethical dilemmas arising from the use of electronic communications in human services, two major limitations require the development of another framework. The first limitation is that none of the above frameworks explicitly include the step of educating those involved in the ethical dilemma about the gaps in ethical principles, institutional policies, and the relevant legislation. In contrast, the INTERNET framework starts the process by having human service professionals identify both institutional policies and relevant legislation. This is essential since human service professionals should be aware of up-to-date information on electronic communication technologies and ethics, institutional policies, and legislation.

The second limitation is that none of the above frameworks have acronyms which elicit associations with human service ethics, values, and perspectives. As discussed, using PRACTICE as the acronym for an ethical framework may help to remind human service workers that they can implement their ethics and values in their host settings. The INTERNET framework presented below uses that acronym for similar reasons. The word Internet and those terms commonly associated with it (i.e., information superhighway, search engines, hackers, surfing the Net) invokes many images and metaphors. However, few if any relate to human service values and ethics. In fact, there are some human service workers who resist using the Internet and related technologies because of concerns about the lack of congruence with their core professional values and ethics (Cwikel & Cnaan, 1991; Rock & Congress, 1999). One step towards decreasing this resistance may be to create new associations with the term INTERNET that would include human service ethical principles and values. Perhaps using the acronym INTERNET for a human service oriented framework for ethical analysis may facilitate the development of these new associations.

The educative step in this process also supports this goal. Human service professionals and their clients who are knowledgeable about gaps in privacy protections for electronic communications may then be empowered to advocate for needed changes. Educating clients about the relevant gaps in institutional policies and legislation may also help facilitate the trust needed for a helping relationship.

Finally, similar to the other three frameworks used in health care, the INTERNET framework is also based on using the five guiding ethical principles that human service professionals are mandated to follow (Gant & Giddens, 1998; Perlin, 1992; Osman & Perlin, 1994). The INTERNET framework is based on a deontological perspective that allows for the inclusion of multiple perspectives and the flexible application of a variety of rules and principles to the ethical conflict (Linzer, 1999).

INTERNET: *A FRAMEWORK FOR ANALYZING ETHICAL DILEMMAS ARISING FROM ELECTRONIC INFORMATION TECHNOLOGY*

The INTERNET framework for ethical analysis is presented below.

I *Identify.* Identify the parties in the conflict and their roles; identify the guiding ethical principles involved (based on their code of ethics); identify the institutional policies and current legislation on use of electronic communication technologies in patient care; identify the congruencies and/or gaps between ethical principles, institutional policies, and current legislation.

N *Needs.* What are the needs of the parties from a biopsychosocial perspective.

T *Terms.* What were the terms of understanding between the parties involved.

E *Elucidate, Educate, and Empower.* Elucidate the ethical conflict. Educate the parties about the congruencies and/or gaps between the ethical principles, the institutional policies, and the current legislation. Empower human service professionals and their clients to enter the current debates about privacy rights and electronic communication technologies.

R *Reconcile* the ethical principles and values involved to create a plan for action.

N *Necessity.* Clarify the necessity for resolution of this conflict (including deadlines).

E *Evaluate* the outcomes and consequences of the conflict.

T *Termination.* Reflect upon how the conflict was terminated.

CASE EXAMPLE

The following example illustrates an application of the INTERNET framework. (Given the complexity of this topic, it is beyond the purview of this paper to analyze all aspects of this case.)

Mary, a 42-year-old breast cancer patient, attends outpatient counseling with Claire, a clinical social worker, at the private hospital where she received her cancer treatment. Mary's mother has recently come to live with her and she is not emotionally ready to inform her about the diagnosis. Mary is quite concerned that her mother may find out anyway now that she lives in her home. Mary asked Claire for reassurance about the confidentiality of her medical records and counseling sessions. Claire assured Mary that everything they discuss is confidential. Mary's medical records are private, and no information can be released without her prior consent.

One day Mary returns home from work to find her mother distraught. While checking the answering machine, Mary's mother replayed a message received earlier from a pharmaceutical company.

They asked Mary if she would be willing to participate in a survey about the quality of life for young women who had been recently treated for breast cancer and were taking a drug manufactured by their company. After hearing the message, Mary was forced to reveal her medical situation. This left Mary and her mother feeling more emotionally distressed–not only about the information conveyed but the manner in which this occurred.

Mary called Claire, demanding to know how the pharmaceutical company had obtained the information without her knowledge or consent. After all, hadn't Claire reassured her that medical records were confidential and wouldn't be released without informed consent? Claire reiterated that she had not disclosed any information in their sessions to outside parties. But, she reminded Mary that she had signed a consent form allowing the hospital to release her medical information in order to receive insurance payments. Upon investigation by hospital administration, it was discovered that the hospital had a contract with a software company that electronically linked databases of patient information to insurance companies, clinical laboratories, and hospitals. This benefited both patients and doctors by cutting costs and increasing efficiency. In exchange for discounted computers, the software company had acquired aggregated patient records, including diagnoses and treatments, which it then compiled and sold to pharmaceutical companies and insurers.

APPLICATION OF THE INTERNET FRAMEWORK

I–Identify: The parties involved and their roles in the conflict; the guiding ethical principles involved; the institutional policies and legislation; the congruencies and/or gaps.

The parties: Mary (the patient), her mother (family), Claire (a hospital employee and clinical social worker), hospital administrators (hospital employees charged with ensuring that the hospital complies with internal and external regulations while maintaining financial solvency), insurance company (a hospital payer), software company (an outside contractor), pharmaceutical company (an outside provider).

The guiding ethical principles involved: autonomy, nonmaleficence, and fidelity.

The institutional policies and legislation: The hospital required that patients sign a release of information so that their medical information could be released to insurance companies and any other providers involved in approving financial reimbursement for care and procedures. As discussed, the hospital also had an internal policy to contract with software companies that eventually resulted in one software company compiling and selling patient information to pharmaceutical companies and insurers.

In terms of the sale or trade of patient databases by the software company, the law is in the process of clarifying privacy rights and the use of medical record information. At present, highly sensitive medical information is routinely shared with third parties uninvolved in patient care (Dickson, 1998). As Mary was not a federal employee or receiving care in a federal institution, any protections afforded by the Federal Privacy Act of 1984 did not apply.

Gaps clearly exist in both the hospital's policies and current legislation (as discussed earlier) regarding the privacy of electronic medical records. These gaps also caused conflicts with the ethical principles of autonomy, non-maleficence, and fidelity.

N–What are the needs of the parties involved (from a biopsychosocial perspective): Mary needed to cope with the psychosocial sequela of her breast cancer and was committed to taking care of her widowed mother. This was manifest, in part, by choosing to delay informing her mother about the breast cancer until a later time. Mary's mother needed to feel that she was not a burden to her daughter. The hospital needed to make sure that prompt filing of insurance claims was done so that financial resources were available for payroll, patient care, and teaching. The software company needed to maximize their profits. The pharmaceutical company needed to conduct market research in order to ensure sales.

T–What were the terms of understanding between the parties involved: Disclosures of information customarily come in the context of a particular relationship, with explicit "contractual" parameters, such as that between therapist and patient. The principle of autonomy and the derived professional value of client self determination dictates respect for the choices of each individual about the uses and disclosures of their own information (Cushman & Detmer, 1997; Welfel, 1998). Therefore, Claire had the professional responsibility to base her relationship with Mary on respect for her autonomy, the obligation to do no harm (nonmaleficence), and to maintain Mary's trust (fidelity).

E–Elucidate the ethical conflict; educate the parties; empower through education. The ethical conflict: The major ethical dilemmas in this case concern the social worker's mandate to respect client autonomy, do no harm, to keep promises and tell the truth. However, these came into conflict with the reality that intimate medical information–such as mental health services–became fodder for examination beyond the practitioner and patient. While the majority of practitioners in managed care settings have their efforts facilitated by electronic medical records, they rarely guarantee that they are able to keep the patient's health information limited to themselves or an identifiable set of others within the practice environment (Strom-Gottfried & Corcoran, 1998; Cushman & Detmer, 1997; Lu, 1997). Clients are compelled to sign consent forms to release information to managed care insurers, which effectively end a client's right to privacy. Yet, ethically and legally human service professionals must protect confidentiality unless the client has consented to do otherwise (Linzer, 1999). This dilemma was exacerbated for Claire because she was not fully informed of her hospital's business practices which led (albeit unintentionally) to the electronic transmission and "barter" of Mary's health data from the software company to the pharmaceutical company.

Educate and empower: Educating clients and staff about why these ethical dilemmas arise and how they relate to conflicts with institutional policies (and legislation) may help to decrease feelings of helplessness engendered by such conflicts. The increased awareness may motivate involved parties to advocate changing policies and legislation. For example, staff should demand that management keep them fully informed of hospital business practices that may compromise the privacy of patient records. All parties involved in the conflict should use their knowledge about privacy rights and electronic communication to promote better protection at the institutional, state and federal levels.

R–Attempt to reconcile the ethical principles and values to create a plan for action: It may not be possible to completely reconcile the ethical principles of autonomy, nonmaleficence, and fidelity with policies that end a client's right to privacy. However, based upon these ethical principles, a plan of action may include human service professionals reviewing detailed release of information forms with clients. These would clearly explain that in a managed-care system, the client and social worker do not control the right to privacy and confidentiality. When discussing the terms of the helping relationship, human service professionals should inform clients that there is no confidentiality under managed care since it may not be possible to obtain reimbursement for treatment without compromising confidentiality. Based on the educative component, the plan of action might include providing clients with information about how to contact legislators regarding the state of privacy rights legislation.

N–Clarify the necessity for resolution of the conflict: One major reason for resolving this conflict is that human service professionals should develop strategies to cope with the split loyalties arising from their need to be loyal to the client (fidelity) and to their employer. Other reasons for resolving this conflict include the need for human service professionals to fully inform clients about the limits of privacy and confidentiality brought on by managed care and electronic medical records.

E–Evaluation of the possible outcomes and consequences of the conflict: While outcomes are difficult to predict, one short-term outcome and consequence may be as follows. Mary might experience an increased psychological burden because of her loss of autonomy (being forced to reveal medical information to her mother), loss of trust in Claire (violation of fidelity), and the resulting psychological harm she suffered (violation of nonmaleficence). Consequently, she might seek help with another provider–perhaps even paying privately in order to avoid dealing with managed care and the "publicness" of her medical records. This financial burden may make it harder to care for her elderly mother without experiencing more emotional strain.

T–Reflect upon how the conflict was terminated: This conflict may have ended with several possible outcomes. For one, the hospital may have to revise its release of information/informed consent procedures so that both providers and clients have a greater awareness of confidentiality issues. Through these efforts, both professionals and clients might become actively involved in advocating for more comprehensive privacy protection of electronic health records.

Through applying this framework, Claire may engage in more realistic discussions with clients about the limits of social worker-client confidentiality. This may prevent miscommunication with clients around the privacy of their medical information, educate those involved about these issues, and enable Claire to better comply with her ethical responsibilities.

CONCLUSION

Ethical dilemmas arising from the use of electronic information technologies in the human services are normative occurrences. Human service professionals may encounter these dilemmas in host settings (e.g., hospitals or corporations), where they have minimal control over how and where their client's medical and social data is stored, transmitted, and used. Despite this lack of control, human service professionals are still mandated to resolve ethical dilemmas in ways that are compatible with their professional codes of ethics, relevant legislation, and agency guidelines. They struggle to reconcile these conflicting pressures is made more difficult by the dearth of legal or ethical precedence around concerns such as invasion of privacy and electronic technology.

Models for ethical analysis, such as INTERNET, are useful in helping human service professionals approach ethical issues in the use of electronic information technology. The framework is designed so that human service professionals will maintain this awareness throughout their analysis. As discussed earlier, privacy, confidentiality, and informed consent are fundamental aspects of the helping relationship. However, in the unregulated virtual world of electronic data collection, storage, and transfer the intent and spirit of these tenets of the helping professions are being eroded. An international debate now rages about how to address these concerns yet not stifle the free flow of information that characterizes a democratic society. Human service professionals must have their voices heard so their core values–service, social justice, and the dignity and worth of the individual–are incorporated into formal policies and legislation.

NOTES

1. For complete statements by NAHDO see their Website at *http://www.nahdo.org*

2. To access the NASW Code of Ethics see http://www.socialworkers.org/pub/naswethics.doc

3. To see the full statement of the Ethics Committee of the American Psychological Association access this at http://www.unn.ac.uk.academics/ss/psychology/resource/apa/ethtel.html

4. To see full statements by the American Psychiatric Association on the practice of telepsychiatry access this at http://www.psych.org/psych/htdocs/prac_of_psych/tp_orgs.html

REFERENCES

Abramson, J. (1990). Enhancing patient participation: Clinical strategies in the discharge planning process. *Social Work in Health Care*, 14 (4), 22-35.

Abramson, M. & Black R. (1985). Extending the boundaries of life: Implications for practice. *Health and Social Work*, 10(3), 165-173.

American Management Association. (1997). More U.S. firms checking e-mail, computer files, and phone calls. [On-line]. Available Internet: http://www.amanet.org/research/default.htm

Beauchamp, T., & Childress, J. (1994). *Principles of biomedical ethics* (4th ed.). New York: Oxford University Press

Beel, N. (1999). Ethical Issues for Counseling Over the Internet: An Examination of the Risks and Benefits. [On-line]. Available online: *http://geocities.com/Athens/Olympus/4609/ethics.html*

Berglund, S. (1997). Legal issues in healthcare and the Internet. *Medicomputer Perspective: Supplement to Computers & Medicine*, 26 (1), 16-21.

Casser, K. (1996). *The Internet and business: A lawyer's guide to the emerging legal issues*. Fairfax, VA: The Computer Law Association, Inc.

Chapin, B. (1987). Autonomy and paternalism: Horns of a dilemma. *Discharge Planning Update*, 8 (1), 23-24.

Cowles, L. & Lefcowitz, M. (1995). Interdisciplinary expectations of the social worker in health care settings. *Health & Social Work*, 17 (1), 57-65.

Cushman, R. & Detmer, D. (1997). Information policy for the U.S. health sector: Engineering, political economy, and ethics. *The Milbank Quarterly: A Journal of Public Health and Health Care Policy*. Available online: *http://www.med.harvard.edu/publication.Milbank/art/index.html*

Cwikel, J. & Cnaan, R. (1991). Ethical dilemmas in applying second-wave information technology to social work practice. *Social Work*, 36, (2), 114-120.

Dickson, D. (1998). *Confidentiality and privacy in social work*. New York: The Free Press.

Dzieglielewsi, S. (1998). *The changing face of health care social work*. New York: Springer.

Freedman, T. (1998). Genetic susceptibility testing: Ethical and social quandaries. *Health & Social Work*, 23 (3), 214-222.

Freudenheim, M. (1998, August 12). Privacy a concern as medical industry turn to Internet. [On-line]. Available Internet: *http://www.nytimes.com/library/tech/98/08/biztech/articles/12healthcare-internet.html*

Gant, L. & Giddens, B. (1998). *Ethical issues, HIV/AIDS, and social work practice: Participant manual*. Rockville, MD: U.S. Department of Health and Human Services.

Gelman, S., Pollack, D. & Weiner, A. (1999). Confidentiality of social work records in the computer age. *Social Work*, 44 (3), 253-261.

Grohol, J. (1999). Best practices in e-therapy: Confidentiality & privacy. [On-line]. Available Internet: *http://www.ismho.org/issues/9901.htm*

Information Infrastructure Task Force (1997). Options for promoting privacy on National Information Infrastructure: Draft for public comment. Information Policy Committee, National Information Infrastructure Task Force.[On-line]. Available Internet: *http://www.iitf.nist.gov/ipc/privacy.htm*

Karger, H.J. & Levine, J. (1999). *The Internet and technology for the human services.* New York: Addison Wesley Longman.

Karger, H.J. & Stoez, D. (1998). *American social welfare policy: A pluralist approach* (3rd ed.) New York: Addison Wesley Longman.

Kitchener, K. (1995). Ethical principles and decisions in student affairs. In J.H. Cannon and R.D. Brown (Eds.) *Applied ethics in student services* (pp 17-29). New Directions in Student Services, No. 10. San Francisco: Jossey Bass.

Levine, J. (1997). *Conflicted helping: The mediator role of social work discharge planners.* Ann Arbor, MI: UMI Dissertation Services.

Linzer, N. (1999). *Resolving ethical dilemmas in social work practice.* Boston: Allyn and Bacon.

Lowenberg, F. & Dolgoff, R. (1996). *Ethical decisions for social work practice,* (5th ed.) Itasca, IL: F.E. Peacock Publishers

Lu, J. (1997). Who's in our genes? Electronic health information and the protection of privacy. [On-line] Available Internet: *http://www-swiss.ai.mit.edu/6805/student-papers/fall97-papers/lu-genes.html*

Macklin, R. (1984). Ethical issues in treatment of patients with end-stage renal disease. *Social Work in Health Care,* 9 (4), 11-20.

Mailick, M. & Ullman, A. (1984). A social work perspective on ethical practice in end-stage renal disease. *Social Work in Health Care,* 9 (4), 21-31.

Manning, S. & Gaul, C. (1997). The Ethics of informed consent: A critical variable in the self-determination of health and mental health clients. *Social Work in Health Care,* 25 (3), 103-117.

McGee, G. (1997). Ethical issues in genetics in the next 100 years. [On-line]. Available Internet: *http://www.med.upenn.edu/~bioethic/library/papers/glenn/100years.html*

Menedez v. Superior Court, 834 P. 2d 786 (1992).

National Association of Social Workers. (1996). *NASW Code of Ethics.* Available on-line: *http://socialworkers.org/pub/naswethics.doc*

Osman, H. & Perlin, T. (1994). Patient self-determination and the artificial prolongation of life. *Health & Social Work,* 19(4), 245-252.

Perlin, T. (1992). The PRACTICE model of analysis for ethical dilemmas in health care. *Health & Social Work,* 17 (2), 205-216.

Perloff, J. (1996). Medicaid managed care and the urban poor: Implications for social work. *Health and Social Work,* 21 (3), 189-195.

Reamer, F. (1986). The use of modern technology in social work: Ethical dilemmas. *Social Work,* 31 (6) 469-472.

Roberts, C. (1989). Conflicting professional values in social work and medicine. *Health and Social Work,* 24 (8), 211-218.

Rock, B. & Congress, E. (1999). The new confidentiality for the 21st century in a managed care environment. *Social Work,* 44 (3), 253-262.

Rose, L. (1995). *Netlaw: Your rights in the online world.* Berkeley, CA: McGraw-Hill

Spielberg, A.R. (1998). On call and online: Sociohistorical, legal and ethical implication of e-mail for the patient-physician relationship. *Journal of the American Medical Association,* 280 (15), 1353-1359.

Spinello, R. (1997). *Case studies in information and computer ethics.* Upper Saddle River, NJ: Prentice-Hall.

Sproull, L. & Faraj, S. (1995). Atheism, sex, and databases: The Net as a social technology. In B. Kahin & J. Keller (Eds.) *Public access to the Internet* pp. 62-81. Cambridge, MA: MIT Press.

Strom-Gottfried, K. & Corcoran, K. (1998). Confronting ethical dilemmas in managed care; guidelines for students and faculty. *Journal of Social Work Education,* (34) (1), 109-119.

Strom-Gottfried, K. (1998). Informed consent meets managed care. *Health & Social Work*, 23, (1), 25-34.

Welfel, E.R. (1998). *Ethics in counseling and psychotherapy: Standards, results and emerging issues.* Pacific Grove, CA: Brooks/Cole Publishing.

The Community Tool Box:
Using the Internet to Support the Work
of Community Health and Development

Jerry A. Schultz
Stephen B. Fawcett
Vincent T. Francisco
Tom Wolff
Bill R. Berkowitz
Genevieve Nagy

Jerry A. Schultz is Courtesy Assistant Professor of Human Development and Associate Director of the Work Group on Health Promotion and Community Development. Stephen B. Fawcett is Professor of Human Development and Director of the Work Group on Health Promotion and Community Development. Vincent T. Francisco is Courtesy Assistant Professor of Human Development and Associate Director of the Work Group on Health Promotion and Community Development. Genevieve Nagy is Community Tool Box Project Coordinator, Work Group on Health Promotion and Community Development. All are affiliated with the Schiefelbusch Institute for Life Span Studies, University of Kansas, Lawrence, KS 66045.

Tom Wolff PhD, is affiliated with AHEC Community Partners Dept. Family Health Community Medicine, University of Massachusetts Medical School, 24 S Prospect, Amherst, MA 01002.

Bill Berkowitz, PhD, is Associate Professor of Psychology, University of Massachusetts Lowell, Lowell, MA 01854.

This work was supported, in part, by grants from the Robert Wood Johnson Foundation, Kansas Health Foundation, and John D. and Catherine T. MacArthur Foundation. We thank those who give guidance to this work, including the Community Tool Box Advisory Board, the writers and partners, and especially, local people doing the work of community health and development.

[Haworth co-indexing entry note]: "The Community Tool Box: Using the Internet to Support the Work of Community Health and Development." Schultz et al. Co-published simultaneously in *Journal of Technology in Human Services* (The Haworth Press, Inc.) Vol. 17, No. 2/3, 2000, pp. 193-215; and: *Human Services Online: A New Arena for Service Delivery* (ed: Jerry Finn, and Gary Holden) The Haworth Press, Inc., 2000, pp. 193-215. Single or multiple copies of this article are available for a fee from The Haworth Document Delivery Service [1-800-342-9678, 9:00 a.m. - 5:00 p.m. (EST). E-mail address: getinfo@haworthpressinc.com].

SUMMARY. Despite limited preparation through formal and non-formal education, local people throughout the world are engaged in the common work of building healthier communities. Some core competencies–including community assessment, planning, mobilization, and evaluation–are needed to address the variety of issues that matter to local communities. This report describes an Internet-based support system for community work known as the Community Tool Box (CTB) [http://ctb. lsi.ukans.edu/]. We examine the idea and origins of the CTB and its core content, access features, and applications. We review evidence for its use, implementation and dissemination strategies, and discuss core values that guide this internet-based work. *[Article copies available for a fee from The Haworth Document Delivery Service: 1-800-342-9678. E-mail address: <getinfo@haworthpressinc.com> Website: <http://www.haworthpressinc.com>]*

KEYWORDS. Internet, community development, support system

Throughout the world, local people come together to address community concerns related to health, development, and their determinants (Fawcett, Francisco et al., in press; Green & Kreuter, 1999; Schorr, 1997). Thousands of partnerships, coalitions, and collaboratives are attempting to improve community well-being and the conditions that affect it. These initiatives are formed based on fundamental commonalties, including the values of civic engagement, trusting relationships, problem-solving, empowerment, and social justice (Fawcett et al., 1996). They share a focus on environmental change, using an ecological perspective to guide local participation in identifying problems and assets, and developing, implementing and evaluating the effects of comprehensive efforts (Epp, 1986; Fawcett, Paine, Francisco, & Vliet, 1993; Fawcett, Paine-Andrews et al., in press; Green & Raeburn, 1988).

Community health and development initiatives exist to solve locally-determined problems, such as substance abuse or inadequate housing, and to enhance community assets, such as caring relationships with children or opportunities for economic well-being. Whether in urban or rural contexts, participants use an array of skills and competencies that are not usually part of formal or non-formal education, such as planning, advocacy, or securing resources. Personal factors of leaders and participants, such as lack of ability to analyze the causes of problems, or limited leadership skills, can impede the problem-solving process. Group factors, such as the presence of strategic plans to reach goals or an inclusive organizational structure, may be important for success. Similarly, organizations with a clear theory of action, such as the Community Health Improvement Process (Durch, Bailey, & Stoto, 1997), may be better able to help guide community-based efforts for change and improvement (Fawcett et al., 1995; Goodman et al., 1998; Schorr, 1997).

Although local people often bring knowledge, experience, and passion to community work, they may lack the array of competencies needed for success. For example, although community members may be skilled in listening or other aspects of community assessment, they may not have experience in strategic planning, evaluation, or securing resources. Such core competencies reflect the common work of promoting community health and development–whether our local purpose is promoting child health or enhancing urban community development (Durch, Bailey, & Stoto, 1997).

As communities face persisting conditions that lead to acute problems, they turn to new resources such as the Internet and other information technology to assist in their problem solving efforts. Some online community support resources provide communication channels (e.g., forums, chat rooms, e-mail) to community members for networking. Most resources offer information for quite specific populations such as people with arthritis or those concerned with environmental issues. Many national websites provide information about the host organization, but offer little supportive material for community practitioners. The development of these resources may cost relatively little, perhaps less than $20,000, or it may exceed a million dollars if extensive programming and content development are required. In most cases, developing these resources requires skilled computer programmers. As the Internet-based resource becomes more complex, the need for a strong development and support team increases (Milio, 1996).

This manuscript describes an Internet-based support system for community work known as the Community Tool Box (CTB) [http://ctb.lsi.ukans.edu/]. Its mission is to promote community health and development by connecting people, ideas, and resources. We examine the idea and origins of the CTB, its core content, access features, and application. Next we review evidence regarding its use, impact, implementation and dissemination. We conclude with some lessons learned, future plans, and core values that guide this work.

THE IDEA OF A COMMUNITY TOOL BOX

We envisioned a literal (or virtual) "community tool box"–a receptacle for practical information and resources–for those doing the work of promoting community health and development. The potential audiences or end users for this resource included community leaders and members (i.e., those doing the work), intermediary organizations (i.e., those supporting it), and grantmakers (i.e., those funding it). We and others engaged in providing technical assistance have difficulty obtaining readily available, easily accessible, and appropriate tools for communities engaged in community health and development. Obtaining such materials can take a significant amount of time. The CTB was developed to help address this problem. We included in the CTB material that we had already developed, with the bulk of material adapted (with crediting) from the work of others.

Origins and Background

With the emergence of the World Wide Web in the early 1990s, we saw possibilities for offering an online (or virtual) "community tool box" with attributes (Engst, 1995) that were responsive to our technical assistance challenge. In 1995, the Work Group on Health Promotion and Community Development at the University of Kansas (the KU Work Group) received a one-year grant from the Kansas Health Foundation to pilot the CTB. The KU Work Group approached AHEC Community Partners of Massachusetts to become a partner in development. The combined KU Work Group-AHEC team brought decades of professional training and experience in supporting a wide variety of community-based initiatives, expertise in behavioral instruction and skill training, and technical competence in building Internet-based resource sites.

The initial grant permitted us to try out and refine the idea, outline a preliminary table of contents for identified core competencies (e.g., community assessment, strategic planning), and generate a modest number of content sections based on a prototype. In 1996, following a brief hiatus in grant funding, we received a two-year demonstration and subsequent two-year development grant from the Robert Wood Johnson Foundation, the primary funding partner. Supplementary grant support from the John D. and Catherine T. MacArthur Foundation helped enhance production of new content. Grantmaking partners appreciated the potential of the CTB for helping support community-based initiatives that were geographically dispersed and whose work unfolded over time with the efforts of multiple generations of leadership.

Some Attributes of a "Tool Box" for Community Work

To be useful, a support system for community work would need several attributes (Fawcett et al., 1995). First, its content had to be *comprehensive*. The breadth of topics should reflect the array of core competencies (e.g., community assessment, leadership development, advocacy, securing resources) associated with the work. Second, the information had to be *readily available*. Since community work is dynamic and unfolding, practitioners must have access to information on a topic (e.g., planning, social marketing) when they actually need it. Third, practitioners benefit from guidance in adjusting how to work in diverse contexts and situations. *Capacity to interact* with others, such as through online forums, could help support the application of a skill in a particular context (e.g., advocating for a policy change in public schools or in a Latino community). Fourth, a support system needs to address the high turnover with both community initiatives and leadership. Widespread availability of a *core curriculum* for the skills of community building would permit new generations of leadership to enhance their competence in promoting community health and development. Finally, a support system should help *reduce the inequities* in capacity for community change and improvement. By permitting free access for those not receiving special funding, a universally available support system could help reduce disparities in resources for community work (Osborne & Gaebler, 1992).

Conceptual Underpinnings for the Core Content

We wanted the core content of the Community Tool Box to reflect a model or framework to guide community practice (Schorr, 1997). The picture of community work that we present is a dynamic and interactive process with six common phases and related core competencies (Fawcett, Paine-Andrews et al., in press):

- Understanding community context (e.g., assessing community assets, conducting public forums);

- Strategic planning (e.g., developing a vision statement, action plan);
- Developing leadership and enhancing participation (e.g., building leadership capacity, organizational structure);
- Community action and intervention (e.g., analyzing problems, designing and choosing interventions);
- Evaluating community initiatives (e.g., documentation of community and systems change, behavioral measures, community-level indicators); and
- Promoting institutionalization of the initiative (e.g., maintaining quality performance, securing grants and other resources).

The choice of content reflects both science-based practice and experiential knowledge among those doing the work. Research with multiple case studies of community initiatives (Fawcett, Francisco, Hyra et al., in press; Fawcett, Francisco, Paine-Andrews, & Schultz, in press) suggested the importance of several key factors in community change (i.e., leadership, having a targeted mission, action planning, community mobilizers, technical assistance, documentation and feedback on community change, and making outcome matter). Similarly, research in behavioral instruction suggested the function (e.g., clear description of the skill, rationales, clear description of the behaviors that make up the skill, models and exemplars, prompts to remind us of key aspects of performance) of key elements of the sections or learning modules' content (Fawcett, Mathews, & Fletcher, 1980). This science base, the experiential knowledge of the team, and its sources of critical feedback (e.g., focus groups with the National Advisory Board and a wide range of community leaders and practitioners) guided content selection and development (Barrett, 1992; Brooks, 1997). An outline of content from a section on "Creating Objectives," an aspect of strategic planning, is offered to help illustrate these features (see Figure 1).

Further, to encourage generalization of the skills to new situations, the examples throughout the section must reflect a variety of issues and contexts for community work. The examples reflect diverse issues in: (a) public health (e.g., teen pregnancy, HIV/AIDS, cardiovascular diseases); (b) development of children, youth, and adults (e.g., substance abuse, violence, education); and (c) community development (e.g., building community organization, mutual aid; advocacy for housing or jobs). They also illustrate application in an array of con-

FIGURE 1. An Example Outline for a "How-To" Section on the Community Tool Box Section on "Creating Objectives"

1. What are objectives?
2. Why should you create objectives?
3. When should you create objectives?
   - Example: A faith community's food drive
4. How do you create objectives?
   - Example: The objectives of the Reducing the Risks coalition
   - Example: The objectives from an initiative to prevent adolescent substance abuse
5. Related topics
6. Resources
7. An illustrative story
8. Checklist
9. Tools
10. Overheads

texts including urban neighborhoods, rural communities, and international contexts; and with people with diverse experiences (e.g., people with disabilities, youth, older adults) and cultural backgrounds (e.g., Hispanic, African American). Although the examples reflect diverse issues, the core material in the CTB is not issue specific. Rather, the focus is on developing the core competencies necessary to address a variety of community concerns.

CORE CONTENT, ACCESS FEATURES, AND APPLICATIONS

The core content of the CTB is the "how-to" tools or sections. These learning modules use simple, friendly language to explain how to conduct activities related to the core competencies for building healthier communities (Fawcett, Francisco et al., in press). Development of new sections is an ongoing process, with the eventual goal of 400 or more discrete learning modules. Information on the CTB remains current through ongoing enhancements in breadth (i.e., new content) and depth (i.e., additional examples and tools). Practical information is readily available to the ever increasing global community with Internet access, and is offered without cost to anyone working to address the concerns that matter to them (Barrett, 1992).

The CTB has several other access features to enhance user ability to connect to people, ideas, and resources. The CTB links to (and describes) hundreds of other web pages and listservs of potential interest to those working to address local concerns. Related sites are searchable by specific category (i.e., community, funding, evaluation, health, education, government, search engines). A troubleshooting guide aids in addressing problems in doing the work. For each of the identified community dilemmas (e.g., not enough people participating) the guide provides clarifying questions and links to how-to information. Forums and chat rooms allow users a place to discuss current issues with which their communities are struggling. We also provide access to the how-to modules through several theories or models of change (e.g., our model–Building Capacity for Community and Systems Change, the Institute of Medicine's Community Health Improvement Process).

Additionally, the CTB assists users in developing useful products to support their work. For example, the online generic grant application allows users to develop a funding request that can be modified for future grant proposals. The grant proposal form offers users introductory information on the grantmaking and grant-seeking process, links users to relevant how-to modules of the CTB to assist with completion of a proposal, and provides links to foundations and other potential funders.

The CTB is also used to support grantmakers in their efforts. For example, in work with the Kansas Health Foundation, the CTB was used to help support a request for proposals (RFP) process and subsequent implementation of a multi-site initiative to prevent adolescent pregnancy. Participants were instructed to use how-to sections of the CTB to help them develop specific components of their proposals and action plans. Similarly, we used the CTB to help support an urban community development initiative funded by the John D. and Catherine T. MacArthur Foundation in mid-south Chicago, and a Turning Point initiative to enhance the public health infrastructure funded by the Robert Wood Johnson Foundation. In these applications, how-to sections of the CTB are linked to components of the initiative's logic model (e.g., for Turning Point, links to the Community Health Improvement Process).

The CTB also offers possibilities for distributed (or distance) learning. For example, we have used the web site as an online text for our undergraduate and graduate level course, Building Healthy Communities, taught from the University of Kansas. In past applications, the course used the Internet and compressed, interactive video and was available to both students and practitioners throughout Kansas. Individuals and organizations at great distances from each other were able to be linked with resources and people from across the state, allowing them to learn from and with others working to address similar concerns. Teaching and public service organizations from other universities have also used readings from the CTB to support students' learning and work related to community health and development.

EVIDENCE OF USE AND IMPACT

Each year the CTB is being used more by a wider range of its potential audience–community leaders and members, intermediary and support organizations, and funders. It remains unclear how the use of the Internet influences the work of building community (Galston, no date). We are interested in understanding whether and how people use the CTB, and if it is meeting their needs.

We estimate use of the CTB by examining the number of "hits" the site received. A hit is an action on the web site such as when a user views a page or downloads a file. Our computer-generated data show sharp yearly increases in the number of hits on the CTB. During the last half of 1995, when the CTB team put online the first few prototype sections, we received only 3,322 hits. In 1996, still early in development and without active promotion of the site, the CTB had 53,469 hits. In 1997, the number of hits increased to 141,860; and in 1998, the number of hits increased to 530,742. By the end of 1999, we expect approximately one million hits.

In addition, the number of users has increased dramatically. The number of discrete user sessions each day rose from 47 in 1997 to over 222 in 1999 (see Table 1). A user session is a session of activity (all hits) for one visitor to the web site. It starts when a user first accesses a CTB page and ends when the user leaves the site. During the session, the user accesses one or more CTB web pages. Most users are from the United States, although a large percentage, nearly half, is from other countries, including Canada, Australia, the United Kingdom, Switzerland, and Germany. Within the United States, more users come from Virginia, Kansas, California, New York, and Texas. Only the top five states are listed in Table 1. Kansas is high on the list because of the extensive work the KU Work Group does with community groups

TABLE 1. Use of the Community Tool Box (1995-99)

Measures	Years				
	1995 (last 6 months)	1996	1997	1998	1999 (first 6 months)
Total Number of Hits	3,322	53,469	141,860	530,742	527,390
Total Number of User Sessions	304	6,495	17,187	33,789	39,733
Hits by States (U.S.)	California Ohio New Mexico Kansas	California Virginia* Ohio Mass. Texas	California Virginia* Kansas Texas Pennsylvania	Virginia* Kansas California New York Texas	Virginia* California Kansas Texas New York
Hits by Country	U.S. (45%) Canada	U.S. (51%) Canada Australia UK New Zealand	U.S. (49%) Canada Australia UK Germany	U.S. (54%) Canada Australia UK Germany	U.S. (67%) Canada UK Switzerland Australia

*Includes a gateway site for America On-Line (AOL).

there. The number of hits from other states may simply reflect their large population size or, in the case of Virginia, because it is the site of a gateway for a network such as America On-Line.

The value of the CTB to initiatives is an important question, but difficult to answer. The number of hits suggests that it is being used extensively. It is unclear whether that is translated into community action and improvement. Anecdotal reports from the CTB guest book [http://ctb.lsi.ukans.edu/] and discussions between our technical assistance staff and community practitioners suggest that CTB use leads to improved action, however. For example, our technical assistance staff for teen pregnancy prevention initiatives using the CTB heavily report community practitioners applying skills (e.g., focus groups, listening sessions) from the CTB in diverse contexts. Similarly, evaluation reports from community participants in our distance learning class using CTB sections to help prepare grant applications report success with funding requests, as well as using other CTB-related skills months after the course ended.

Those providing technical assistance in the KU Work Group report that the intensive use of the CTB was associated with reduced start-up time for implementing comprehensive community initiatives. They also note increases in the amount and efficiency of technical assistance they have been able to provide.

User interests and contexts are highly diverse as well. Examples of issues to which users are applying the CTB tools include substance abuse, teen pregnancy, housing, education, mental health, youth violence, environmental health, child abuse and neglect, rural health, urban community development, and promoting independent living for older adults. A sampling, from our guestbook and other communications (i.e., e-mail messages, phone calls, discussions at conferences), of past users illustrates this diversity. It includes school children in Pennsylvania working to save a bog, an AIDS activist in Philadelphia, a social worker in the Men's Movement, a regional community development office in South Africa, a charitable organization working for the poor in Pakistan, a minority health worker in Texas, an Ann Arbor coalition working to end violence against women, those involved in democracy building in eastern Europe, and a nonprofit organization working to obtain permanent housing for migrant farm workers.

SOME CHALLENGES IN THIS WEB-BASED WORK

This section outlines several key challenges and adjustments in this effort to build an online support system for community initiatives.

Increasing Access and Awareness of the Web Site as a Resource

Any Internet resource, no matter how well developed, is useless unless those who could benefit from it can access it. This is a fundamental challenge for the CTB because it is designed for use by community-based organizations (CBOs) including grassroots neighborhood groups and non-governmental organizations (NGOs). Two barriers had to be overcome before the CTB could be of use.

First, access to the Internet itself presented the most obvious barrier to use. Some grassroots organizations do not have access to the Internet, which precludes their use of *any* Internet-based tools. When we started developing the CTB in 1994, access to the Internet was a major barrier we felt would diminish over time. Internet use has mushroomed in the United States so that nearly every school, public library, and public health department has access (Engst, 1995; U.S. Department of Education, 1998). Studies suggest that Internet use is increasing rapidly and will reach half of America's households by shortly after 2000, but there remain great disparities between the haves and the have nots (Hoffman & Novak, 1998; McConnaughey, Lader & Chin, 1998). Although racial and age disparities may diminish significantly, current Net users are still higher income earners, have higher education, and are younger than those yet to come online.

Second, an organization may have access to the Internet, but be unaware that the CTB exists on it. Search engines such as AltaVista, Lycos, MSN, and Infoseek provide one strategy for regular Internet users to connect with the CTB. When "Community Tool Box" is entered, the search results include the homepage of the CTB. This is less useful than it appears, however, since the typical community practitioner is not usually looking for the title of the CTB, but rather some subject of interest such as advocacy or leadership. But, if you type the word "advocacy" in the AltaVista search engine, for example, you will hit over 60,000 web pages that include the word advocacy. Accordingly, unless the CTB becomes a brand name with wide user recognition, Internet search engines may be of limited use in contacting it.

A more successful strategy for increasing awareness of the CTB has been to identify potential early adopters of community health and development information and promote it through communication channels they regularly use–conferences, journals, newsletters, and related sites on the World Wide Web. Professional organizations and national initiatives whose constituents were ready to use this information became our primary target audience for informational messages.

Professional conferences associated with community health and development provide an interested audience for the CTB. We regularly demonstrate the use of the CTB at professional conferences. Where computer lab facilities are available, demonstrations and training sessions are offered as we did at the 1997 Biennial Meeting of the Society for Community Research and Action. We have held sessions at the annual American Public Health Association meetings and demonstrated the CTB at the Robert Wood Johnson Foundation's exhibition booth at these meetings. We have presented introductory or training sessions at numerous regional or special initiative conferences as well. When attendance of CTB staff at conferences is not possible we send brochures and an exhibit for display. Descriptions and reviews of the CTB have also been included in professional journals, newsletters, and listservs.

Other sites on the World Wide Web offer another important channel for promoting use of the CTB. We regularly establish linkages with pertinent sites. For example, we have been linked to the web pages for the American Public Health Association and the Coalition of Healthier Cities/ Communities. Hundreds of other web sites have links to the CTB.

We also constantly use the CTB in our own work providing technical assistance to state and community initiatives in Kansas, Massachusetts, and nationally and globally. The CTB is now integrated into the development and support of all initiatives we work with. It becomes the first level of technical assistance for new and ongoing initiatives. To build capacity, we encourage members and leaders of in local initiatives to turn first to the CTB as problems are confronted, and then to contact us directly if that is insufficient.

Alliances with strategic partners have also been used to promote widespread use of the CTB. These usually are funded initiatives that seek support for multisite (or multistate) efforts. With support from funding partners, we create and maintain customized portals or gateways to CTB sections and tools. For example, we have partnerships with several Robert Wood Johnson Foundation-supported initiatives including Turning Point, a national and state-based initiative to restructure public health, and the Access Project, a national initiative attempting to increase access to health care for the uninsured. By using the partner's model of change to serve as a gateway to the tools, we create and maintain an online support system for initiatives that involve multi-site efforts at local, state, and national levels.

Creating Material for the Web

Putting large amounts of information on the Web presents challenges regarding ownership, production, and proper use of material. First, use of materials written and prepared by others turned out to be too complicated and potentially expensive to pursue. To use copyrighted materials we had to negotiate use and fees with publishers and sometimes the writers. Rather than rely on published materials we decided that writing (adapting) our own material for the CTB was the best approach.

Second, we had to develop a system to support content development. Each section that is written is based on research and reviews of the literature. We chose a style that was easy to read, designed for the Web, practical and user-friendly. We always reference the material that the sections may be based on and welcome collaboration with other writers. Writing this quantity of material required a team of writers, and where possible, we hired writers for topics they had written on elsewhere or for which they had special skills or experience. All sections are also closely edited by at least one person with expertise in that topical field. During 1998, for example, the team of writers–consisting of one full-time writer and several part-time writers and editors–could produce about five how-to sections each month. It has taken some time, but we now have a significant database of original materials that practitioners are finding valuable for their work.

Finally, we had to stipulate appropriate use of the CTB material we created. Since the site and material is considered intellectual property (of the authors and the University of Kansas), its redistribution or use for material gain is prohibited without compensation. But, individuals are encouraged to print and use CTB sections in their work. We simply request crediting of the CTB as the source.

Passive Information versus Interactive Support

The how-to sections of the CTB are easily accessible, but as passive sources of information. The users must search for and find the information that is most useful to them. There are several tools to assist the user in finding needed CTB material available (e.g., search engine, Table of Content). Although we have written the materials as jargon-free as possible, the user should be somewhat familiar with the language of community health and development. In addition, to maximize use of the tools, users need to understand their current community situation and identify the information they need.

With the exception of the Troubleshooting Guide, the CTB offers little help with this. Although the current version of the CTB is somewhat limited in helping people understand their situation or identify the information they might need, we are planning to create workspace on the CTB that will support practitioners and provide orientation, guidance, and critical assessment of their situation. Once the issues are identified the user will be presented with models, advice, and consultation that will support the development of products (e.g., community assessment, strategic plan) used to build healthier communities. The use of some of the components of the workspace will be free, while the use of other components that may require direct staff time may require a fee.

Another objective of the CTB is to connect people who engage in this common work. The World Wide Web has the capacity to bring together people who share common experience as well as bring novices in touch with those who have greater expertise or experience. This could be done through e-mail and forums in the CTB that focused on applying CTB materials to work in the community. To date, these channels have not been used extensively in the CTB, primarily because we have not been able to commit staff time to moderating forums. We have created generic and unmoderated forums on the CTB for the general user, but they have not produced a coherent discussion of issues.

Supporting the Online System Over the Long-Term

The costs of maintaining the CTB include staffing, especially writers for content development, and support for technological infrastructure, user service, administration, and marketing. The writing is a very time-consuming and labor intensive activity. For each section the writers have to research the topic, conduct interviews with practitioners, and the sections have to be passed through several writer-editor iterations. Each section may have input from several writers and editors before it is placed in the online database.

In addition, infrastructure costs can increase quickly. Initially, during the start-up phase, the CTB could use a personal computer as the server. But, as use increased, a higher capacity server was required. To enhance content development database programming became more sophisticated, allowing creation and maintenance of how-to sections online. The equipment costs quickly ran into the tens of thousands of dollars. Programmers are currently writing custom programming for the database, which adds tens of thousands of dollars more. Our staff, fortunately, included those with skills in computer programming, handling maintenance of the equipment, and troubleshooting technical problems. Typically, organizations would have to hire a computer specialist.

We provided limited technical support for those trying to use the site. This entailed responding to approximately 10-15 phone calls, e-mails and other requests for assistance each month. As the site's breadth, depth, interactivity, and use increased, this capacity needed to be enhanced. The administration and marketing of the CTB also requires ongoing support. In addition, the work of the writing team and the project staff has to be coordinated. What is more, the marketing of the site requires the often time-consuming identification of prospective users, plus (electronic) mailings, travel to conferences, and collaboration with a variety of partners. The number of staff varies from year to year and much of the research and development of content for the CTB is undergirded by other projects we are involved in, requiring flexible staffing. This project requires a strong multiskilled development team that consists of coordinators, writers/editors, computer programmer, web site manager, administrator and support staff (Milio, 1996).

Governmental agencies and private foundations that value the customized use of its content to build capacity for local, state, and national initiatives may support the future development of the CTB. Foundations have found using the CTB especially helpful in building capacity for community leadership in geographically dispersed sites. Government initiatives (e.g., public health programs, youth development initiatives) are also beginning to use the CTB to support their efforts. Interactive features may require a fee for use to recoup some of the development costs. In addition, we will continue to seek foundation support for core development of content. Our goal continues to be to offer as much free and practical information as possible.

CONCLUSION

In conclusion, we outline our lessons learned, some future plans, and the community-building values that guide this work.

What We are Learning

Our experience over the first five years of development of the CTB has led to a better understanding of the process of creating and maintaining an online support system for building healthier communities. These lessons are outlined under the categories of creating content, developing technology, and promoting its use.

Creating Content

- Create a framework for content (e.g., a working table of contents) that is carefully critiqued by a variety of outside reviewers (end-users) before drafting content. Once you commit to a framework, it becomes both logistically and psychologically hard to change extensively.
- Assemble a writing and editing team that combines topic-area expertise with ability to write for the nonprofessional reader, ideally within the same person.
- Make sure that any writer's draft contribution is thoroughly reviewed by and discussed with at least one editor, before any draft section gets posted online.
- Accept the reality that ongoing changes in the site will always be necessary.

Developing the Technology

- Create practical material and tools with the end-user in mind.
- Develop your information database (i.e., core content and access features) first, then develop the computer technology to support it.
- Develop computer programming that makes development (e.g., creation, deletion, modification of information) of the database manageable.
- To enhance access (including for those with visual impairments), keep graphics, animation, and other high bandwidth-using features to a minimum.

Promoting Use of the Online Information Technology

- Make the information available (e.g., through web site links, conference presentations) to those who are ready to use it.
- Reduce the costs in time and effort of using the site (e.g., ease of navigation, fewer clicks to get to information).
- Write with a viewer reading a monitor screen in mind.
- Make it easy to print or download documents.
- Provide support for those who encounter difficulties using the site.
- Integrate use of the site into initiatives as they unfold and develop.

- Partner with others to complement available supports for doing the work.

Some Future Plans

Predicting the future of the CTB is a daunting task, since it is intimately tied to what one can imagine about the future of the Internet over the next decades. Even in the short period of time that we have been developing the CTB we have had to make constant adjustments as the field has undergone rapid changes. For example, where we worried about gender imbalance in the use of the Web in our first years of development, recent data indicate that women are rapidly increasing their presence on the Web (McConnaughey, Lader, & Chin, 1998). The view of the future of the CTB includes a look at the content, interactivity, users, usages, and potential partners.

New writing will continue to develop the breadth of tools available, filling out the planned sections identified for the web site. Such extension and revision to embrace additional audiences (e.g., other ethnic groups, global communities) and issues (e.g., educational reform, environmental justice) will be a natural and ongoing part of our work in the future.

Building in interactivity is the next CTB challenge, as it is for many other Internet sites. To help address this, we may develop an expert guidance or mentoring function, where any community practitioner or general user can e-mail a question on community health and development and receive a specific personalized e-mail reply. In developing this concept, we have engaged relevant associations of community practitioners, such as the Society for Community Research and Action.

Enhanced interactivity of the CTB will move the site beyond passive access to vast amounts of material and move towards greater engagement with the user. Increased activity by the user is already present in sections such as writing a grant proposal where the user actively adds their own material to the grant development template and emerges with a grant proposal as a final product. More sections like this will be added. To increase experiential knowledge and mutual support, interactivity will go beyond this to include networking among users working together on similar products. A proposed online workspace will allow colleagues at various sites to work together on a joint project on the CTB. Thus, the CTB will become not only a source of information for community developers but also a source of support, linkages, and collaboration.

As we develop the CTB, we have proceeded with the belief that the web will become increasingly not only widely available, but also an integral part of peoples' lives. The issue of greatest concern for us has been the inequitable distribution of access to the Internet especially for low-income and disenfranchised populations. If our goal is to get tools for community development into the hands of those who have least access to formal technical assistance, can we succeed if low-income folks do not have equal access to the Web?

The future of the CTB will ride on our capacity to find creative ways to reach the isolated community change agent in rural communities and inner cities across the United States and globally (Milio, 1996; Mitchell, Sanyal, & Schon, 1996; Stoecker & Stuber, 1997). One continuing strategy for doing this involves partnering with organizations and initiatives that already link to grassroots leaders engaged in the work of community change and improvement.

In the United States, and globally, collaborative approaches are becoming the cutting edge of numerous movements for human and community development. In public safety, we see the development of community policing; in education, it is school/community partnerships often focused around parent involvement; in public health, it is collaborative partnerships for population-based health; and in municipal government, it is focused on rebuilding social capitol and promoting civic involvement.

All these new approaches and movements require people with the skills and know-how to bring about change in programs, policies, and practices in communities. Unfortunately, most formal and non-formal education systems fail to provide this type of training in practical citizenship. So, on a continuing basis, people all across the country and world seek solutions without the training and without the local access to help (Sclove, 1995). This is an ongoing and critical role for the CTB and other online supports for community building and change.

Enhancing Community-Building Values

As this article concludes, it may be helpful to reflect critically upon the relationship between Web-based innovations such as the CTB and the values we espouse. Such reflection takes on added significance because at the core of those values is promoting vibrant community life, in face-to-face rather than electronic transactions, and in geo-graphic rather than virtual communities.

More specifically, among our primary professional values are the strengthening of personal competence, the building of local capacities, the empowerment of disenfranchised groups, the expression of diversity, and the stimulation of citizen participation. One question then becomes whether such values can be adequately served over the Web (Galston, no date). A related question is how effective such Web-based mechanisms are in relation to other non-online forms of communication.

To the first question, our answer is a swift and simple "yes." Building personal and community competence is intrinsic to the CTB's mission. Many current CTB sections give implicit or explicit guidance on promoting cultural diversity; others discuss such topics as involving community members and mobilizing residents to act. Providing practical skills and encouraging their use are what our sections are about. We believe community-building values are both implicit and explicit in CTB content, as much as any words can reasonably allow. These values are also considered intrinsic to the professional discipline with which the authors are affiliated–public health, community psychology, community development, and applied anthropology.

The second question, comparing service to community-building values over the Web to other options, is more challenging and harder to answer unequivocally. We believe that community values are best developed in person-to-person interactions, in flesh-and-blood communities. They are often best promoted over coffee or tea, in casual conversations, by handwritten notes, through subtle nonverbal cues when passing on the sidewalk. Small personal affirmations, repeated over time and space, gradually build trust, community cohesion, and the ability to act in concert.

The Web does these things poorly, if at all. Its messages traditionally are inflexible, invariant, blind to individual users. But community builders need feedback and dialog. The community-building impact of the web, certainly for geographic communities, must therefore be more indirect. The CTB is one online means to an off-line end. The user-blind and invariant aspects of the Web can be at least partially overcome. One way to maximize appeal for all users is to pay more attention to writing style. We have developed a writer's guide, and we use it. To quote that guide: "We have to grab the skeptical viewer's attention and make sure it stays grabbed. Otherwise, they'll surf, and we're sunk." In other words, we want our style to be friendly, inclusive, supportive, motivating, and graceful, even elegant, so that the style itself expresses the community values we believe in and keeps users coming back.

The compensating advantages, of course, are speed, accessibility, breadth, and depth. A community-enhancing communication over the Internet can instantly reach a potentially-unlimited audience and provide fine-grained detail, without barriers of location, eligibility, or cost. An additional advantage, is one of revision. Face-to-face messages may be unclear, incomplete, inaccurate, and/or insensitive (and sometimes the message may simply not be heard). Web-based messages, however, can be created in quiet contemplation, when full concentration can be given to the task at hand. They can be drafted and redrafted, shaped until every element is in just the right place, and then revised again if necessary. Careful text can move people as careless speech cannot.

The jury is still out on how more interactive features will work in practice. But we are certain that in a short time the CTB will be a different web site. We also know that currently there are no other web sites that offer the comprehensive one-stop-shopping for generic, cross-cutting community building information that the CTB does. Through extending our content breadth and depth, adopting the best interactive practices, our community values will be better expressed. More human and community development professionals of all stripes will find a welcoming electronic home. And we will come closer to reaching the maximum deliverable capacity of any computerized resource site for improving daily community life.

REFERENCES

Barrett, E. (1992). *Sociomedia: Multimedia, hypermedia, and the social construction of knowledge.* Cambridge, MA: MIT Press.

Brooks, D.W. (1997). *Web-teaching: A guide to designing interactive teaching for the World Wide Web.* New York: Plenum Press.

Durch, J. S., Bailey, L. S., & Stoto, M. A. (Eds.) (1997). *Improving health in the community: A role for performance monitoring.* Washington, D.C.: National Academy Press.

Engst, A. C. (1995). *Internet starter kit.* Indianapolis: Hayden Books.

Epp, J. (1986). Achieving health for all: A framework for health promotion. *Health Promotion, I,* 419-428.

Fawcett, S. B., Francisco, V. T., Hyra, D., Paine-Andrews, A, Schultz, J. A., Russos, S., Fisher, J. L., & Evensen, P. (in press). Building healthy communities. In A. Tarlov (Ed.), *Society and population health reader: State and community applications.* New York: The New Press.

Fawcett, S. B., Francisco, V. T., Paine-Andrews, A., and Schultz, J. A. (in press). Working together for healthier communities: A research-based memorandum of collaboration. *Public Health Reports* (Special Supplement).

Fawcett, S. B., Mathews, R. M., & Fletcher, R. K. (1980). Some promising dimensions of behavioral community technology. *Journal of Applied Behavior Analysis, 13(3)*, 505-518.

Fawcett, S. B., Paine, A. L., Francisco, V. T., and Vliet, M. (1993). Promoting health through community development. In D. Glenwick and L. Jason (Eds.), *Promoting health and mental health in children, youth, and families* (pp. 233-255). New York: Springer Publishing Company.

Fawcett, S. B, Paine-Andrews, A., Francisco, V. T., Schultz, J., Richter, K. P., Berkley Patton, J., Fisher, J. L., Lewis, R. K., Lopez, C. M., Russos, S., Williams, E. L., Harris, K. J., and Evensen, P. (in press). Evaluating community initiatives for health and development. In I. Rootman & D. McQueen et al. (Eds.), *Evaluating health promotion approaches*. Copenhagen, Denmark: World Health Organization–Europe.

Fawcett, S. B., Paine-Andrews, A., Francisco, V. T., Schultz, J. A., Richter, K. P., Lewis, R. K., Williams, E. L., Harris, K. J., Berkley, J. Y., Fisher, J. L., & Lopez, C. M. (1995). Using empowerment theory in collaborative partnerships for community health and development. *American Journal of Community Psychology, 23*, 677-697.

Fawcett, S. B., Paine-Andrews, A., Francisco, V. T., Schultz, J. A., Richter, K. P., Lewis, R. K., Harris, K. J., Williams, E. L., Berkley, J. Y., Lopez, C. M., & Fisher, J. L. (1996). Empowering community health initiatives through evaluation. In D. Fetterman, S. Kaftarian, & A. Wandersman (Eds.), *Empowerment evaluation: Knowledge and tools for self-assessment and accountability* (pp.161-187). Thousand Oaks, CA: Sage Publications.

Galston, W. (no date). (How) does the internet affect community? Some speculations in search of evidence [Online]. Available: *http://www.ksg.harvard.edu/visions/galston.htm*, [1999, January 28].

Goodman, R. M., Speers, M. A., McLeroy, K., Fawcett, S., Kegler, M., Parker, E., Smith, S., Sterling, T., and Wallerstein, N. (1998). Identifying and defining the dimensions of community capacity to provide a basis of measurement. *Health Education & Behavior, 25*, 258-278.

Green, L. W. & Kreuter, M. W. (1999). *Health promotion planning: An educational and ecological approach*. 3rd ed. Mountain View: Mayfield.

Green, L. W., & Raeburn, J. M. (1988). Health promotion: What is it? What will it become? *Health Promotion, 3*, 1551-159.

Hoffman, D. L., & Novak, T. P. (1998). Bridging the racial divide on the Internet. *Science, 280*, 390-391.

McConnaughey, J. W., Lader, W., & Chin, R. (1998). Falling through the net II: New data on the digital divide. National Telecommunications and Information Administration [Online]. Available: *http://www.ntia.doc.gov/ntiahome/net2/falling.html*.

Milio, N. (1996). *Engines of empowerment: Using information technology to create healthy communities and challenge public policy*. Chicago: Health Administration Press.

Mitchell, W., Sanyal, B., & Schon, D. (1996). High technology and low-income communities: Prospects for positive use of advanced information technology [Online]. Available: *http://web.mit.edu/sap/www/high-low/*, [1999, January 28].

Osborne, D. & Gaebler, T. (1992). *Reinventing government: How the entrepreneurial spirit is transforming the public sector.* Reading, MA: Addison-Wesley Publishing.

Schorr, L. B. (1997). *Common purpose: Strengthening families and neighborhoods to rebuild America.* New York: Anchor Books, Doubleday.

Sclove, R. E. (1995). *Democracy and technology.* New York: The Guilford Press.

Stoecker, R., & Stuber, A. C. S. (1997). Limited access: The information superhighway and Ohio's neighborhood-based organizations. *Computers in Human Services, 14,* 39-57.

U. S. Department of Education, National Center for Education Statistics. (1998). Internet access in public schools. NCES 98-031, Office of Education Research and Improvement, Issue Brief, March.

Promoting Computer-Mediated Communications in Community Coalitions

Paul K. Dezendorf
Ronald K. Green

SUMMARY. Community coalition participants are adopting new communication tools. This article identifies issues involving adoption of one type of communication tool, computer-mediated communications (CMC), based on a review of relevant literature and a recent exploratory research study of CMC adoption by community coalitions. Suggestions for aiding adoption and anticipating problems are presented and some social justice and professional value issues are highlighted. Human service professionals whose work involves community coalitions may find the theoretical background and practical advice useful in anticipating and responding to CMC changes in coalitions. *[Article copies available for a fee from The Haworth Document Delivery Service: 1-800-342-9678. E-mail address: <getinfo@haworthpressinc.com> Website: <http://www.haworthpressinc.com>]*

KEYWORDS. Community coalitions, computer-mediated communications, innovation diffusion, computers, Internet

---

Paul K. Dezendorf is Chair, Department of Social Work, Winthrop University, Rockhill, SC 29733.

Ronald K. Green is Visiting Professor, School of Social Work, East Carolina University, Greenville, NC 27858.

[Haworth co-indexing entry note]: "Promoting Computer-Mediated Communications in Community Coalitions." Dezendorf, Paul K., and Ronald K. Green. Co-published simultaneously in *Journal of Technology in Human Services* (The Haworth Press, Inc.) Vol. 17, No. 2/3, 2000, pp. 217-236; and: *Human Services Online: A New Arena for Service Delivery* (ed: Jerry Finn, and Gary Holden) The Haworth Press, Inc., 2000, pp. 217-236. Single or multiple copies of this article are available for a fee from The Haworth Document Delivery Service [1-800-342-9678, 9:00 a.m. - 5:00 p.m. (EST). E-mail address: getinfo@haworthpressinc.com].

217

Participants in community coalitions have been using computer-mediated communications (CMC) tools to facilitate communications between individuals and within groups, and also provide access to information, e.g., e-mail, listservs, and archives. These communication tools were developed in 1971 (Chesebro & Bonsall, 1993) and have been used to facilitate collaboration and community-wide change efforts since 1978 (Rapaport, 1993; Rheingold, 1993). These tools can still address coalition communication needs even given current Internet-based innovations, e.g., compressed video, Internet-based telephony, etc. However, while CMC tools appear beneficial for coalitions, the authors believe that most human service professionals may underestimate the changes in coalitions that might result from adoption of CMC tools. Research has demonstrated that organizations in general are commonly changed by adopting CMC tools and are often transformed, e.g., flatter organizational structure leading to changes in lines of authority (see Fulk & Steinfield, 1990; Jessup & Valacichi, 1993; Lucas, 1996). As a result, coalitions, a major tool for social workers, appear likely to be significantly affected.

Despite the apparent importance, there is little community coalition-specific practice experience or research available regarding CMC tools. In response, this article describes the importance of communications to coalitions, the nature of CMC, and the utility of innovation diffusion theory to understanding the adoption of CMC by coalitions. An exploratory study of CMC in community coalitions is presented. The results of the study and theoretical discussion are used to develop guidelines for encouraging adoption of CMC tools and possible problems resulting from their adoption. The article also highlights some professional value issues raised by the use of CMC.

COALITIONS AND COMMUNICATIONS

Coalitions, groups of organizations united to achieve common goals by means of collaborative action, are a major tool used to intervene in the community. Such interventions involve multiple sectors of the community, e.g., government units, faith communities, grassroots organizations, and others. Cooperative interaction among them is often referred to as collaboration (see Andrews, 1990). One approach to collaboration is the formation of coalitions (Gray, 1985; Hagebak, 1982; Weisner, 1983). In general, coalitions allow an organization to address community-wide issues without having the sole responsibility for action. This sharing of responsibility and initiative increases efficiency and provides for an economy of scale in gathering and using resources, e.g., coalitions are one way agencies compensate for cutbacks in funds (Roberts-DeGennaro, 1996; Weisner, 1983). The rational for using coalitions for collaboration includes providing a supportive environment for action and empowerment, mutual problem-solving, improved decision-making, increased respect for participants, and addressing changes on an ecological basis (Benard, 1989).

Communication in coalitions is very important (Mizrahi & Rosenthal, 1992; Roberts-DeGennaro, 1986). Communications appears as a common issue throughout studies of coalition assessment and is possibly the most fundamental function of a coalition (Butterfoss, 1993). Coalition communications can be viewed as either internal or external. A typical internal communications goal is accessing the resources of coalition participants. External communications similarly provide participants with access to resources by allowing resource exchange between participants and others, e.g., neighborhood associations and civic groups (Chavis, Florin, Rich, & Wandersman, 1987).

COMPUTER-MEDIATED COMMUNICATIONS (CMC)

Tools for internal and external coalition communications are increasing in number, availability, and use. This change is driven by the rise in importance of information in society, advent of computers, and at present the development of networks among these computers (Beamish, 1995; Drucker, 1993). This evolution has brought about the development of computer-mediated communications tools for use on these networks. Computer-mediated communications (CMC) is essentially the application of data-processing technology to improving interpersonal relations (Chesebro & Bonsall, 1993).

CMC is characterized by four qualities that play important roles regarding potential changes in coalitions. These qualities are interactiveness, demassification, asynchronicity, and anonymity (Rogers, 1986; Williams, Rice & Rogers, 1988). For example, e-mail displays asynchronicity in that sending and receiving may be performed at different times convenient to the participants. Demassification refers to the ability to use CMC with sub-groups within an audience, e.g., multiple listservs for subgroups perform demassification functions when they operate in coalitions. Anonymity in CMC can be seen in public posting of notices without overt identification of the sender as in the electronic equivalent of an office suggestion box. Interactiveness refers to the ability of CMC to change with the needs of the participants, e.g., Web sites can provide specific areas for conferences as needed.

The use of CMC, much more than previous media such as telephones or radio, brings about changes in participants and their social systems (Chesebro & Bonsall, 1993). CMC has become "at once a technology, medium, and engine of social relations." (Jones, 1995, p. 16). Those who regard CMC as a substitution of one medium for another, a cheaper way to send a letter for example, are very likely to underestimate the potential for changes in their organizations due to the use of CMC tools.

CMC Benefits

The potential of CMC tools has received increased attention in recent years (see Finn, 1996; Finn & Lavitt, 1994). In administrative practice, these tools offer improved efficiency in internal agency processes, external relations, and outreach to constituent groups (Dezendorf, Falk, Klein, & McCurry, in press). Internal efficiency benefits which have begun to be seen in health and human service agencies include improved management information systems, clinical diagnosis and tracking methods, and more efficient organizational processes. External relations efficiencies include sharing data, pooling information sources, and maintaining close contact with partner organizations. Constituency relations benefits include more rapid dissemination of information and increased potential for dialog. In community practice, CMC tools offer the opportunity to construct community support networks that allow improved client access to services, empower clients, and extend individual and community resources (Dezendorf & Green, in press). Finally, these tools offer a means for assisting social change by raising consciousness and empowering groups (Hiltz & Turoff, 1993; Jones, 1995) and thus should contribute to policy practice.

CMC Problems

The potential problems resulting from use of these tools is also beginning to come to light. Areas of particular concern from the authors' perspective include unintended secondary effects, opportunity costs, goal displacement, and technology dependence. Secondary technology effects are unforeseen and detrimental changes to either the user or society in general that result from the adoption of technology (Tenner, 1996). For coalitions, one secondary effect of increased e-mail may be a decrease in face-to-face meetings and thus a reduction of the attractiveness of coalition participation for some persons.

Opportunity costs are the costs of not pursuing a particular alternative. Organizations may incur opportunity costs in adoption of CMC by acquiring expensive (and soon obsolete) "cutting edge" technology rather than using those funds to improve their staff's ability to use existing technology. Opportunity cost problems have become increasingly important for human service organizations due to rapid rate of technological changes.

Adoption of CMC tools also may displace goals, i.e., users reduce their attention to existing organizational goals due to increased attention to goals related to the technology. One example may be seen in the tendency of CMC tool users to focus on the instrumental uses of the technology (such as producing reports) rather than the changes in interpersonal relationships due to use of machine-based communications and consequent changes in organizational culture.

A final problem is technology dependence. For example, technicians may gain power and influence agency goals, alter priorities, and reallocate resources due to the organization's dependence on their unique knowledge and skills.

Why Are CMC Tools Adopted?

A necessary first step in understanding a coalition's use of CMC is to ascertain why CMC tools are adopted. Innovation diffusion theory (see Rogers, 1983) provides analytical frameworks for describing and predicting the adoption of CMC tools by coalitions. Of the various approaches, perhaps the most direct one for use with community coalitions is to identify characteristics of successful innovations and compare them with the perceived characteristics of the CMC tools proposed for coalition adoption.

Rogers himself suggested specific characteristics of successful innovations for use in evaluating electronic communications (Rogers, 1986; Williams, Rice & Rogers, 1988). Of these, six characteristics that were found to be a useful framework for examining whether or not CMC tools may be adopted by a coalition are relative advantage, compatibility, complexity, trialability, observability, and tangible benefits (Dezendorf, 1998). The relative advantage of an innovation is the degree to which an innovation is superior to the one it supersedes. The characteristic of compatibility describes the degree to which an innovation is consistent with the values, experience, and needs of the potential adopters. The complexity of an innovation refers to the degree to which an innovation is relatively difficult to understand. Trialability describes the degree to which a subject may experiment with an innovation with a low level of commitment to long-term use. Observability is the degree to which the prospective user easily sees an innovation in use. Tangible benefits are substantive and relevant rewards to the user for use of the innovation.

Theoretically, the more these characteristics are perceived, the more likely coalition participants may be to adopt CMC tools. When these characteristics are evaluated along with other factors, such as the availability of equipment or policies of member organizations, this approach provides a reliable means to predict the likelihood of adoption and forecast adoption problems.

A STUDY OF CMC TOOL ADOPTION

An opportunity to apply this framework came about as the result of a Centers for Disease Control (CDC) funded trial of CMC tools (SIP 12G, 1995). The trial was designed to explore the potential for CMC tools to aid collaboration among professionals involved in cardiovascular health issues. Participants from across the country were recruited at cardiovascular health conferences and with cardiovascular health-related groups. The participants were provided access to a BBS that was called the Cardiovascular Health Network (CVHN). The CVHN provided these participants with an opportunity to interact using CMC tools of e-mail, listserves, and information archives. The CVHN used widely distributed and accepted CMC software published by SoftArc, Inc. (SoftArc, 1994) and could be accessed through the Internet and national toll-free telephone numbers.

Aside from the immediate CDC trial goals, the investigators were interested in better understanding why and how CMC tools might be used in community coalitions as preparation for future coalition research. The CVHN participants, all experienced users of CMC and well-grounded in community coalitions, offered a fortuitous opportunity for a qualitative study. As a result, the investigators decided to explore why and how e-mail, listservs, and information archives are likely to be used for CMC communications among participants in community coalitions by means of interviews with the CVHN participants.

METHOD

Participants

A convenience sample of CVHN participants was recruited. All participants in the CVHN trial who logged into the BBS and used the system during a 90-day period were identified. CVHN personnel and CDC staff were excluded. Only two participants were unable to cooperate in the study. The remaining participants, 36 in all, became the respondents in the study. These respondents were knowledgeable of and had experience with CMC tools. Each respondent also had extensive experience with community coalitions. Of these respondents, 26 (72%) were female. Three-quarters held masters degrees and six of the nine others held doctoral degrees. Most were employed in government settings (86%) with two in health care and three in academic settings. Approximately equal numbers were health educators (44%) or administrators in health and human service agencies (42%). Most of the subjects (86.1%) performed work that gave them a detailed understanding of community coalitions, e.g., community health education specialists whose primary job function is support of community coalitions in a geographic area. The other respondents were employed in research or teaching and had experience as a member of coalitions as well as knowledge of coalitions in their professional areas, e.g., they worked with coalitions in their research studies or taught about coalitions in their courses. Every respondent was asked detailed questions probing their education and skill level with CMC tools. Each respondent had extensive experience with these tools, with a minimum length of use of three years, and every respondent was currently using the three CMC tools as part of their daily job responsibilities.

Procedures

Respondents, however, did not share a common terminology or perspective regarding coalition operations. To offset this problem, respondents were provided a scenario of a hypothetical community coalition. The scenario described a formally structured and issue-oriented community coalition of 15 organizations. The groups within the coalition included a steering committee of representatives from each organization, an executive committee of five persons from the steering committee, and ten committees and task forces carrying out projects, programs, and tasks. The coalition was described as depending on member and non-member organizations for funding, facilities, and personnel. Support of elected and appointed officials, key constituency groups, and the public had to be maintained for the coalition to be successful. As a result, internal and external communications were essential.

The respondents were told that some participants of the coalition were interested in adopting electronic communications. The study respondents then were asked to assume the role of a member of the coalition and provide their assessment of the perceptions of typical coalition participants regarding the attributes of CMC tools of e-mail, listserves, and information archives and the utility of these tools for the coalition. Respondents were asked to answer questions from a semi-structured interview schedule. For example, respondents were asked "What advantages will coalition participants see in (e-mail, listserves, information archives)?" Each question was asked for each CMC tool. Respondents were not limited in terms of time. Respondents also answered questions regarding their experience and skill with CMC tools, demographic information, and opinions regarding the scenario. Responses were tape recorded, transcribed, and analyzed. The analysis of their responses was structured according to Yin's case study analysis framework (Yin, 1993) using pattern matching. Pattern-matching is one of the thirteen tactics for generating meaning suggested by Miles and Huberman (1994) and one of the most desirable strategies for case study analysis according to Yin (1989).

RESULTS

Among the results, two areas of particular interest were identified: approaches for encouraging adoption and problems resulting from adoption of CMC.

Guidelines for Encouraging Adoption

Overall, respondents believed that coalition participants would adopt CMC tools due to their relative advantages. The primary advantages seen by respondents were the features of the tools (simplicity, ease of use, convenience, and speed) and to a lesser degree the ability of these tools to improve the quality of group discussions or the effectiveness in reaching out to constituent groups, e.g., clients, public officials. These advantages were not outweighed by concerns with value conflicts or complexity. While the ability to observe or try CMC tools was seen as limited, these limitations were judged as likely only to slow down the rate of adoption rather than halting adoption. The tangible benefits seen by respondents were primarily those involving improvements in coalition organizational processes and not improvements in program outcomes or long-term community changes.

Relative advantage: Respondents in the study believed that adoption would be aided by stressing the relative advantages that coalition participants are most likely to understand and accept, and thus attention should first be given to features (speed, convenience) rather than benefits (improving the quality and quantity of information). The primary feature to address was identified as ease of use; gaining general agreement on ease of use aids acceptance of the concepts of simplicity and convenience. In speeding adoption, respondents suggested initiating adoption with a one-to-one CMC tool (e-mail) followed by one-to-many (such as listserves) and finally the use of CMC tools to access archives of information.

Conflicts with coalition values: A low level of value conflicts characterizes successful innovations. Congruence between group values and the innovation accelerates the adoption process. Most coalition participants may well have a difficult time identifying congruence between group values and CMC tools. Coalition participants instead may tend to identify conflicts and use these conflicts to justify not adopting CMC tools. Study results suggested persons seeking to encourage adoption should identify latent and manifest conflicts early in the adoption process rather than "selling" CMC tools as supportive of coalition principles such as representativeness. The four conflicts found in the study most likely to be raised by participants in community coalitions were the loss of benefits from face-to-face communications, problems created by a verbatim record of communications, possible fragmentation of communications, and a decrease in confidentiality.

Complexity: A low level of perceived complexity characterizes successful innovations. Study results suggested that coalition participants are most likely to perceive complexity due to personal issues of their own rather than the actual complexity of the technology. Some of the contributing factors identified in the study as contributing to perceived complexity were lack of reason to use, age, rural location, social status, and computerphobia. The actual complexity of the CMC tools also may be an obstacle. Some of the dimensions that were of concern to respondents included degree of sophistication, frequent changes in hardware and software or problems with documentation. Participants' concerns should be addressed on a case by case basis. As complexity tends to be perceived most highly prior to actual use, approaches that engage participants in actual trials of the technology appear to be the most appropriate choice.

Trialability and observability: Even given relative advantage and low conflict with values, adoption may not occur or occur slowly without trialability and observability. Study results suggested actual trials rather than other approaches (such as vicarious modeling or reduction of cognitive dissonance) due to the nature of objections. Ideas suggested by respondents included provision of technology at coalition meetings, including CMC tools in training sessions, integrating tools into coalition communications, and requiring CMC tools in grant proposals. To aid adoption, observability should be combined with trials, e.g., having the coalition chair bring a laptop to meetings or bringing state agency personnel in to demonstrate technology.

Respondents suggested that adoption could be encouraged by focusing on the strengths and addressing objections in four settings: at coalition activities, in the participants' workplace, at community locations, and at participants' residences. The most advantageous setting for encouraging adoption of CMC tools was seen at coalition activities. The study results suggested the utility of using CMC tools for communications involving coalitions meetings to aid adoption, e.g., minutes, notes, and documents for review. Outreach communications came next in terms of potential interest, e.g., listservs or web sites. Storage uses for coalition materials (such as volunteer lists or press clippings) and community information such as statistics and directories also have potential to encourage adoption by coalition participants.

Use of community locations, such as libraries, was seen as of particular benefit in rural locations, low-income settings, or where participants gather due to social patterns, e.g., senior centers. These types of settings offer opportunity to take classes, use terminals in public libraries, or even visit local agencies to observe and use CMC tools. For example, adult day care facilities in some settings offer terminals allowing caregivers to experiment with access to the care facility's web site and thus encourage CMC tool use to access the facility and thus increase client use.

The third most useful setting for encouraging use, based upon the study, is in the participant's home. Use may be encouraged by identification of web sites and listserves that are attractive to participants. One of the most useful approaches may be the establishment of a web site for the coalition with links to other sites of interest for coalition participants.

The least advantageous location for encouraging adoption of CMC was seen as participant workplaces. The two possible approaches in this setting were encouraging participants to elect to take training in CMC tools and to use electronic communications in the course of their work. As the range of options for many coalition participants regarding training and use of CMC tools at work is limited, this approach appears to be of use primarily for professionals in coalitions who often have limited need for additional exposure.

Tangible benefits: Respondents saw most coalition participants as believing that CMC tools may provide tangible benefits for process (such as correspondence and meetings) but not believing that CMC tools may change program impacts or improve long-term outcomes, e.g., health status. Most likely types of process benefits were in the areas of administration, finances, membership, communications, and community relations.

Study results indicated that the benefits for coalition administration included improvement in meetings due to better-informed participants, improved appearance of communications products, and faster decisions regarding routine matters. Finance benefits include reductions in expenses and possibly increases in revenues, primarily due to improved success in identifying and obtaining grants. Membership benefits that might be stressed include increased recruitment of coalition participants, improved communications leading to a higher level of cohesion among the participants, increased cooperation in executing projects, increased accountability in team projects, and improved individual competence with technology. Community benefits include increased influence of the coalition in the community and increased public recognition.

Very low levels of belief existed among respondents regarding the possibility of improvements in program impacts or long-term outcomes, such as teen pregnancy rates. Objections based on this perceived lack of benefits to impacts and outcomes might be rebutted by focusing on process benefits and by allowing coalition participants to discover for themselves the benefits in impacts and outcomes.

Problems Associated with Adoption

Potential problems with adoption were identified in the study. Six issues appear to be of particular concern: lack of resources, personal barriers, loss of face-to-face communication, marginalization of some coalition participants, and changes in coalition strategy and mission.

Resource barriers: Belief in lack of resources as a barrier was the most common one among study respondents. However, this belief appeared intuitive rather than based on empirical information, e.g., respondents usually mentioned only a single personal problem. The belief in lack of resources by the respondents appears greater than the lack identified in academic publications (see Rand, 1995). This might be addressed by presentation of factual information regarding national trends related to the rapid growth of Internet accessibility.

Personal barriers: Respondents provided the most emotional responses regarding personal barriers. There appeared to be a general belief that computerphobia, or fear of the computer itself, was endemic among coalition participants and constituted a major barrier to adoption. Addressing this concern can be done through case examples of individual coalition participants overcoming personal barriers.

Loss of face-to-face communications: Many respondents believed that adoption of CMC tools would lead to a reduction in face-to-face communications with resulting adverse impacts on community coalitions. Their responses appeared driven by a subjective and emotional concern with the loss of face-to-face communications rather than quantifiable losses, e.g., reduced creativity and networking. This issue can be addressed by introducing CMC tools as a complement rather than as a substitute for in-person gatherings.

Marginalizing coalition participants: CMC tools have the potential for bringing into coalitions persons otherwise barred due to transportation or other problems. However, CMC tools also were seen as potentially marginalizing some participants due to their lesser capacity to use these tools, e.g., those with less computer skills, lower literacy level, and those who rely more on verbal rather than written discussion. This problem is more complex than the preceding three issues. Potential marginalization of coalition members due to use of CMC tools should be identified in advance along with appropriate responses. Potential responses might include computer skills training, literacy improvements, or substitution of voice-activated word processing software instead of keyboards.

Changing strategies: CMC tools increase the ability of a group to deal with information and thus alter organizational structures and processes. One issue raised by respondents in the study was that coalitions might shift their focus toward obtaining, processing, and providing information to other groups in place of providing direct service. This issue might be addressed by communicating the consequences of potential changes to coalition participants.

Changing mission: The most complex and perhaps the most fundamental issue raised in the study were possible changes in coalition mission. The growth of information technology has lead to the development of virtual communities, i.e., communities existing electronically rather than in a spatial setting (see Jones, 1995). Study respondents voiced concern that present geographically-based community coalitions might be affected by the growth of virtual communities. They suggested that the growth of virtual communities might lead coalitions to move their focus away from spatial communities. This issue might be addressed by distribution of information regarding virtual communities and the disposition of resources between spatial and non-spatial coalitions among coalition participants.

DISCUSSION

Social workers are faced with a range of challenges and opportunities, both now and in the future, regarding the use of CMC in building and maintaining of coalitions. Social workers should be aware of these challenges and be prepared to turn challenges into opportunities. This study suggests that there are three major challenges to the adoption of CMC by community coalitions at present. The first centers on issues of access, given that many people lack Internet access and an interactive interface device such as a personal computer. The second challenge is the willingness of coalition participants to use this new medium even where access is available, e.g., study respondents saw computerphobia as a major barrier. The third major challenge is the low skill level of social workers regarding information technology.

Lack of access is a threshold issue for coalition adoption of CMC tools. Although the 1996 Telecommunications Act set as national policy the goal of universal access to the Internet (Telecommunications Act of 1996), this goal is unlikely to be met in the near future although the issue may be resolved over time. This may be indicated by the high rate of growth in Internet use; by 1998, 1.3 million people a month were gaining access to the Internet (The Industry Standard, 1998).

While Internet access is increasing, perhaps a greater challenge is whether participants in coalitions are willing to utilize CMC tools to enhance their communications. There appear to be three strategies regarding CMC tools. One approach is to forgo the use of CMC. Despite the short-term advantages of avoiding conflict with those who resist the innovation, the long-term loss of CMC tool benefits may outweigh the long-term problems of CMC use. An intermediate approach is use of parallel communications channels, a "hybrid" solution, to serve both CMC users and non-users. However, additional resources are required to maintain parallel communications channels. In addition, CMC is a different medium and some types of process and outcomes may not be the same for users of traditional communications as opposed to CMC tools, e.g., some types of communications may bypass certain types of coalition participants.

A final approach would be to limit participation to those willing to use CMC. This strategy of complete changeover is based on the premise that resisters will adopt if use of CMC tools was the only way in which they could participate in the coalition. This strategy requires an investment in training and consultation to aid resisters to overcome their problems with the use of CMC tools. In the experience of the authors in bringing new information technology into organizations, virtually all people will, with help, overcome resistance to use of CMC tools.

The third challenge, developing social worker competence with CMC tools, is the most important and problematic. Social workers must take greater responsibility than in the past for developing their skills with these tools and human service organizations must support them with in-service training. Social work educators need to greatly supplement course content and continuing education providers must take similar actions.

Professional Value Implications

These three challenges have professional value implications. In social work, the practitioner is responsible for helping the client gain "access to needed information," insuring "meaningful participation in decision making," promoting "responsible self-determination," enhancing the client's "capacity and opportunity to . . . address their own needs," in engaging clients as "partners in the helping process," and in "challeng(ing) social injustice" (National Association of Social Workers, 1997). These ethical principles strongly suggest that an important consideration in the development of coalitions is the involvement of clients and client groups as part of the coalition. What then are the implications of the use of CMC with client constituents?

Those responsible for coalition development must ensure that CMC is readily available to all having a vested interest in the activity of the coalition. Fortunately, there are a number of models of how communities have opened Internet access to low-income residents. For example, in Cleveland the Greater Cleveland Neighborhood Centers Association in collaboration with the city, the public libraries, Ameritech, and Cleveland State University developed a model that provided Internet access to low-income residents through portals available in neighborhood centers, public libraries, and city recreation centers (Cleveland Neighborhood Link Project, 1998). One of the advantages of providing Internet access in a public building is that staff can be made available to facilitate the training and consultation needed to overcome any resistance the client participant brings to CMC. As long as this type of support is built into the coalition development effort, client/participant resistance to CMC can be overcome.

Those responsible for coalition development also must ensure that the staff is competent to provide support to client/participants utilizing CMC. Professional social workers have an ethical obligation to "continually strive to increase their professional knowledge and skills," (National Association of Social Workers, 1997) and in this era of information technology all social workers have an obligation to understand and have skill in using CMC tools that support their practice. By utilizing the power of CMC, social workers can help operationalize for the client the ethical principles listed above. Social workers can provide clients the opportunity to secure information that effects their lives and provide access to and involvement in decision making. For example, social workers can use CMC to share with clients the possible impact of funding decisions and give them the capability to input their views into coalition decision making. CMC also provides a means to helping identify and organize others with similar concerns and to address issues of social injustice through organized communication with public policy decision-makers.

Limitations of the Study

The study attempted to increase understanding of the questions that should be asked in future studies by speaking with persons close to the phenomenon. Such exploratory studies are the most limited types of case studies due to the intimate examination of empirical information with minimum encumbrance (Yin, 1993). Accordingly, the results from this study should not be taken as indicating causality but as illuminating issues and avenues for further research. The nature of CMC further constrains the study. CMC is rapidly evolving (see Bryant, 1994) which makes future predictions of use problematic (Rand, 1995).

The choice of a hypothetical coalition rather than actual community coalitions limited the empirical details so valued by qualitative researchers (Boyatzis, 1998). However, coalitions may be characterized in a variety of ways and no generally accepted definition exists as coalition research is characterized by "disciplinary and organizational fragmentation" (Andrews, 1990). Accordingly, the use of a brief scenario appeared more practical for the intended use of providing an initial exploration of how and why CMC tools could be used in coalitions.

The nature of the CVHN respondents also limited the study. While their responses illuminated a great many issues for future research, their input can not be taken as representative of coalition members in general. Similarly, non-users were not represented and thus the non-adoption perspective was limited. The study was also limited regarding socio-economic and demographic parameters. For example, only one of thirty-six respondents was an African-American, which is particularly troubling given the suggested difference among computer users by race (Novak & Hoffman, 1998). Finally, the study only examined one type of innovation diffusion analysis, characteristics of successful adoption, and did not include other approaches such as stages of adoption in organizations or external influences such as technological availability and use by related organizations. Use of additional types of analysis would provide an understanding of the influence of declining prices for equipment, increased advertising by computer networks, and other external influences.

Future Challenges

Technology appears likely to challenge social workers for at least the next generation. One future challenge appears likely to be to identify and incorporate new technologies into community practice given the increasing rate of technological change. For example, even as coalition participants adopt tools such as e-mail, listservs, and archive resources, the challenges of video-conferencing, voice recognition and virtual reality interventions will soon be here (see Holden, Bearison, Rode, Rosenberg, & Fishman, 1999; Turkle, 1996). A major problem facing the social work profession is the apparent inability to incorporate current changes into practice before the next major change occurs. As a result, social workers may be in the position of falling further behind the technology curve rather than catching up for some time into the future.

Of these future challenges, the greatest one appears to be the upcoming development of a single digital "pipe" to all residences and workplaces. This change may mean devices like interactive TV will become a reality and with it the capacity to bring CMC into everyone's living room. As a result, all coalition participants and all those served, as well as the various constituencies would be open to a vast range of communications tools. This change will require that social workers become proactive in integrating changes in technology with their practice.

CONCLUSIONS AND RECOMMENDATIONS

Baccalaureate and masters programs should make immediate and substantial changes to their course content that reflects the shifts among the types of communications used in society and the particular applications for each type. Most programs focus on primary uses of new technology (such as sending e-mail) but fail to assist students in understanding the systemic effects (such as changes in coalition diversity).

Social workers involved with community coalitions should learn to work with CMC tools in order to understand and predict the problems and benefits of CMC. For many social workers, such ability will come through their use of consultants. At present, computer consulting services once only available to few organizations are now actively marketed to social work organizations (see Dezendorf, Falk, Klein, & McCurry, in press). Whatever means they use, social workers should give careful attention to the social justice and equality implications of information technology's impact on community coalitions. In this way social workers will be in the best possible position to ensure maximum benefits for community coalitions.

REFERENCES

Andrews, A. (1990). Interdisciplinary and interorganizational collaboration. In L. Ginsberg et al. *Encyclopedia of social work* (18th ed., Supp. 1990, pp. 175-188). Washington, DC: NASW Press.

Beamish, A. (1995). *Communities on-line: A study of community-based computer networks.* Unpublished master's thesis, Massachusetts Institute of Technology, Cambridge, MA.

Benard, B. (1989). Working together: Principles of effective collaboration. *Prevention Forum, October*, 4-9.

Boyatzis, R. E. (1998). *Transforming qualitative information: Thematic analysis and code development.* Thousand Oaks, CA: Sage Publications.

Bryant, A. D. (1994). *Creating successful bulletin board systems.* Reading, MA: Addison-Wesley.

Butterfoss, F. (1993). *Coalitions for alcohol and other drug abuse: Factors predicting effectiveness.* Unpublished doctoral dissertation. University of South Carolina, Columbia.

Chavis, D., Florin, P., Rich, R., & Wandersman, A. (1987). *The role of block associations in crime control and community development: The block booster project.* New York: Ford Foundation.

Chesebro, J., & Bonsall, D. (1993). *Computer-mediated communication: Human relations in a computerized world.* Tuscaloosa, AL: University of Alabama Press.

Cleveland Neighborhood Link Project. (1998). Neighborhood partners. <http://little.nhlink.net/nhlink/nhl_part.htm> (1999, May 10).

Dezendorf, P. K. (1998). An exploratory case study of electronic bulletin board system diffusion among participants in community coalitions. Unpublished doctoral dissertation, University of South Carolina, Columbia.

Dezendorf, P. K., Falk, D., Klein, M., & McCurry, G. (in press). Electronic social work and agency effectiveness: Three perspectives. In S. Wimpeheimer & A. Savage (Eds.), *Social work management 2000.* Washington, DC: National Network for Social Work Managers.

Dezendorf, P. K. & Green, R. K. (in press). Using electronic social work to serve the rural elderly population. In I. Carlton-LaNey, R. L. Edwards, and P. N. Reid, (Eds.), *Preserving and strengthening small towns and rural communities.* Washington, DC: NASW Press.

Drucker, P. M. (1993). *Post-capitalist society.* New York: HarperCollins.

Finn, J. (1996). Computer-based self-help groups: On-line recovery for addictions. *Computers in Human Services, 13(1),* 21-41.

Finn, J., & Lavitt, M. (1994). Computer-based self-help groups for sexual abuse survivors. *Social Work with Groups, 17(1/2),* 21-46.

Fulk, J. & Steinfield, C. (1990) (Eds.). *Organization and communication technology.* Newbury Park, CA: Sage Publications.

Gray, B. (1985). Conditions facilitating interorganizational collaboration. *Human Relations, 38(10),* 911-936.

Hagebak, B. R. (1982). *Getting local agencies to cooperate.* Baltimore: University Park Press.

Hiltz, S. R., & Turoff, M. (1993). *The network nation: Human communication via computer* (Rev. ed.). Boston, MA: MIT Press.

Holden, G., Bearison, D., Rode, D., Rosenberg, G., & Fishman, M. (1999). Evaluating the effects of a virtual environment (STARBRIGHT World) with hospitalized children. *Research on Social Work Practice, 9,* 365-382.

The Industry Standard. (1998). Behind the numbers: Internet population estimates. <http:// 209.1.23.84/metrics/display/0%2C1283%2C1761%2C00.html> (1999, May 5).

Jessup, L. M., & Valacichi, J. S. (Eds.)(1993). *Group support systems: New perspectives.* New York: McMillan.

Jones, S. G. (1995). Understanding community in the information age. In S. G. Jones (Ed.), *Cybersociety: Computer-mediated communication and community* (pp. 10-35). San Francisco: Sage Publications.

Lucas, H. C. (1996). *The T-Form organization: Using technology to design organizations for the 21st century.* San Francisco: Jossey-Bass.

Miles, M. B., & Huberman, A. M (1994). *Qualitative data analysis: An expanded sourcebook,* (2nd. ed.). Newbury Park, CA: Sage Publications.

Mizrahi, T. & Rosenthal, B. (1992). Managing dynamic tension in social change coalitions. In T. Mizrahi & J. Morrison (Eds.), *Community organization and social administration: Advances, trends, and emerging principles.* New York: The Haworth Press, Inc.

National Association of Social Workers. (1997). *Code of ethics.* Washington, DC: NASW Press.

Novak, T. P., & Hoffman, D. L. (1998). Bridging the racial divide on the Internet. *Science, 280 (5362),* pp. 390-391.

Rand Corporation (1995). *Universal access to e-mail: Feasibility and societal applications.* Santa Monica: Rand Corporation.

Rapaport, M. (1993). *Computer-mediated communications: Bulletin boards, computer conferencing, electronic mail, and information retrieval.* New York: John Wiley & Sons.

Rheingold, H. (1993). *The virtual community: Homesteading on the electronic frontier.* Reading, MA: Addison-Wesley.

Roberts-DeGennaro, M. (1986). Factors contributing to coalition maintenance. *Journal of Sociology and Social Welfare, 31,* 248-264.

Rogers, E. M. (1983). *Diffusion of innovations* (3rd ed.). New York: McMillan.

Rogers, E. M. (1986). *Communication technology: The new media in society.* New York: The Free Press.

SIP 12G (1995). *SIP 12G: Electronic CVD bulletin board.* Unpublished grant application. Prevention Center, School of Public Health, University of South Carolina, Columbia.

SoftArc, Inc. (1994). First class client/server [Computer software], Scarborough, Ontario, Canada: Author.

Telecommunications Act of 1996, Pub. L. 104-104, 110 Stat. 56 (1996).

Tenner, E. (1996). *Why things bite back: Technology and the revenge of unintended consequences.* New York: Random House.

Turkle, S. (1996). *Life on the screen: Identity in the age of the Internet.* New York: Simon & Schuster.

Weisner, S. (1983). Fighting back: A critical analysis of coalition building in the human services. *Social Service Review, 57,* 291-306.

Williams, F., Rice, R. E., & Rogers, E. M. (1988). *Research methods and the new media.* New York: The Free Press.

Yin, R. K. (1989). *Case study research: Design and methods.* Newbury Park, CA: Sage Publications

Yin, R. K. (1993). *Applications of case study research.* Newbury Park, CA: Sage Publications.

Offering Social Support via the Internet:
A Case Study
of an Online Support Group
for Social Workers

Andrea Meier

SUMMARY. Human service professionals have begun to explore the Internet's potential as a therapeutic medium for individuals, families and groups, but we still know very little about the ways that Internet-mediated communication affects interventions. This paper uses examples from a recent study of a short-term, listserv-based support group that helps social workers cope with job stress to discuss issues related to the use of online support groups. *[Article copies available for a fee from The Haworth Document Delivery Service: 1-800-342-9678. E-mail address: <getinfo@haworthpressinc. com> Website: <http://www.haworthpressinc.com>]*

KEYWORDS. Online support groups, job stress, social workers

INTRODUCTION

Human service professionals in many disciplines have benefited from the Internet's flexibility and speed as a communication channel.

Andrea Meier, PhD, is affiliated with the School of Social Work, University of North Carolina, Chapel Hill, Chapel Hill, NC 27599.

The author extends her appreciation to the 52 participants in the study who took the risk of volunteering to participate in an untried intervention, and especially to the 19 members who completed the study.

[Haworth co-indexing entry note]: "Offering Social Support via the Internet: A Case Study of an Online Support Group for Social Workers." Meier, Andrea. Co-published simultaneously in *Journal of Technology in Human Services* (The Haworth Press, Inc.) Vol. 17, No. 2/3, 2000, pp. 237-266; and: *Human Services Online: A New Arena for Service Delivery* (ed: Jerry Finn, and Gary Holden) The Haworth Press, Inc., 2000, pp. 237-266. Single or multiple copies of this article are available for a fee from The Haworth Document Delivery Service [1-800-342-9678, 9:00 a.m. - 5:00 p.m. (EST). E-mail address: getinfo@haworthpressinc.com].

Recently, they have begun to explore its potential as a therapeutic medium. Some have begun to offer individual, family and group counseling using e-mail (Ainsworth, 1999; Colon, 1998; Markowitz, 1999; Osterman, 1997). Self-help organizations have established online groups to enable members to stay in touch with each other (Hensley & Hensley, 1999; Medara, 1999). Despite the excitement over the Internet's potential benefits, we currently know little about designing effective interventions that incorporate this new technology. To make the best use of these innovations on behalf of consumers, human service professionals need to be knowledgeable about how the forms and contexts of online support groups are changing and the ways that they are being used as interventions. This paper reviews research on online support groups and discusses issues in the systematic design and implementation of online group interventions targeted at a specific group, social workers with occupational stress.

All online groups are referred to generically as "forums," but groups may be organized as "newsgroups," "bulletin boards," "conferences," "mailing lists," "discussion groups," or "chat groups" (Internet.com, 1999). Members of newsgroups, bulletin boards, mailing lists and conferences communicate without having to be online at the same time ("asynchronously"). Chat group participants communicate in "real time" ("synchronously"), so they must all be online at the same time to read each other's messages.

These Internet-mediated communication technologies have enabled the development of a variety of group social structures and interaction styles to suit the preferences of different users (see Figure 1). Each type of communication has its advantages and disadvantages. Members of groups using asynchronous communication can write messages of unlimited length and explore issues in depth because they do not compete with each other for "air time." Chat group members enjoy the immediacy of the responses they can get from other group members "real time" (Southwick, 1999). Members of groups that use asynchronous communication must be able to cope with the uncertainty over who will respond to their messages and the timing of those responses. Chat group members must learn how not to be distracted when multiple strings of text appear on their screens as several members reply simultaneously. They also have to be satisfied with conversations that are lively but cover subjects in less depth (Southwick, 1999).

FIGURE 1. Features of Online Groups: Technology and Social Structure

Group Characteristic	Type of Group			
	Newsgroups	Bulletin boards & conferences	Listservs	Chat Groups
Timing of communication	Asynchronous	Asynchronous	Asynchronous	Synchronous ("real time")
Access to messages	Usenet host computer	Internet Service Provider's host computer, or website	Messages sent to host computer are automatically distributed to listserv subscribers	Requires users to have special software for "real time" interactions
Moderated or unmoderated	Both	Both	Both	Both
Membership	Open membership	Open membership	closed or open membership	closed or open membership
Group size	Unlimited	Unlimited	Range widely in size	Up to 12 people
Designated group facilitator?	No	Usually do not have designated facilitators; May have visiting experts participate to answer questions	Usually do not have designated facilitators	Usually do not have designated facilitators; May have visiting experts participate to answer questions
Type of "session"	Ongoing; 24-hour access	Ongoing; 24-hour access	Ongoing; 24-hour access	Scheduled; time-limited

No single Internet registry catalogs online groups, so obtaining an accurate count of the number of online groups is difficult. To obtain an up-to-date count of the number of listservs, the author conducted a search for listservs over the Web using the L-Soft search engine (www.lsoft.com/catalist.html) to find all listserv groups that used List-Soft's proprietary listserver software. This search identified over 151,000 such groups, of which 24,352 were accessible to the public (L-Soft International, 1999). Liszt.com (*www.liszt.com/news*), another Web search engine used to find online groups, currently links users to 30,000 Usenet newsgroups and 25,000 chat groups (Liszt.com, 1999). In addition to all of these, there are many groups that are accessible only to America On-Line® (AOL), Compuserv®, or other commercial Internet service subscribers.

All groups offer members companionship and opportunities to share ideas and information about common interests (Northen, 1988). Social support groups provide members opportunities for emotional ventilation and validation in addition to these other functions (Schopler & Galinsky, 1993). Researchers have begun to distinguish two different types of social support groups (Humphreys & Rappaport, 1994). Mutual aid groups are organized by members who recognize that they have a problem in common. The help they offer is reciprocal, so, over time, all members play both helper and helpee roles. Mutual aid groups do not have professional facilitators while support groups are professionally organized and/or professionally led.

Based on these definitions, how many online groups are support groups? In April 1999, the author's keyword search using the descriptor "support group" on three Web search engines produced lists of listserv groups, bulletin boards and conferences that ranged in size from 210 groups to 52 groups (see Figure 2). Most of these groups appear to be mutual aid groups rather than support groups. While some may have expert participants to answer members' questions and list owners who will intervene if members become unduly provoc-

FIGURE 2. Variability in Results of WWW Searches for Online Support Groups

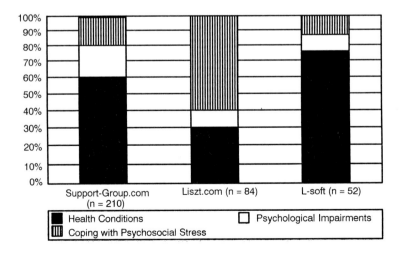

ative in their messages, there are few online social support groups with active, ongoing professional facilitation (King & Moreggi, 1998).

Online social support groups can be categorized according to the problems they address, such as diseases and physical impairments, psychological disorders (including addictions), and coping with psychosocial stress. The three Web search engines had different search protocols, so the lists of listserv groups, bulletin boards, and newsgroups they produced varied widely within in each of these three categories (see Figure 2). Overall, health-related groups were found most frequently and those focusing on psychological disorders were found least often.

Accessing online support groups. Until recently, most people subscribed to Internet services so they could use e-mail. In the past two years, however, "surfing" the World Wide Web has become the most common way of using the Internet (Graphic Visualization & Usability Center, 1998). As the survey of online support groups above demonstrates, the Web has also made it much easier to find online support groups, increased the number and types of communication channels, and expanded the range of available services and content. Some self-help organizations, such as Alcoholics Anonymous, GriefNet, and 4SelfHelp.com, have made it easy to access support through their Web sites. Many sponsor topic-focussed discussion forums and/or chat groups, and provide links to reliable sources of information (Alcoholics Anonymous, 1999; GriefNet, 1999).

RESEARCH ON ONLINE SUPPORT GROUPS

Technological advances are spurring human service providers to invent innovative ways to use online groups to benefit clients. Social group work researchers who wish to systematically investigate the feasibility, appropriateness, and effectiveness of different kinds of online groups are challenged to keep up with the innovations that are going on all around them. Technological developments consistently outpace researchers' ability to study their processes and impacts (Eng, Gustafson, Henderson, Jamison, & Patrick, 1999). While there is great interest in the therapeutic use of online groups, the review of the literature shows that this field of research is clearly in the early stage of its development.

To date, relatively few articles on online support groups have been published in conventional or online professional journals. Those reports that have been published address widely scattered topics. Some have surveyed online therapeutic group resources (Cutter, 1996; Stofle, 1999), or reviewed issues in the use of online groups in human service practice (Bowman & Bowman, 1998; King & Moreggi, 1998; Schopler, Abell, & Galinsky, 1998; Stofle, 1999). Studies of specific groups have drawn from such diverse populations. Berman, (1996) and Meier (1997; 1999) both studied groups composed of social workers. Some researchers have studied groups of people who are living with life-threatening, physical conditions such as cancer (Fernsler & Mancester, 1997; Weinberg, Uken, Schmale, & Adamek, 1995), amyotrophic lateral sclerosis (Feenberg, Licht, Kane, Moran, & Smakith, 1996) or HIV (Gustafson et al., 1999). Others have studied groups composed of people coping with emotional difficulties, such as obsessive-compulsive disorders (Stein, 1997), and survivors of alcoholic families (Phillips, 1996) and sexual abuse (Berman, 1996; Finn & Lavitt, 1994). Some investigators have done studies with different kinds of existing groups (Finn, 1996; Finn & Lavitt, 1994; Stein, 1997), or on groups that they themselves have facilitated (Colon, 1998; Meier, 1997). Most of the groups studied were listservs, possibly because listserv technology has been in existence longer than chat group software. A few have compared Internet-mediated (IM) support groups to face-to-face (FTF) groups (Cutter, 1996; Phillips, 1996).

We know little about the relative benefits and risks of participation in online groups. We do know that online groups can make it easier for people to obtain support if (a) they live in rural areas, (b) have restricted physical mobility, or (c) are homebound because of their caregiving responsibilities, or (d) are living with a rare disease with no access to a nearby community of people coping with the same condition (Colon, 1998; International MS Support Foundation, 1999; White & Madara, 1999). Online support groups can provide their members with many kinds of support such as (a) opportunities for emotional ventilation and validation (Fernsler & Mancester, 1997; Meier, 1999; Winzelberg, 1997), (b) information from other members and encouragement to seek out FTF therapies (Stein, 1997; Winzelberg, 1997), and, in some groups, (c) access to experts who are brought online to answer specialized questions (International MS Support Foundation, 1999). Some studies have found that participation in online groups is associated with statistically significant improvements, such as reduced stress in teenage mothers (Dunham et al., 1998), improved quality of life in HIV+ patients (Gustafson et al., 1999), and prolonged sobriety in drug addicts (King, 1994).

Potential Risks

Although human service professionals have expressed their concern with the potential risks and liabilities of online support groups, we still do not have much documented evidence to justify these concerns. To date three main categories of risks have been identified. Some risks arise out of the uncertainty inherent in members' IM self-representations, including the difficulty of (a) verifying that group members are who they claim to be and have not misrepresented their problems (Sagen, 1995, January), and (b) responding with the appropriate kind of direct aid when group members experience crises but do not reside in the same locality (Meier, 1999). Other risks are rooted in the nature of IM interactions. Members may: (a) feel dissatisfied because they do not receive the number and kinds of responses they hope for (Dunham et al., 1998; Meier, 1999); or (b) find that spending a lot of time engaged in Internet-based activities has shrunk their FTF social networks, leaving them more depressed and lonelier than they had been before they joined the group (Kraut et al., 1998). A third type of risk arises from the difficulty of protecting members' confidentiality. Despite the use of group norms for confidentiality and technological procedures to prevent non-members from reading members' messages, online group members' privacy is still vulnerable to (a) invasions by computer hackers and mass mailers ("spammers"), (b) accidental violations due to members' thoughtlessness in leaving onscreen or printed messages where passersby can read them, or (c) their forwarding messages to other online acquaintances without first asking the sender's permission.

This review of the literature suggests that we already know enough about benefits of online support groups to justify further exploration of this kind of intervention. Because almost all of the studies of specific groups mentioned above used small samples and descriptive methodologies, however, it is unwise to generalize from currently available findings. Researchers and professional in the human services clearly need to do more research and accumulate more practical experience if online group interventions are to be integrated into human service practice. Much work is needed to determine which of our assumptions about FTF group composition, structure, process and content are applicable to IM groups. This study, focusing on a listserv-based support group for social workers, is one of the first to embark on this mission.

ONLINE INTERVENTIONS
FOR SOCIAL WORKERS' STRESS

When social workers and their colleagues in the other human service disciplines become overstressed by work, they often minimize or deny their distress. They are ashamed of their vulnerabilities and fearful of the professional consequences of admitting to their problems (Deutsch, 1985; Guy, Poelstra, & Stark, 1989; Swearingen, 1990). The little empirical data available on help-seeking among workers in these occupational categories indicates they are reluctant to seek help for work-related stress and, when they do, they are more likely to seek individual therapy rather than join support groups (Guy et al., 1989; Reamer, 1992).

If human service professionals generally do not participate in FTF stress management support groups, what would make an IM support group more attractive to them? Internet-mediated support groups can provide support in a way that is energy conserving and easily accessible. Members with Internet access from home do not have go elsewhere to obtain support. With asynchronous communication, they do not have to add another event to their overloaded schedules; they can communicate with other group members whenever they choose. Online support groups offer members opportunities to discuss their problems in private without having to engage in more emotionally intense FTF interactions (Phillips, 1996; Schopler et al., 1998).

In this study, the author investigated whether practicing social workers would find a listserv-based group a satisfying and helpful way to explore their job stress and coping issues. Most public listserv groups are ongoing, have open membership, and have no professional leaders. In this case, the intervention protocol was designed to parallel the structure of a conventional FTF stress management group to make it easier to compare FTF and online support groups. In the study, the group lasted only ten weeks. Members were specifically recruited for the group and the group size was limited to 30 members. It was led by clinical social worker who had extensive experience facilitating FTF, job-stress management support groups.

Members of the listserv group interact with each other only through their written messages. In this respect, a listserv support group is roughly analogous to an intensive journaling workshop (Progoff, 1975). In journal workshops, participants write non-judgmentally about their life experiences and the meanings they ascribe to them. Participants are then invited to share their narratives by reading them aloud to others in the group. As they compose and share their narratives, workshop members reframe their life experiences. According to anecdotal reports, many participants have found that the writing exercises helped to relieve physical and emotional suffering from trauma, increased their sense of control over their lives, and increased their self-esteem (Evans, 1999; Peterson, in press; Progoff, 1975). While journal workshop participants can choose the aspect of their life they want write about, group members in the author's study were asked to focus on their work-related concerns.

Research Questions

Figure 3 describes the research questions posed by this study. These include questions related to the feasibility, process and participant satisfaction of the online group. The study also included an experi-

FIGURE 3. Intervention Feasibility: Research Questions

Feasibility Component	Research Questions
Research Implementation	• Will it be feasible to recruit social workers for a study of online stress management support group using the Internet as the only the communicatons channel? • If so, what are their demographic, socio-psychological, and professional characteristics?
Group Structure, Discussion Content, and Process	• Will members participate enough to sustain a listserv-based support group for 10 weeks? • If a group of social workers is given the chance to discuss the stress they experience at work and how they coped, what do they choose to talk about? • Did the group achieve social cohesion?
Outcomes	• To what extent and in what ways did group provide social support? • To what extent and in what ways were members satisfied with the experience? • To what extent was participation in the group associated with reduced occupational stress and psychological strain, and increased coping resourcefulness?

mental assessment of the strength and direction of the association between participation in the group with degree of occupational stress, psychological strain, and coping.

METHOD

Participants

The first goal of the study was to test the feasibility of recruiting social workers using the Internet as the only communication channel. When the author began to plan this project in April 1997, there was no data available on how many social workers used the Internet. Consequently, there was no way to predict the size of the population, so the recruiting "net" had to be cast widely. Volunteers were recruited nationally by posting announcements about the study to forty-four listserv groups that had a total of 5,727 subscribers. These included twenty-six groups that addressed topics of interest to practicing social workers and eighteen "social work-specific" groups sponsored by NASW or its state chapters.

Selection criteria. This study targeted masters-level social workers who were in full-time practice and who had computers and Internet access at home. There were four reasons for these selection criteria. First, social workers who worked full-time were most likely to be experiencing work-related strain. Second, there were no research funds available to provide participants with computer equipment or pay their Internet access fees, so they had to have already invested in them. Third, it was also impossible to provide hands-on technical assistance in using these technologies, so participants had to be reasonably competent computer and Internet users. It was assumed that participants who had their own computers and were already members of other listserv groups would have the necessary competencies. Fourth, even if participants had Internet access from their computers at work, it was assumed that they would feel less distracted and more comfortable about disclosing personal information writing from home. Participants were specifically asked not to use their work computers to communicate with the group to avoid the ethical conflicts of using office computers for personal use as well as potential violations of confidentiality.

Recruitment activities. Recruitment was a two-stage process. All social workers who responded to the initial announcements posted to the listserv groups were sent a second e-mail message containing more information about the study and the text of the project's informed consent statement. They were asked to review this information, contact the author by e-mail if they had questions about the project, and then confirm by e-mail that they were still interested in participating. All volunteers who sent back confirmations were sent the two pre-group, paper-and-pencil data collection instruments and a paper version of the study's informed consent statement. Volunteers who completed and returned all of these materials were considered part of the study's participant pool.

The recruiting target was sixty participants. However, the author encountered many delays and obstacles, and ultimately never succeeded in recruiting the entire sample. It took two waves of recruiting messages, in May and again in July, to recruit fifty-two participants. At the end of July, the author stopped all recruiting efforts after she concluded that the risk of losing the people who had already volunteered outweighed the advantages of spending more time attempting to recruit eight more members. At the end of July, these fifty-two participants were randomly assigned to the Intervention Group or a non-treatment Control Group. Intervention Group members participated in the ten-week online support group. Control Group members received no treatment of any kind: they were only required to complete all of the pre-group questionnaires and the post-group standardized stress and coping instrument. Participants were considered to have completed the study if they returned their completed post-group surveys. All those who completed all their questionnaires received a thirty-dollar stipend.

Data Collection

A multistage data collection process was used to collect qualitative and quantitative data. Quantitative data were collected by administering four paper-and-pencil questionnaires. The first two were administered by mail before the group started and the last two immediately after it ended. The qualitative data collected included all e-mail messages related to the recruitment and implementation of the group and the author's field notes, and the Group Leader's process notes. The e-mail messages included all the messages group members sent to the group over the ten weeks; messages they wrote privately to the Group

Leader and the author (who served as the group's technical assistant); and those the Group Leader and author exchanged in their discussions of implementation issues.

Baseline data collection. To characterize the social workers who were Internet users and willing to participate in an online support group, a comprehensive, background information questionnaire (BIQ) was developed for the study. This instrument was administered by mail to all study participants before the group started. It was composed of seventy-nine multiple-choice and Likert-type items used to collect information on members' sociodemographic characteristics; professional education and training; type of employment working conditions and job satisfaction; satisfaction with family relationships and caregiving responsibilities; health and mental health status; and experience with and attitudes toward computers and the Internet.

Members also completed the standardized Occupational Stress Inventory (OSI) prior to the start of the group (Osipow & Spokane, 1987). The OSI is used to measure participants' levels of occupational stress, psychological strain, and coping resourcefulness. It was given at the start of the group and immediately after it ended. All the subscales have acceptable to good reliability with Cronbach alphas ranging between .71 to .94.

Post-group data collection. During the week after the end of the group, Intervention Group members completed a comprehensive satisfaction survey and a second administration of OSI. The satisfaction survey, also developed for this study, contained 83 items. Seventy-five of them were multiple-choice and Likert-type items and eight were open-ended. The multiple-choice questions covered members' satisfaction with: various aspects of the group experience; coverage of various discussion topics; the group's informativeness; the group's discussion format; the perceived helpfulness of the leader and other members; and level of technical support. There were also questions concerning the group's time burden; and members' level of comfort with IM communication. To make it easy for members to respond to the eight open-ended questions about what they liked most and least about the group experience, these questions were sent to them in an e-mail message. The OSI was administered a second time to both the Intervention and Control Groups to determine whether participation in the group was associated with reduced job stress, psychological strain and increased coping resourcefulness levels.

Analytic Strategies

The quantitative data from the background information and satisfaction surveys were analyzed using descriptive statistics. The pre- and post-group OSI data for the two groups were compared using the non-parametric, Wilcoxon-Matched-Pairs Signed Ranks Test. (Significance levels were set at.10 to compensate for the study's low statistical power.) The statistical analyses were performed using SPSS (SPSS Inc., 1993) while the qualitative data analysis application, NUD.IST 4 was used to perform all the qualitative analyses (SCOLARI, 1995).

RESULTS

Intervention Group Composition

The analyses of the background information survey and the initial OSI data were used to answer the second Implementation question about the group members' sociodemographic and work characteristics and the stressors that affected them.

Sociodemographic characteristics. The Intervention Group was primarily female (84%). The median age 43 years, but members ranged in age from 24 to 69 years. Almost all were of European-American descent (95%); one was a Latina. Members were scattered across eleven states with a majority (57%) living on the East Coast. Over two-thirds of the members (68%) were married; a few were divorced (21%). Most had at least one child under the age of 18 (84%) and aging parents (95%).

Job characteristics. Most members were seasoned professionals. The median number of years they had worked in the field was 11.5 years, but their work experience ranged widely, from less than one year to 30 years. Most (79%) worked in private-sector agencies; only a few (21%) worked in publicly funded organizations. Only three (21%) were in private practice. Members' median work-week was 40 hours long, but some members reported that they often worked up to 65 hours per week. The median salary for the group was $37,000, but members' wages ranged between $20,000 and $100,000.

Computer and Internet experience, skills and attitudes. Intervention Group members were active computer and Internet users. Most (89%)

used a computer both at work *and* at home, however, most (79%) only had access to the Internet and the World Wide Web from home. The median amount of time they spent online each week was five hours, but their weekly Internet use ranged from 1 hour to 15 hours. Four members also ran their own online groups and spent the most time online. Almost all the group members (95%) rated themselves as having good to excellent computer and Internet skills. All of them valued both technologies highly as professional tools.

Stressors

Physical health problems. Most members (89%) rated themselves in good to excellent physical health. Six members rated their health as only fair. Although they were working full time, some members reported that they had to cope with physical disabilities and chronic illnesses including sleep apnea and morbid obesity, hypothyroidism secondary to cancer, and irritable bowel syndrome.

Mental health problems. Many members reported that they had been under considerable strain. Nearly half of them (47%) had been treated for depression or anxiety disorders in the past two years. Those members who had received psychological treatment had only participated in individual psychotherapy and received psychotropic medications; none had participated in FTF support groups.

Family stressors. Many members also reported stress from domestic sources. Nearly half of them (47%) were dissatisfied in their relationships with their spouses; nearly the same number (42%) were dissatisfied in their relationships with their parents, and over a quarter (27%) reported troubled relationships with their children. Nearly one-third of the members (32%) reported that they were actively involved in caring for chronically or mentally ill relatives in addition to their routine family commitments.

Professional stressors. Members' answers to the BIQ indicated that many members were experiencing work-related stress. Over a third of the members were juggling two part-time social work jobs. Although nearly all of them used computers at work, over half (53%) reported that the technical training they were provided to use this technology was inadequate. Nearly half of the members (44%) reported they were dissatisfied with the salary they received for their professional work.

Members' pre-group OSI scores provided other evidence of members' struggles with job stress. A majority of members had high scores on three of the six Occupational Role Questionnaire scales: Role Ambiguity (84%), Role Boundaries (74%) and Responsibility (52%). These scores can be interpreted to mean that a majority of members felt uncertain about what was expected of them in their jobs, frustrated by conflicting supervisor demands, and blocked from achieving their personal and professional aspirations. On the Personal Strain Questionnaire, over two-thirds of the members (68%) scored high on the Vocational Strain scale. High scores on this scale indicate alienation from work, diminished performance, problems with concentration, and increased absenteeism.

On the Personal Resourcefulness Questionnaire, a majority of members had high scores on all four scales, indicating well-developed capacities for using self-care, rational-cognitive strategies, recreation and social support to cope. It is telling that, despite their knowledge and use of these coping strategies, many members were still experiencing problems with occupational stress and psychological strain.

Group Process

Group process refers to the rate and frequency of members' interactions and the extent to which those interactions contribute to the development of group cohesion and the attainment of group goals (Northen, 1998; Toseland & Rivas, 1995). In this study, group cohesion was assumed to be a function of member participation levels, the types of members' interactions with each other and with the Group Leader, and the topic(s) they discussed.

Member participation levels. The first group process question asked whether members would participate enough to sustain a listserv-based support group for 10 weeks. However, no research has been done to determine the minimum number of active members or the rate of messages needed to keep online group members engaged. It was assumed that some minimum number of members had to write in regularly to keep the group viable. To insure that there would be enough activity, members were asked to write at least one message per week. Member activity levels were analyzed in terms of the total number of messages over ten weeks, the number of messages sent each week, and the number of members who sent at least one message per week (e.g., "active members").

Members sent a total of 294 messages. The median number of messages sent in a week was 37, but weekly message totals ranged from seventy-seven in Week 6 to eighteen messages in Week 10 (see Figure 4). The number of active members gradually decreased from twenty-three to eleven over the first 7 weeks, rising again to with thirteen in the final two weeks. In face to face and online groups, some members are always much more active than others (Hare, 1976). In this study, five members (26%) sent 50% of all the messages. Members' participation rates were not uniform over the ten weeks. Some members who wrote only occasionally in the early weeks of the group became more active later on. There was only moderate compliance with the requirement to post at least one message a week. Only 12 members (65%) sent at least one message per week. However, 14 of them (78%) *averaged* at least one message per week.

"Lurkers" vs. Dropouts. Internet-mediated communication poses problems for group leaders who must be concerned with member

FIGURE 4. Comparison of the Total Number of Messages Sent Each Week and the Number of Active Members*

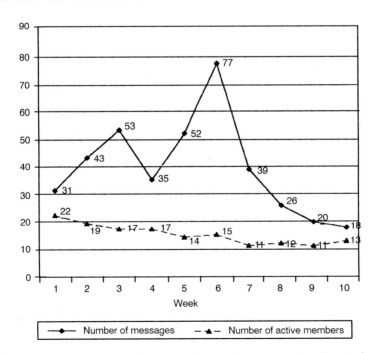

* Active members refers to all members who wrote at least one message in a given week.

retention. Unless members post messages, there is no way to know how they are feeling about the group. Online group members who read others' messages without contributing comments of their own are known as "lurkers." Because of the uncertainty over who was lurking in the group, members were considered to be active unless they explicitly asked to be dropped from the study. Some members did become disengaged and stopped writing when the discussion went in directions that no longer interested them, but only one member asked to be dropped from study.

Lurking is not necessarily a sign of alienation. Some lurking members wrote privately to the Group Leader to say they were too exhausted or sick to write messages to the group, but they appreciated being able to read about other members' experiences. Some others made only minimal contributions in the early weeks of group. They later wrote in their satisfaction surveys they had been overwhelmed by the number of messages and anxious about how they would appear to others. As the number of messages decreased and they become more comfortable with the group's process, these shyer members began writing several messages each week.

Group Leader's role. All support groups aim to improve members' coping skills and to empower them to solve their own problems. The facilitator supports the group's development by encouraging members to share in setting the group's goals (Northen, 1988). In this study, the Group Leader performed these leadership functions. She also prompted members to explore themes in more depth, raise new concerns, and share their perceptions of the ways that IM communication affected their experience of the group. When participation levels dropped, she asked them to comment on how to make group process more satisfying.

Discussion themes. The study's second question on group process explored what group members chose to talk about in their discussions. The discussion protocol followed a pattern similar to that of a FTF support group. During Week 1, members introduced themselves and discussed group norms for "netiquette" and confidentiality. Over the next three weeks, they described how macro-level changes, agency operations, and professional role characteristics contributed to their job stress, and how they coped. Members varied in the frequency with which they responded to the group's e-mail, so themes from one week were often carried on into discussions during succeeding weeks. After a sharp drop in the number of messages in Week 4, the Group Leader suggested a mid-term assessment and invited members to discuss how to make the group more satisfying. A lively discussion ensued about the group's process and goals. Afterwards, members decided to shift the focus of the discussion to more personal concerns. While they continued to write about professional role stress issues over the next three weeks, members wrote more about their problems balancing work and family obligations, and their health, marital, and parenting problems. As in FTF groups, members dealt with termination issues during the final two weeks. They discussed what they liked and disliked about the group and their feelings about its ending. Unlike most FTF groups, members were offered the option of continuing on as a leaderless group. During those weeks, members also discussed whether enough of them wanted to keep the group going to make it possible to continue.

The qualitative analyses revealed that the group discussed many different types of stressors and coping strategies (see Figure 5). Members wrote the most comments about professional role stress and coping. Comments about personal, family, and health stressors and coping

FIGURE 5. Stress and Coping Themes: Comment Frequencies

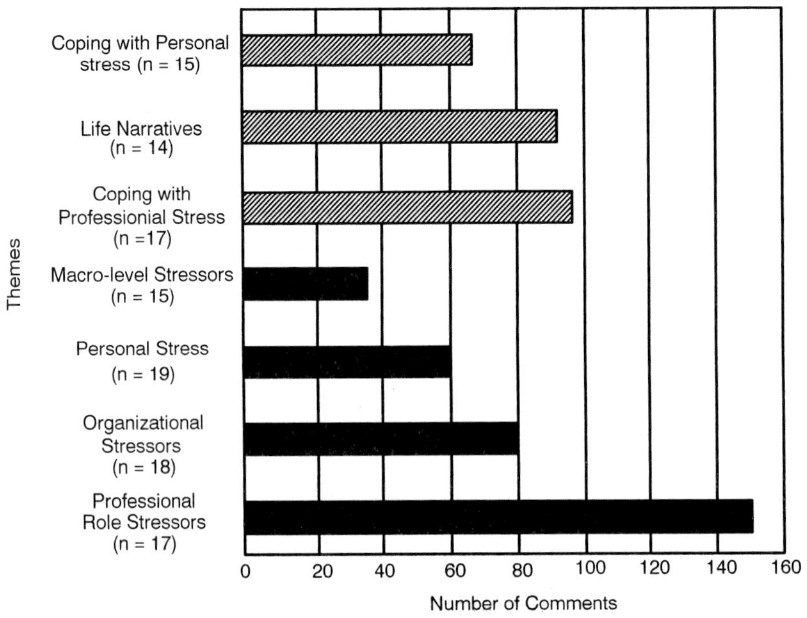

were less frequent, in part because these issues were only raised in the later weeks of the group after a number of members had already withdrawn from the study or had become inactive. The author had assumed that members would write only about current situations and events in their lives. However, the thematic analyses revealed that members also wrote "life narratives" in which they recounted how they had managed to overcome stressful situations in the *past*. These narratives, which increased in frequency until Week 7, often appeared in response to another member's description of a current problem.

Group Cohesion

The third research question on group process explored whether the group was able to achieve social cohesion. This characteristic of viable groups occurs as members get to know each other, discover their shared interests, and learn how to work together to achieve shared goals (Northen, 1988). In cohesive groups, members participate more actively, are more willing to assume leadership roles, and express more satisfaction with the group (Northen, 1988). They are also more likely to show diminished psychological distress, improved self-esteem, and self-confidence (Toseland & Rivas, 1995). In this study, cohesion was considered a surrogate indicator for intervention effectiveness because members of a cohesive support group would also be more likely to experience the psychological benefits of social cohesion that could help to alleviate job strain. In the study, group cohesion was conceptualized as: members' responsiveness to each other; their perceptions of similarity to each other; and the degree to which they wanted to continue on as a group (Northen, 1988).

Member responsiveness. This construct was operationalized as the number of messages in which members commented about each others' messages and members' strategies to make their messages more personal. The Group Leader repeatedly encouraged members to comment on each other's messages so that message senders would know how their messages affected their intended recipients. By Week 2, members began to include comments and the rate of messages using this format increased over time until almost all messages contained such responses. Also starting in Week 2, some members began to include subheadings to cue their readers whether their comments were directed to the group as a whole or to specific individuals. When directing a comment to a specific person, members would begin a new paragraph with that person's name. Over time, messages with multiple subheads became the norm and, by the end of the group, all members were using this format. In their messages, some members commented that the use of subheads made it easier to know when someone had responded to their earlier messages and made the discussions seem more intimate.

Perceived similarity. In cohesive FTF groups, members perceive each other as similar enough in their experiences to identify with each other's needs and aspirations (Northen, 1988). In the satisfaction survey, members were asked to rate their levels of agreement to five statements about the overall similarity of their experiences to other group members, and the ease with which they could relate to others' work and family experiences, and their mental and physical health problems. Items were based on a 4-point Likert scale from "strongly agree" to "strongly disagree." Only about half of the members (53%) agreed that they perceived their experiences as similar overall. In follow-up questions on more specific kinds of experiences, however, at least two thirds of the members agreed that their experiences with mental and physical health problems and work were similar. A majority of members (58%) agreed that their family experiences were similar.

Despite these indications of solidarity, members in the study had mixed responses to diversity in the group. In their e-mailed responses to an open-ended question in the satisfaction survey, some members wrote that they appreciated learning about the range of social workers' experiences. Private practitioners reported that they had problems relating to the concerns of members who worked in public agencies. Some members felt overwhelmed and helpless when confronted with the crises of the members who were much more emotionally needy.

Desire to continue in the group. When members are satisfied with a FTF group, they typically are reluctant to see it disperse (Northen, 1988). In this group, thirteen members (68%) expressed interest in continuing on in the group–among these were several members who had "lurked" for most of the time. These thirteen members later demonstrated their commitment to the group by continuing on for another ten weeks as a leaderless group. These findings confirmed the other two indicators that the group had achieved cohesion.

Outcomes

Social Support. One goal of the group was to provide members with support. The first outcome question examined the extent to which the group achieved this goal. The group's supportiveness was assessed qualitatively using content analyses of members' e-mail messages, and quantitatively on the satisfaction survey. Members' messages were analyzed for the frequency of comments in which they explicitly requested support, offered support, or acknowledged that the support they received had been helpful (see Figure 6). Nine members made a total of 17 requests for support. These requests occurred mostly during the first five weeks of the group and mostly concerned work-related problems. There were a total of 209 supportive comments.

The qualitative analysis found that the more than half of the comments (54%) offered emotional support and validation, slightly more than a quarter (29%) expressed encouragement, while less than one-fifth (17%) offered advice and information. The number of supportive

FIGURE 6. Exchange of Social Support

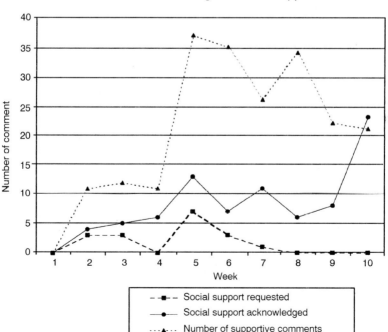

comments increased dramatically in Week 4 and stayed relatively high for the rest of the group. Members also offered support even when it was not explicitly requested–usually in response to members' reports of their family or health problems. Others in the group commented that they also found this encouragement and advice helpful. These comments may explain the finding that eighteen members wrote a total of eighty-three comments acknowledging the helpfulness of various messages.

In their satisfaction surveys, a majority of members rated the group as helpful in clarifying their professional values (69%) and as a source of useful feedback for improving coping (63%). Members found the group somewhat less helpful as a source of information about resources to enhance coping; only about half of the members (53%) reported that the group was good source of such information.

Members also confronted the real limitations of IM support groups. During Week 8, one member reported that she had just been diagnosed with cancer. Members commented that, although they felt emotionally connected through e-mail, this announcement forced them to realize how geographically distant they were from one another. Many wrote about how frustrated they felt, knowing about the crisis but unable to respond with casseroles and other help that they would have provided to a friend who lived nearby who was experiencing similar problems.

Member Satisfaction

To be feasible, most members must feel satisfied with the group's discussion content and process. In the satisfaction survey, members were asked to rate the strength of their agreement with statements about their satisfaction with different aspects of the group on a four-point scale ranging from "strongly disagree" to "strongly agree." Most members (74%) agreed that they had been satisfied overall with the group and that it had lasted about the right number of weeks (79%). Most members (90%) agreed that having a group leader had been helpful, especially in facilitating the changes in the agenda midway through the group. Over three-quarters of the members (79%) were satisfied with the range of topics discussed, and a majority of members agreed that the appropriate amount of attention had given to 12 out of 13 items listing stress and coping themes. The one topic that a majority of members (58%) felt had not been discussed enough was problems related to computerization in the human services.

Because the group relied on IM communication, it was important that the technology did not act as a barrier to participation. On the satisfaction survey, members rated their agreement to statements on the ease of IM communication. Almost all agreed that it had been easy for them to communicate their thoughts and feelings in writing (90%) and via e-mail (95%). A majority also agreed that they had been comfortable knowing that others in the group could contact them via e-mail (74%) and with being unable see the group members with whom they were corresponding (58%). Members reported in their e-mail responses to the satisfaction survey that they liked the convenience and privacy of being able to participate in the group from home.

Members were not totally satisfied with their experience in the group. On the four-point scale, members rated their agreement to statements that the group's size, volume of messages, and amount of time needed to participate were "about right." Sixteen members (84%) disagreed with the "size of group" item; 14 (74%) disagreed with "number of messages" item; and 8 (42%) disagreed with the "amount of time" item. These responses coincide with findings from the qualitative analysis that members complained repeatedly about how corresponding with the group took too much time because the group was too big and the volume of messages too great.

Stress Reduction Effects

The main purpose of this highly exploratory study was to explore the feasibility of a facilitated, listserv-based support group for social workers, rather than its effectiveness in reducing stress. The small sample size and relatively weak intervention made it unlikely that any effects would be detected. Not surprisingly, analyses of the pre- and post-group OSI data found no statistically significant changes in members' levels of occupational stress, psychological strain, or coping resourcefulness.

DISCUSSION

The Internet's rapid evolution has created opportunities for support group interventions, but it also has sparked a multitude of questions about the nature, feasibility, processes and effectiveness of such interventions. The author's study examined the factors that contributed to the feasibility of one kind of group, a listserv-based group targeted at social workers. The results show that it was possible to recruit stressed social workers to participate in the study using only the Internet as the communication channel, but also that this type of recruitment process for an online group can be complicated and time consuming. Study findings also support the use of ecological perspectives on job stress. Most participants were experiencing considerable strain from work, including stress caused by computerization of their agencies. Many were also struggling with family and personal problems, but none of them had sought help from face-to-face support. More work is needed to determine how prevalent this combination of stressors and pattern in the use of support services is among social workers.

We still have much to learn about the structure and processes of effective online support groups. In this case, despite a large group and a high volume of mail, the 10-week listserv-based group proved to be feasible. Once the group started, some members became inactive but few members dropped out because they felt alienated from the group. Establishing norms for participation levels helped to insure an adequate flow of messages, but these norms did not need to be rigorously reinforced. In fact, if all members had been regular correspondents, members would have suffered more from message overload than they did. Findings from the study suggest that short-term, listserv-based groups may be similar to FTF groups in that they function better if they composed of approximately twelve members, but more work is needed to confirm whether this size of group promotes adequate participation levels without creating message overload. Study findings also suggest that IM groups are similar to FTF groups in that some members are much more active than others and that individual participation levels change over time. The IM channel enabled exhausted and sick members to stay connected with their peers, and gave shyer members opportunities to "observe" the group until they felt safe in joining in the discussion.

When the group shifted emphasis midstream from professional to family and personal concerns, some members became disengaged while others participated more. More research needs to be done to determine how to match different discussion formats with different members' needs. For example, some social workers might be more interested in an IM group that provided them with clinical supervision as well as opportunities to discuss job stress issues. Others who were experiencing more non-work-related stress may be more attracted to a freeform group in which discussions of work and personal concerns could be interspersed.

A few members had crises that threatened to overwhelm the group's capacity to respond. The background information questionnaire and pre-group OSI identified some members who were experiencing high levels of strain, but other crises could not have been predicted. Future studies need to improve strategies for pre-screening potential group members to help them decide whether an online group would meet their needs, possibly by combining background questionnaires with pre-group, telephone interviews with the Group Leader. These kinds of assessments might also be done online on an individual basis. More extensive pre-group contacts would make it easier for the Group Leader to know in advance which group members are likely to need a lot of direct support or are experiencing major life crises. Further research is needed to determine what background information on members is needed to help the Group Leader facilitate the group, and what methods will work most reliably to collect this data.

Overall, the Group Leader's role in this kind of online group appears to be similar to leadership in a FTF support group. The leader can expedite the initial agenda setting process and help the group modify the agenda as new needs emerge. Leadership activities can include keeping track of who is in the group, reaching out privately to those who become inactive, and encouraging them to stay connected. If a member goes into crisis, the Group Leader can encourage other members to explore their feelings about the situation and acknowledge feelings of helplessness. He or she can then facilitate discussions on how to cope with helplessness, and help members set reasonable expectations for the amount and kind of support the group can provide. In this group, members were more satisfied when the Group Leader used a more egalitarian facilitation style, but this may reflect the fact that many members were experienced group leaders themselves. Future studies need to explore relationships between the Group Leader facilitation styles, member characteristics and member satisfaction.

Members were able to overcome the uncertainty introduced by asynchronous IM communication to form a cohesive group. They were inventive in finding ways to respond to each other's needs for more personalized communication. This group was homogenous in terms of members' professional training and credentials, but quite heterogeneous in members' work settings, family situations, and health and mental health status. Over the course of the group, some of these differences became problematic. Composing a group is always as much art as science (Northen, 1988) but more research is needed to determine if there are key dimensions in which IM support groups need to be homogeneous.

The group achieved its goal in that most members reported that it provided them with support in coping with work and family stressors. Because social workers are more comfortable offering support than asking for it, it is not surprising that there was an imbalance between the number of requests for help and the number of offers of support. What was unexpected were the high number of comments acknowledging support even when the message was not directed at the person who acknowledged it. For many, simply being able to read other members' narratives about the past and present stressors in their lives and how they coped was helpful. Further studies are needed to determine whether this pattern in the exchange of social support is replicated in other IM groups composed of social workers or other human services professionals.

Although there was strong evidence of social cohesion, comparisons of the pre- and post-group OSI data did not find that participation in the group was associated with changes in members' occupational stress, psychological strain or coping resourcefulness. The lack of positive findings on the OSI may be more indicative of the low statistical power of the study as much as the ineffectiveness of the intervention. Alternatively, lack of change may be a function of measuring too soon after the end of the group. Many members were coping with entrenched and complex situations that would have taken more than the ten weeks to resolve. Further research is needed to determine the reason(s) for lack of positive change in the study's outcome measures. This may be due to deficiencies in the intervention, the appropriateness of the outcome measures, the measurement methods, or the timing of the data collection.

CONCLUSION

The Internet is transforming our personal lives, our work as human service professionals, and the lives of our clients. We need to be on the alert for ways that we can incorporate this technology into practice for their benefit and for ourselves. As with any innovation, we are attracted by the benefits of IM interventions while the empirical demonstrations of effectiveness and the potential drawbacks take time to become apparent. This study provides examples of both benefits and drawbacks. These mixed findings demonstrate more research is needed to document for whom and under what circumstances online groups are effective interventions. Internet users will undoubtedly continue to form their own groups without the benefit of professional leadership, and professionals will seek to use IM groups as part of their service repertoire. For now, however, human services professionals who use IM groups in their practice or who wish to refer clients to leaderless support groups should consider IM groups an experimental procedure and inform clients of this fact during the recruitment process.

REFERENCES

Ainsworth, M. (1999). The ABC's of Internet therapy. Retrieved April 29,1999 from the World Wide Web: www.metanoia.org/imhs/

Alcoholics Anonymous. (1999). Online Intergroup of Alcoholics Anonymous: Retrieved June 15, 1999 from the World Wide Web: http://www.12steps.org/Brochure/menubord/menu.htm.

Berman, Y. (1996). Discussion groups on the Internet as sources of information: The case of social work. Aslib Proceedings: Retrieved May 16, 1999 from the World Wide Web: http://www.aslib.co.uk/proceedings/1996/feb/1.html.

Bowman, R. L., & Bowman, V. E. (1998). Life on the electronic frontier: The application of technology to group work. *Journal for Specialists in Group Work*, 23(4), 428-445.

Colon, Y. (1998). Chat(ter)ing through the fingertips: Doing group therapy online: Retrieved July 9, 1998 from the World Wide Web: http://www.echonyc.com/~women/Issue17/public-colon.html.

Cutter, F. (1996). Virtual psychotherapy: *PsychNews International: An Online Publication*. Retrieved April 29, 1999 from the World Wide Web: http://www.cmc.com/pni13b.htm.

Deutsch, C. (1985). A survey of therapists' personal problems and treatment. *Professional Psychology: Research and Practice, 16*, 305-315.

Dunham, P. J., Hurshman, A., Litwin, E., Gusella, J., Ellsworth, C., & Dodd, P. W. D. (1998). Computer-mediated social support: Single young mothers as a model system. *American Journal of Community Psychology. Vol 26*(2), Apr 1998, 281-306.

Eng, T. R., Gustafson, D. H., Henderson, J., Jamison, H., & Patrick, K. (1999). Introduction to evaluation of interactive health communication applications. *American Journal of Preventive Medicine, 16*(1), 10-15.

Evans, C. H. (1999). Awakening behind the walls in an Intensive Journal Workshop: Dialog House. Retrieved July 29, 1999 from the World Wide Web: http://www.intensivejournal.org/Fir/Evans_article.htm.

Feenberg, A. L., Licht, J. M., Kane, K. P., Moran, K., & Smakith, R. A. (1996). The online patient meeting. *Journal of Neurological Sciences, 139*(Supplement), 129-31.

Fernsler, J. I., & Mancester, L. J. (1997). Evaluation of a computer-based cancer support network. *Cancer Practice, 5*(1), 46-51.

Finn, J. (1996). Computer-based self-help groups: On-line recovery for addictions. *Computers in Human Services, 13*(1), 21-41.

Finn, J., & Lavitt, M. (1994). Computer-based self-help for survivors of sexual abuse. *Social Work with Groups, 17*(1), 21-46.

Graphic Visualization & Usability Center. (1998). GVU's 8th WWW User Survey: Retrieved October 30, 1998 from the World Wide Web: http:// www.cc.gatech. edu/gvu/user_surveys/survey-7-10/general_bullets.html.

GriefNet. (1999). Welcome to GriefNet: Retrieved July 15, 1999 from the World Wide Web: http://griefnet.org/home.html.

Gustafson, D. H., Hawkins, R., Boberg, E., Pingree, S., Serlin, R. E., Graziano, F., & Chan, C. L. (1999). Impact of a patient-centered, computer-based health information/support system. *American Journal of Preventive Medicine, 16*(1), 1-9.

Guy, J. D., Poelstra, P. L., & Stark, M. (1989). Personal distress and therapeutic effectiveness: National survey of psychologists practicing psychotherapy. *Professional Psychology: Research and Practice, 20*, 48-50.

Hare, A. P. (1976). *Handbook of small group research.* New York: Free Press.

Hensley, A., & Hensley, A. (1999). Support-Group.com: Retrieved April 28, 1999 from the World Wide Web: http:// www.Support-Group.com.

Humphreys, K., & Rappaport, J. (1994). Researching self-help/mutual aid groups and organizations: Many roads, one journey. *Applied and Preventive Psychology, 3*, 217-231.

International MS Support Foundation. (1999). International MS Support Foundation: Retrieved July 20 from the World Wide Web: http://www.msnews.org.

Internet.com. (1999). PC Webopaedia Definitions and Links: Retrieved May 26, 1999 from the World Wide Web: http://webopedia.internet.com/Internet_and_Online_ Services/Newsgroups/forum.html.

King, S. A. (1994). Analysis of electronic support groups for recovering addicts. *Interpersonal Computing and Technology: An Electronic Journal for the 21st Century, 2*(3), 47-56.

King, S. A., & Moreggi, D. (1998). Internet therapy and self-help groups: The pros and cons. In J. Gackenbach (Ed.), *Psychology and the Internet: Intrapersonal, interpersonal, and transpersonal.* San Diego, CA: Academic Press, Inc.

Kraut, R., Lundmark, V., Patterson, M., Kiesler, S., Mukopadhyay, T., & Sherlis, W. (1998). Internet paradox: A social technology that reduces social involvement and psychological well-being? *American Psychologist, 53*(9), 1017-1031.

Liszt.com. (1999). Liszt's Usenet Newsgroups Directory: Retrieved April 28, 1999 from the World Wide Web: http://www.liszt.com/news/.

L-Soft International. (1999). CataListm the official catalog of LISTSERV lists: Retrieved April 18 1999 from the World Wide Web: http:// www.lsoft.com/catalist.html.

Markowitz, L. (1999). Therapy.com: Can computers replace the therapist's couch?: Utne Reader Online: Retrieved April 28, 1998 from the World Wide Web: http://www.utne.com:80/lens/bms/82bodytherapycom.html.

Medara, E. (1999). How to develop an online support group or web site: Retrieved June 15, 1999 from the World Wide Web: http://mentalhelp.net/selfhelp/strtonln/online.htm.

Meier, A. (1997). Inventing new models of social support groups: A feasibility study of an online stress management support group for social workers. *Social Work with Groups, 20*(4), 35-53.

Meier, A. (1999). *A multi-method evaluation of a computer-mediated, stress management support group for social workers: Feasibility, process, and effectiveness.* Unpublished dissertation, University of North Carolina, Chapel Hill.

Northen, H. (1988). *Social work with groups.* (2nd ed.). New York: Columbia University Press.

Osipow, S. H., & Spokane, A. R. (1987). *Occupational Stress Inventory manual*: Research edition. Odessa, FL: Psychological Assessment Resources, Inc.

Osterman, C. (1997). Psychologist takes couch on-line with Internet therapy: Retrieved May 20, 1998 from the Word Wide Web: http://www.openminds.com.

Peterson, V. (in press). Journal Stories 1-4. *Holistic Depth Psychology.*

Phillips, W. (1996). A comparison of online, e-mail and in-person self-help groups using Adult Children of Alcoholics as a model (Vol. 1999): Rider University Psychology Department. Retrieved April 29, 1999 from the World Wide Web: http://www.rider.edu/users/suler/psycyber/acoa.html.

Progoff, I. (1975). *At a journal workshop: The basic text and guide for using the Intensive Journal process.* New York: Dialogue House Library.

Reamer, F. G. (1992). The impaired social worker. *Social Work, 2*(2), 165-70.

Sagen, D. (1995, January,). Sex, lies and cyberspace. *Wired,* 78-84.

Schopler, J. H., Abell, M. D., & Galinsky, M. J. (1998). Technology-based groups: A review and conceptual framework for practice. *Social Work, 43*(3), 254-267.

Schopler, J. H., & Galinsky, M. J. (1993). Support groups as open systems: A model for practice and research. *Health and Social Work, 18*(3), 195-207.

SCOLARI. (1995). *QSR NUD.IST* [qualitative data analysis program]. Thousand Oaks, CA: SCOLARI.

Southwick, S. (1999). LisztIRC: A Brief Intro to IRC: Retrieved May 24, 1999 from the World Wide Web: http:// www.liszt.com.

SPSS Inc. (1993). *SPSS Base 6.1 for the Power Macintosh* (Version PMC 6.1) [Statistics application]: SPSS Inc.

Stein, D. J. (1997). Psychiatry on the internet: Survey of an OCD mailing list. *Psychiatric Bulletin, 21,* 95-98.

Stofle, G. S. (1999). Thoughts about online psychotherapy: Ethical and practical considerations: Retrieved April 30, 1999 from the World Wide Web: http://members. aol.com/stofle/onlinepsych.htm.

Swearingen, C. (1990). The impaired psychiatrist. *Psychiatric Clinics of North America, 13*(1), 1-11.

Toseland, R. W., & Rivas, R. F. (1995). *An introduction to group work practice.* (2nd ed.). Boston: Allyn and Bacon.

Weinberg, N., Uken, J., Schmale, J. D., & Adamek, M. (1995). Therapeutic factors:

Their presence in a computer-mediated support group. *Social Work with Groups,* *18*(4), 57-69.

White, B. J., & Madara, E. J. (1999). American self-help clearinghouse: Self-help source book online: Retrieved April 28, 1999 from the World Wide Web Available: http://mentalhelp.net/selfhelp/.

Winzelberg, A. (1997). The analysis of an electronic support group for individuals with eating disorders. *Computers in Human Behavior, 13*(3), 393-407.

The Nature and Prevention
of Harm in Technology-Mediated
Self-Help Settings:
Three Exemplars

Vincent R. Waldron
Melissa Lavitt
Douglas Kelley

SUMMARY. This paper argues that in addition to the substantial benefits they provide for members, on-line support groups create the potential for harm. Qualitative discourse analysis methods are used to examine messages exchanged in three distinct groups comprised of sexual abuse survivors, persons with disabilities, and parents. Examples of on-line practices with the potential to be harmful to individuals, dyadic relationships, and the larger group are identified. Several protective practices used by these groups that appear uniquely adapted for on-line support environments are also documented. Tentative guidelines are suggested for human services professionals interested in developing on-line support groups or referring clients to existing groups. The paper concludes with a discussion of the need for more research and a caution about the ethical responsibilities of researchers and practitioners who

Vincent R. Waldron, PhD, is Associate Professor of Communication Studies, Melissa Lavitt, DSW, is Associate Professor and Chair of Social Work, and Douglas Kelley, PhD, is Assistant Professor of Communication Studies, all affiliated with Arizona State University West.

Address correspondence to: College of Human Services, Arizona State University West, 4701W. Thunderbird Rd., Phoenix, AZ 85069.

[Haworth co-indexing entry note]: "The Nature and Prevention of Harm in Technology-Mediated Self-Help Settings: Three Exemplars." Waldron, Vincent R., Melissa Lavitt, and Douglas Kelley. Co-published simultaneously in *Journal of Technology in Human Services* (The Haworth Press, Inc.) Vol. 17, No. 2/3, 2000, pp. 267-293; and: *Human Services Online: A New Arena for Service Delivery* (ed: Jerry Finn, and Gary Holden) The Haworth Press, Inc., 2000, pp. 267-293. Single or multiple copies of this article are available for a fee from The Haworth Document Delivery Service [1-800-342-9678, 9:00 a.m. - 5:00 p.m. (EST). E-mail address: getinfo@haworthpressinc.com].

267

venture into this rapidly developing context of human service work. *[Article copies available for a fee from The Haworth Document Delivery Service: 1-800-342-9678. E-mail address: <getinfo@haworthpressinc.com> Website: <http://www.haworthpressinc.com>]*

KEYWORDS. Internet, support groups, communication, harmful effects

INTRODUCTION

The proliferation of on-line self-help in the form of listservs, bulletin-boards, chat-rooms and related electronic forms of communication creates a vast new reservoir of social support in our culture. When compared to the traditional methods of communication used by human service professionals, these electronic types of support make information, advice and emotional assurance available to more people, more quickly, with arguably fewer barriers to access. Indeed, recent research has documented wide acceptance by the general populace. One survey indicated that nearly 31 million people had recently used electronic sources to obtain information about health or psycho-social concerns (Green & Himelstein, 1998). Service providers have responded to this groundswell of interest. For example, mental health professionals increasingly view Internet-based information and dialogue as an important opportunity for delivering services (Lamberg, 1997). Researchers have begun to describe the myriad human service applications of the Internet, including on-line support groups serving sexual abuse survivors (Finn & Lavitt, 1994), breast cancer patients (Sharf, 1997), hemophiliacs (Scheerhorn, 1997), home caregivers (Brennan, Moore, & Smythe, 1992; Brennan & Fink, 1997), single young mothers (Dunham et al., 1998), people with physical disabilities (Braithwaite, Waldron, & Finn, 1999), and parents (Mickelson, 1998).

Because of these unmistakable trends, human service professionals should be, and in many cases are, in the forefront when it comes to developing electronic support systems and touting their benefits. However, electronic forms of support also harbor the potential for harm (Finn & Lavitt, 1994). Electronic media can render obsolete the protections traditionally offered to members of face-to-face support groups. One implication is that human service professionals must develop an understanding of the types of harm that clients might experience in mediated environments. As participants and designers of mediated support systems, these professionals may be called upon to select technology features, develop rules of use, and create access procedures that make electronic support environments safer. Unfortunately, research to date has been primarily focused on the availability, usage patterns, and nature of on-line support services. Relatively little research has illustrated how interactions in electronic support groups may actually be harmful to participants.

This paper describes both the potential for harm and the protective features of on-line support groups. After a brief discussion of the unique characteristics of electronic social support, we introduce the reader to three active electronic support groups that provide the basis of our analysis. They serve populations with potentially distinct support needs: parents, persons with severe physical disabilities, and sexual abuse survivors. Based on our analysis of the messages exchanged among group members, we present a typology of potential harm. We then discuss the protections provided in our three sample groups. Finally, we present guidelines for human service professionals working in mediated support environments.

Social Support in Mediated Relationships

On-line self-help groups provide opportunities for the creation of expanded social support networks. They are a tool for overcoming barriers to group participation, including the lack of local groups, transportation or scheduling problems, rarity of disease, and mobility limitations due to severe physical disability. The relationships developed through these channels are potentially different from those developed through face-to-face contact. In this regard, Walther (1995, 1996) identifies three types of technology-mediated interaction, hereafter referred to simply as mediated interaction. First, *impersonal* communication occurs when mediated interactions are narrowly task-focused, as when a request for information yields a factual response. On-line reservation systems fit in this category. Second, mediated interaction is *interpersonal* when its characteristics resemble that of typical face-to-face communication. That is, its level of sociability, emotional tenor, conformity with politeness rules and social norms, and level of intimacy would be considered appropriate if conducted in analogous face-to-face contexts. E-mail discussions among co-workers tends to be of this type, in part because they are subject to monitoring and influenced by workplace roles and rules. However, a third form of interaction, that which Walther calls *hyperpersonal*, intensifies characteristics of "normal" interaction, and tends to be viewed as highly desirable by on-line participants. The emotionally intense communication observed among members of some illness-related communities (e.g., Scheerhorn, 1997) appears to be of this type.

Hyperpersonal communication develops in part because of the limited nonverbal, historical and contextual information available in mediated contexts. In this environment, message senders are able to carefully manage the presentation of self. Lacking an external reality against which perceptions might be checked, message recipients can develop idealized perceptions of their fellow interactants. The asynchronous nature of mediated communication and the limited cues available (primarily the often carefully-crafted written messages of fellow participants) can create a kind of feedback loop that intensifies and magnifies the interpersonal experiences of participants. Hyperpersonal interaction is not inherently harmful, but its effects on support-group members, particularly those who are psychologically vulnerable, should be the subject of scrutiny by human service professionals and researchers.

In addition to noting the potential for hyperpersonal communication, researchers have engaged in a dialogue about the negative and positive effects of technology-based support services (Street, Gold, & Manning, 1997). On the positive side, users of electronic support groups can, and sometimes do, expand their network of friends (Parks & Floyd, 1995) and at least one study (Katz & Aspden, 1997) concluded that the Internet can enrich the social relationships of users. Group identity and members' sense of mutual obligation may be heightened and friendships can develop more quickly (Kurtz, 1997). Ironically, it may also be easier to abandon mediated relationships, because members can easily disappear into cyberspace without fear of being held accountable by other members.

E-mail can be sent any time of day; can be sent from home; and is relatively unaffected by biases due to appearance, age, race, and social status. Because comments can be prepared off-line before being posted, they can be more reflective than those offered in face-to-face, real-time communication (Brashers, Adkins, & Meyers, 1994). Moreover, the Internet can be a critical source of social support and advice for those who might otherwise be isolated. Studies have documented these benefits for house-bound caregivers (Brennan et al., 1992) and hemophiliacs living in rural areas (Scheerhorn, 1997).

On the negative side, a recent exploratory study provides some evidence that use of Internet-based communication systems is associated with subsequent reductions in family communication, a decline in the size of the local social network, increased loneliness, and increased depression (Kraut et al., 1998). One explanation is that Internet-based communication replaces strong social ties with weaker ones. Strong ties are complex relationships that provide strength and support along multiple dimensions (emotional, informational, tangible assistance). Communication across strong ties tends to be frequent, varied, and adapted to the relational history and larger contexts within which a given interaction takes place (Krackhardt, 1994; for a discussion of weak ties, see Granovetter, 1973). Persons rely on strong ties for favors and historical perspective–two social resources that may be less easily provided by electronic friends. However, we interpret Kraut et al. results with caution. Participants in the Kraut et al. study were not members of online support groups. More needs to be known about how Internet-based relationships are supplemented by face-to-face contacts. The motives and knowledge levels of users and the extent to which alternate sources of social support are available to them may ultimately determine the effects of Internet-based communication.

Much of the research to date has concerned itself with the quantity of Internet use and the types of social support provided by online groups (Braithwaite et al., 1999). Although suggestive, this work is limited by its failure to consider the quality of communication in on-line support groups. In particular, discussions of harmful and protective features of these support groups would be enhanced by qualitative data demonstrating the types of on-line behavior exhibited in real groups. In this regard, researchers studying face-to-face communication have called for more research on the discourse patterns through which effective and ineffective social support is enacted (Burleson, 1994). Moreover, those investigating social support in mediated settings have called for more exemplars of the natural patterns of talk used in electronic groups (Brashers et al., 1994).

ELECTRONIC SELF-HELP:
THREE EXEMPLARS

In this paper, we present a qualitative analysis of the potentially harmful and protective practices of three distinct on-line self-help groups. The group names used below are fictional.

"SupportNet": Participants of SupportNet are persons with disabilities who share and receive advice and emotional support in a "conference" (bulletin-board) format. Some members are home-bound or have limited mobility, but the group's published description also invites those who are challenged by emotional or mental limitations to join the discussion. SupportNet members post messages to local Bulletin Board Systems (BBS) and they are distributed through regional and national hubs that carry the conference. Similar groups are available through Usenet on the Internet. Message traffic is monitored by a system moderator, in this instance a student-volunteer who runs SupportNet as part of a larger project designed to make recycled computer technology available to persons with disabilities.

"ParentNet": The second group we examined is a parent support group with the self-described objective of raising of happy, healthy children. Membership in this on-line support group is free and there are no professionals monitoring bulletin board content, although volunteer moderators are enlisted for this purpose. The group's easily accessible web site contains message boards dealing with a variety of issues, such as pre-pregnancy, family types and styles, postpartum depression, breastfeeding, potty training, miscarriages, and violence-proofing children.

"SurviveNet": The third group we examine is an Internet-based mediated self-help group for survivors of sexual abuse. The moderator is an active part of the discussion, although her qualifications are not stated. There is an extensive set of rules governing the behavior, language, and topics of participants. The purpose of the group is to provide a safe haven for the discussion of issues related to surviving childhood sexual abuse.

We have chosen these three groups for several reasons. First, two of them are quite familiar to us because our previous research has involved detailed analysis of the messages exchanged among group members (Braithwaite et al., 1999; Finn & Lavitt, 1994). Second, the groups serve members with distinct social support needs. ParentNet provides considerable parenting advice and information to its users, but the social support that is exchanged is less emotional and relationally intense, when compared to the other groups. Interaction on ParentNet is more often of the interpersonal or impersonal types, described by Walther (1994). In contrast, SupportNet members appear to use the net to create emotionally intimate relationships that might otherwise be unavailable, in some cases due to the social isolation imposed by physical challenges. Members share stories about their medical and psychological challenges and advice about medical treatments and coping strategies. Discussion on SurviveNet in intended to promote understanding, healing, and coping with the psychological trauma associated with sexual abuse. Both of these latter groups exhibit considerable amounts of hyperpersonal interaction. As indicated by their discourse, members of these groups shared a strong group identity, idealized other members, used emotionally-charged discourse, and were highly enthusiastic and committed. Magnification and intensification, both discussed by Walther, were obvious in the frequent use of expressive verbal content and associated punctuation (e.g., *"I love you guys!!!!!!!!!!!!!"*).

Another reason for selecting these three groups is that they appear to represent different stages in the "evolution" of on-line support. At the time we observed it, SupportNet had the feel of a "grassroots," informal support network, having sprung from the personal energies of one highly committed volunteer. Some of the users were relatively inexperienced in the use of technology. The group discussed a broad range of topics and few "rules of use" had evolved or been imposed by the moderator. The moderator received frequent inquiries from members, but was not highly involved in regulating discussion. Parent Net represents the opposite end of the spectrum, having developed formal guidelines for users, a variety of protective features, and offering a host of specific subtopical discussion boards from which participants can choose. SurviveNet lies between these informal/formal extremes. This mediated group resembles group therapy rather than a conversation or structured information exchange. Therefore, self-disclosure is valued, but established boundaries regulate the types of disclosure permitted.

HARM IN ON-LINE SUPPORT GROUPS

Despite our intention of examining these groups for potentially harmful practices, we should note that all three provide members with considerable social support (for discussions of social support benefits, see Braithwaite et al., 1999; Dunham et al, 1998; Finn & Lavitt, 1994). It is not our intention to malign these groups or to claim that members *are* being harmed by participating. Rather we hope to identify the *potential* for harm in such groups, and then to discuss the mechanisms these groups use (or could use) to protect members.

Drawing on the literature pertaining to self-help groups (e.g., Thomas, 1995; Wasserman & Danforth, 1988), advantages and disadvantages of mediated communication compared to face-to-face forms (e.g., Chesebro & Bonsall, 1989; Leets & Giles, 1997; Walther, 1994, 1995, 1996, 1997; Walther, Anderson, & Park, 1994) and the role of communication technology in health promotion (Street, Gold, & Manning, 1997), we argue that harm can occur at individual, relational, and group levels. We focus on types of harm that are more likely in electronic support environments as compared to traditional face-to-face support groups. Typically researchers have only speculated about the possibilities for on-line harm (Braithwaite, Waldron, & Finn, 1999; Mickelson, 1998; Walther, 1996), rarely documenting actual instances of its occurrence. But, from this previous work we expected harm to take the form of violations of privacy, the increased potential for misunderstanding, disinhibited communication, rapid and wide distribution of inaccurate information, "cyber-addiction," misrepresentation of identity, the emergence of unanticipated or burdensome member obligations, faulty or missing communication procedures and rules, ignorance of technology, and on-line harassment or stalking.

Using the broad categories of harm described above (individual, relational, and group) as our guide, we used the methods of qualitative discourse analysis (Tracy, 1991) to locate samples of the talk exchanged in the three support groups. Individual members of the research team reviewed the messages, isolating those that initially appeared to represent any type of potential harm previously identified in the literature. As is typical of discourse analysis methods, we sampled messages until we reached the point of redundancy (no additional types of harmful messages could be located). These were then discussed with other members of the research team and an initial, mutually-acceptable category system was created. The system was applied, expanded, and revised through discussion and repeated categorization, until all members were satisfied that the coding system accurately captured the types of harm observed in each group.

It is inconsistent with the purpose of qualitative discourse analysis to make claims about the frequency or statistical representativeness of observations. However, we did review extensive amounts of on-line interaction and feel reasonably confident that we have identified kinds of harm that are typical in these particular groups. Our analysis of SupportNet is based on a full month's worth of messages posted to the bulletin board. In a previous analysis, these data were determined to include nearly 1,500 distinct support messages (Braithwaite et al., 1999). In addition, we examined 250 messages exchanged on 12 of ParentNet's subtopic bulletin boards and 900 messages exchanged by SurviveNet members over an approximately four-month period.

To illustrate the types and form of potentially harmful on-line practices we provide selected quotes from members. However, to protect the identities and rights of group members these quotes are edited and fictionalized. All member and group names and all identity-compromising comments have been changed to protect the participants. In no case is a member's actual utterance reproduced in its original form. But, we have made every effort to preserve the original meaning.

Harm to Individuals

We counted as harm to individuals those exchanges of messages that might lead a single message sender or recipient to experience psychological distress, embarrassment, disillusionment, alienation, or other negative internal states.

Misunderstandings. The potential for misunderstanding may be heightened in mediated settings. Communicators are hampered by limited message cues and the lack of immediate nonverbal or verbal feedback (Walther, 1997). For example, one contributor to ParentNet felt her comments were misunderstood by a number of readers:

> Many of you missed the context of my message and thought it criticized your personal parenting style. I should have made it clearer but I have been distracted over the last few weeks by other things happening in my life. Let me try it another time. . . .

We saw a number of similar instances in which the emotional tone of a message was misread, presumably due to the limited message cues available for receivers (compared to face-to-face communication). In some cases, new members were unaware of the emotions used in mediated environments to convey emotional states (for a review, see Kurtz, 1997). The practical effects of this were evident in exchanges in which an original message sender complained that group members were "overreacting" to a previous message's level of despair, taking the message out of its context, or misinterpreting a previous comment as a personal attack, rather than simply an "observation." We believe these kinds of misunderstandings are more likely in mediated support groups. Moreover, the asynchronous nature of electronic communication may delay the process of repairing the damage done by misunderstandings. In face-to-face communication, remediation can happen immediately (obviously, it does not happen in many cases). In the example above, as time passed, members apparently "stewed" over what they perceived as an attack on their parenting values. As a consequence, the message sender, unable to log on for several weeks due to personal issues, was greeted with a large number of hostile responses.

Excessive dependence. It appeared from their discourse, that some members of SupportNet become excessively dependent on the network. Electronic communication and the maintenance of network relationships apparently became too time-consuming. For example, Sara found that she needed to spend more time and effort in the "real world" and posted this rationale for leaving the group:

> E-mailing with the group is taking too much time from the rest of my life and I simply must focus on other things. The Net has been a way to avoid my other problems and I have been doing too much of that . . . I can't seem to do small amounts of e-mail, so I will have to do none at all. I will definitely miss the group, but I really have other things waiting for me.

This response to Sara, from Ken, a frequent correspondent, reveals that members can be pressured by their electronic peers to remain in the group: *"There must be some other way!!!!! Please don't leave the group! Please!!!!"*

Members sometimes joked about their reliance on SupportNet. Jill noted: *"I was thinking about starting a 12-step support group for anonymous 'message addicts.' Whenever you wanted to e-mail, you'd send a message your 'sponsor.'"*

On-line emotional distress. We observed on-line incidents with the potential to be psychologically traumatic for some members. Others indicated that members were experiencing levels of emotional distress that required a level of intervention beyond that available in cyberspace. For example, one thread on SurviveNet pertained to a participant's suicidal feelings. The member described a state of emotional confusion and loneliness and indicated that he/she had taken a substantial dose of a prescription drug and was considering taking more.

A "spoiler" (header) warned group members that the thread contained suicidal thoughts and feelings. While this may serve as a protective strategy to some vulnerable members, we would argue that the Internet is not the place to deal with a potential drug overdose. The content of this and (a few) other messages indicated that the individual was experiencing acute distress that required more direct intervention. Group members did not acknowledge this in a timely fashion. As Kurtz (1997) notes about electronic support systems, it is possible that a member in emotional distress could post a cry for help that will be missed or ignored by the anonymous mass of subscribers.

Members of SurviveNet are, in general, a psychologically vulnerable group. Group rules do not permit sexually explicit material because the content may cause significant emotional distress to participants. A message from the moderator, however, noted the a barrage of sexually explicit advertising was requiring the group to reform under another address.

When we searched for this sexual abuse recovery group, we, too, found obscene and sexually explicit messages and ads interspersed with genuine postings. SupportNet had similar problems, and ultimately changed its name and description at one point because members were unintentionally reading messages from an alternate lifestyles BBS with a name similar to that used by SupportNet. Members apparently found the content to be unpleasant and embarrassing.

These problems illustrate that on-line support groups, in comparison to face-to-face groups, may require additional training for members. In addition, we see evidence that monitoring the message flow in a large mediated support group may be more cumbersome than in face-to-face groups. At least in the groups we observed, moderators were unable to read every message and screen out those that were offensive. On ParentNet, which attempted to monitor messages, monitors made clear that high levels of message traffic, and limited amounts of time, made monitoring imperfect.

Loss of anonymity/confidentiality. It is possible, perhaps likely, that new members of on-line support groups may be unfamiliar with the technology and its implications for the communication process. They may not know that confidentiality is hard to preserve, if not impossible, in mediated environments. We saw examples of privacy violations that may have been unintentional, but created the potential for unwelcome personal contact.

For example, on SupportNet one member was delighted to discover that another lived close by. In his excitement he (perhaps inadvertently) revealed that a third member also lived nearby, identifying the location quite specifically. This information became accessible to anyone who read the message. Sometimes members appeared to forget that their "confidences" were essentially broadcast to all users of the BBS. For example, this comment was made in apparent seriousness:

> Please help me out Jane. Don't let everyone know that I did you this favor, 'cause right now I can't do the same thing for everybody in the group.

Another member revealed potentially damaging information about his employer's financial situation:

> I'm doing a project at the moment for the [reveals name of city] drug prevention program, which helps people to stop abusing cocaine, and get their lives back to normal. They have lost a lot of money, so I am not sure when my work there will be done.

In addition, members of these groups copied and forwarded messages to other individuals and groups. Some search engines (e.g., Dejanews) are explicitly designed to search Usenet posts for names or content. All of this means that compared to face-to-face groups, ostensibly private information shared within the context of the mediated support group may be more rapidly, widely and publicly distributed.

Barriers to external medical and therapeutic expertise. A positive feature of mediated support groups is their potential to "democratize" healthcare, aiding members in their search for alternate sources of information and opinion and thus empowering them to question the advice of traditional health experts (Scheerhorn, 1997). The groups we examined unquestionably provided this kind of empowering environment for members. We wondered, however, if the mediated environment also created opportunities for misrepresentation of expertise.

Only ParentNet facilitated access (through an e-mail link) to externally-verified content experts or trained therapists. Moreover, the backgrounds, knowledge, and experiences of fellow members may be less discernable in cyberspace. As Walther (1996) has noted, idealization of group members is more likely in mediated settings, because impressions are based primarily on texts created by members–more limited contextual or historical information is available in most cases. The combined effects of these two factors could be a tendency to overvalue advice received in an electronic group, while undervaluing external expertise.

Illustrating this theme was a question posted on SurviveNet concerning the long-term physical effects on a child of unwanted sexual touching. In response, one member made the dubious claim that unwanted stimulation of sexual parts of the body at an early age can lead to long-lasting changes in the brain. The originator of the query did not question this claim, nor did other group members. However, it seems at least possible that speculation about biological effects of sexual abuse provoked unfounded anxiety for this person and for others in the group as it was passed about. In a face-to-face support environment, it seems likely that the expertise of the person offering this information could be at least verified through investigation of the source's background. The checking of source credibility may be hampered in cyberspace.

Members of all three groups frequently expressed their complaints about medical or social service providers or their own physical conditions, sometimes "one-upping" each others' tales of misery. One possible outcome of this magnification effect was a kind of "me too" contagion, with members confirming each others' fears. For example, in several postings to SupportNet, Jay reported that he was suffering from a psychological disorder although it was undiagnosed by the doctors he had visited. Another member responded with a post in which several vague symptoms were described. This prompted Jay to "diagnose" a similar problem. Several rounds of commiseration followed. A third member who joined the conversation was also diagnosed by Jay as having this disorder, but she sharply corrected him: "*I don't have [the disorder]!*"

This series of exchanges provide some evidence that diagnoses can "spread" through an electronic support network, as members speculate about one another's health problems based on limited information.

We don't mean to suggest that these speculations were invalid in Jay's case, but they appear to be based on limited diagnostic information, unchecked by an external source of expertise, and fueled in part by an intense, hyperpersonal sense of empathy and mutual support among members.

Relational Harm

We defined as relational harm those messages or interactions that might have negative effects for multiple parties and the relational qualities that bound them.

Harm to "external" relationships and displaced aggression. Support group members sometimes shared secrets or asked for advice about their relationships outside the network. For example, some shared marital problems or criticized their spouses in their postings. Correspondents then offered diagnoses of relational problems and frequently supported the member's interpretation of the situation. Postings of this type create the possibility for several types of relational harm. First, relational intimacies were sometimes shared in this public forum, without the knowledge of the spouse, but with potentially negative consequences for the spouse's reputation. Second, it appeared that anonymous communication with a very supportive electronic audience may, in some cases, have replaced more difficult face-to-face interactions with the spouse. After detailing his marital problems, Cedrick shared this over SupportNet:

> My wife just wouldn't understand some of these things that I have told you about . . . I wouldn't want her to have to worry about them.

Emotional hostility developed in outside relationships sometimes "spilled over" into the mediated environment. Although this could happen in face-to-face groups, the audience for such revelations is substantially larger and the lack of immediate relational consequences in cyberspace may make members uninhibited about delivering relational "cheap shots" (see Leets & Giles, 1997). Messages describing guilt over extramarital affairs were sometimes posted to a ParentNet message board concerning adultery. In response, one member, who was the self-described victim of an adulterous relationship, used the bulletin board to accuse his own spouse and the sender of the original message of behaving like prostitutes. The message continued:

> Accept my apologies for the choice of words, but I found out recently that my partner was involved with someone else. Just like you, she claimed to have a lot of complaints that lead her to adultery. You fool yourself to think you haven't harmed him permanently.

Premature intimacy and emotional intensity. There is ample evidence in the discourse we observed of emotional magnification, previously reported to be more common in mediated relationships (Walther, 1995, 1996). Linguistic intensifiers like *"super," "really,"* and *"great"* are used frequently to create this effect. Some examples: *"I'm super glad you are here . . . "* and *"I am soooooooo darned excited [to hear from you]!"* Emotional magnification may have the unintended effect of accelerating relational intimacy (see Kurtz, 1997). A potential harmful consequence may be that face-to-face relationships, characterized by more routine discourse, might seem dull by comparison.

In general, hyperpersonal communication, so common in the discourse we observed, is characterized by unrealistic relational perceptions, fed by the careful management of the self and the idealization of other members. The intensively attractive qualities of mediated support relationships might explain why Internet users may neglect close local ties with family and friends (Kraut et al., 1998). It is possible that the social support obtained in these idealized relationships may not "transfer" well to the more complex but also more routine world of face-to-face relationships.

Access and availability in mediated relationships. Members of these groups often expressed an obligation to "be there" for others and communicated their confidence that others would do the same: *"Thank you for sticking by me . . . I think of you often and wish you all the best . . . Our group will stay together and cheer each other on"* [ParentNet].

What seemed to distinguish these groups from their face-to-face counterparts was the apparently expanded definition of what "being there" meant. In contrast to members of face-to-face support groups, many of which gather at prearranged times, members of these electronic group exchanged support on a frequent and varied schedule, day or night. We observed that some group members read and posted e-mail daily, sometimes many times a day. Members sometimes repri-manded each other, usually in jest, for not responding quickly enough. Others expressed guilt or frustration when the pace of their partner's support messages exceeded their capacity.

> I DO know you asked [for my opinion] a long time ago . . . I feel awful about not getting back to you . . . We have been busy with family gatherings and my health problem is affecting my typing [ParentNet].

Members of SupportNet, who sometimes described being house-bound and socially isolated because of limitations on physical mobil-ity, were among the most frequent message senders. We found in some exchanges of messages evidence of an apparent "mismatch" between the frequency, depth, and length of support messages delivered by these users and the responses of those who were less dependent on electronic communication. This is inherently harmful to neither party, but it may explain the apparent irritation in messages like that quoted above. Electronic communication expands access to a network of supportive relationships but it may also require members to renegoti-ate the communicative norms that govern those relationships.

Potentially unsafe relationships. As is characteristic of hyperperso-nal communication, SupportNet members self-disclosed private and emotional information early in their relationships–sometimes with very limited knowledge of their correspondents. It is possible that this practice leads to a false sense of trust (see Parks & Floyd, 1995 for a discussion of on-line relational dynamics). In some cases, these ex-changes lead to offers to meet in an unmediated environment. Al-though not inherently harmful, these discussions rarely concerned precautions that might be customary in unmediated relationships. For example, there was rarely discussion of meeting in a public place, or meeting in the presence of friends, or planning a graduated series of meetings. "If it is more difficult to assess wealth and status electroni-cally, it is also more difficult to judge honesty. An emotionally vulner-able population may be at special peril here" (Kurtz, 1997, p. 194).

From reading only a few posts (on SupportNet) by Mary, about her recent emotional hardships, Jack felt comfortable suggesting: *"We should get together some time."* But in this case, Mary communicated a desire to progress more slowly: *"Maybe we should send snail mail first."* When Julie, on SurviveNet, asked whether others experienced sexual abuse by a female who was not their mother, she received several replies from others who had similar experiences. One respondent shared her history of sexual abuse by both male and female perpetrators and invited Julie to contact her by e-mail or in a chat room. This respondent appears quite enthusiastic in her attempts to make herself available to Julie: *"I want to talk with you sweetie. Watch out for yourself and you can be sure that you are one of my family."*

Our point in both these examples is simply that on the basis of one or two brief messages members of these networks are referring to each other with pet names ("sweetie") and being invited to form close bonds, that in "real life" relationships take time and the development of trust. The hyperpersonal nature of mediated communication creates the impressions that such relationships are safe. Practitioners who have experimented with on-line groups question this assumption, particularly when emotionally vulnerable clients are involved (Kurtz, 1997). In contrast, face-to-face relationships are often (not always) initiated with people who are in some way connected to members of our immediate social networks (friends, work associates) and some measure of safety is derived from the potential to reduce uncertainty about the potential partner.

Harm to the Group

We observed some instances of harm that affected all participants or stemmed from violations of group norms.

Infiltration and hidden identities. It is relatively easy for unwanted participants to infiltrate on-line support groups. This was illustrated dramatically on SurviveNet, when a (self-identified) sex offender infiltrated the discussion, offering comments that minimized the suffering experienced by the members and disrupted the discussion. This individual used an electronic identity that referred to pedophilia and defended adult/child sexual contact. As one might imagine, this was particularly distressful to members.

It is easier in mediated groups for users to hide or misrepresent their identities, a practice that would likely be considered unethically deceptive in some face-to-face groups. A discussion among self-identified parents of illicit drug use by teenagers apparently experienced this form of deception. One of the discussants finally "re-identified" as a teen who had used drugs.

I will let you know that I have been hiding something. I am really a teenager and I know what I am talking about because I ran away from home and did drugs and now I am just fine. I get along with my mom and dad now. You people need to realize that illegal drugs are not the big thing you think they are.

Technological failure/complexity. Group discussion can be interrupted or halted by technology failure. Indeed, "erratic performance of telephone-line technology can strain the patience of people already emotionally stressed" (Kurtz, 1997, p. 193). Members of SupportNet repeatedly complained about problems accessing the national discussion because of problems locating and maintaining access through local feeds. Members of SurviveNet and SupportNet reported difficulties in accessing the correct electronic addresses, due to naming confusions and similarities. As discussed earlier, in attempting to access the SurviveNet discussion, a member of our research team accidentally retrieved messages from groups devoted to discussions of explicit sex and pornography. On ParentNet members had the option of using private e-mail, but messages went unread. Members reported being unsure about how to use it.

Members also complained about the inability to connect with the net because of technology limitations. Many members of SupportNet used donated, older computers with limited processing capacity. Due to physical disabilities, some members had trouble typing quickly enough to keep up with the message flow. Members sometimes expressed frustration at being disconnected from what had become an important source of social support in their lives. For example: *"We have had a breakdown on our board again . . . So, I have gone with no mail for two or three days . . . it makes me so mad . . . aargh!!!"*

PROTECTIVE FEATURES
OF ELECTRONIC SUPPORT GROUPS

Protection in face-to-face support groups is often the responsibility of a formal leader or moderator if one exists. This function involves setting limits, creating and enforcing norms, interceding, and making suggestions. In self-help groups without a professional leader, the sense of mutuality enhances trust and becomes a source of reassurance and protection. Because sharing is at the heart of the mutual aid experience, certain guidelines and rules for sharing have evolved in these types of groups. For example, in most 12-step groups "no one may interrupt, advise, confront, or question another person's sharing" (Thomas, 1995, p. 246). Finally, in traditional mutual-aid groups, anonymity and confidentiality of group process also serve as valued sources of protection. *Alcoholics Anonymous*, as well as other 12-Step groups, view anonymity as the cornerstone in building an atmosphere where members can safely self-disclose (Thomas, 1995).

In electronic environments, some traditional protections can be easily adapted. For example, rules regulating communication can be set forth in "FAQs." However, new forms of protection can be offered. For example, the moderator may exert a stronger influence when a listserv model is used. Messages may first go through the moderator, who conceivably can block or edit messages and monitor the list of participants. In another example, mediated support systems create the opportunity to forewarn participants about the theme of the message. Members who may be harmed by certain discussions can avoid potentially harmful messages by looking at the message heading.

In examining our three sample groups, we found that ParentNet, and to some extent SurviveNet, have pre-established formal protections for members. To the extent that the protection was provided on SupportNet, it tended to emerge informally from the interactions and mutual concern of members and the moderator. Here we review primarily those protections that are especially adapted to the mediated environment.

Ground Rules for Electronic Communication

Users of ParentNet were asked to follow a series of guidelines and communication rules, some of which reflected the unique characteristics of mediated support environments. These were easily located by users who sought them because they were referenced by a heading on the group's main web page. One of these guidelines discouraged members from revealing any personal information about themselves or their families because of the public nature of the ParentNet message board.

SurviveNet offered communication guidelines that seemed specially crafted to protect emotionally vulnerable members in cyberspace. Guidelines relate to the following topics: electronic harassment, topic and language restrictions in "public" messages, and suicidal messages. For example, group members were encouraged to use spoilers (message headers) to warn of suicidal, religious, depressing, or "triggering" messages. They were cautioned against posting material that may be inappropriate for children (because the age of the recipient cannot be determined in cyberspace). In this case, the "children" were the young personality alters of those with multiple personalities or children with computer access in the homes of adult members.

Active Monitoring and Editing of Message Traffic

As indicated above, leaders of ParentNet warned users that they would block certain kinds of personal messages. This active approach provides protection unavailable in face-to-face groups. In SurviveNet, the moderator would often be the first one to respond in a gentle and caring way to a distraught member. She sometimes took advantage of the capacity provided by SurviveNet to trace threads of conversation between two members and intervened to give advice or suggest resources. SupportNet was minimally supervised by a "host," a college student who introduced new members. She shared details of their disabilities and their level of expertise with the technology. In doing so, she eased the process of on-line participation, and kept the network from being unintentionally exclusive once original members had established relationships.

Peer Monitoring

ParentNet recruited and trained peer leaders from the community of users as a way to manage the large flow of messages. This is a significant protection because, as we noted before, the sheer volume of message traffic generated in on-line groups can overwhelm the moderator. Peer leaders monitored message boards devoted to specific subtopics (e.g., childbirth). As this (fictionalized) solicitation suggests, peer leaders accepted significant responsibility for keeping the environment supportive and monitoring the rules.

> *Our volunteer peer leaders are the foundation for ParentNet! As a peer leader, you get to play "talk show host"–you keep the chat interesting, give your spin to the topic, keep everyone feeling comfortable, and make sure everyone plays according to the rules.*

Expanded Access to Decision-Making Information and Resources

ParentNet included an e-mail feature that allowed members to gather information directly from content experts. In addition, we saw evidence in all three groups of members accessing information that might not be available to them. On SupportNet, members frequently shared specific references to medical specialists. In some cases, material from other on-line sources (e.g., on-line medical magazines) was copied and distributed to the group. Although some of these practices raise copyright issues, there seems little doubt that this exchange of information broadens member access to important medical resources, particularly when geographic or socio-economic factors limit such access through traditional channels (Scheerhorn, 1997). We saw many instances where members expressed their belief that they had made better decisions about their health, treatment options, finances, and other important matters because of participation in the group.

Reporting Violations

ParentNet featured an explicit procedure for reporting violations of its rules and guidelines to group moderators. This involved all members in policing the support group's postings. According to the rationale provided by creators of ParentNet moderators, this self-policing was needed because moderators need help with the cumbersome task of monitoring the large volume of messages.

Confidentiality protections: ParentNet urges members to realize that their messages are public and warns that members' words may be quoted in newsletters, newspaper columns, and books written by the site managers. It promises to be "sensitive" in this effort and to try to contact the member by e-mail before quoting. Messages *are* identified by the name used by the member on the message board.

PRELIMINARY GUIDELINES
FOR HUMAN SERVICE PROFESSIONALS

The practice of mediated social support is expanding more rapidly than the body of research evaluating its effects. Our own investigation is only a preliminary effort to document harmful and protective practices and stimulate discussion by researchers and practitioners about how to best utilize on-line support. Although our knowledge about "what works" in mediated groups is far from definitive at this point, human services professionals will no doubt find themselves increasingly confronted by the need to offer reasonable and prudent advice to their agencies and clients. Against this backdrop, we suggest the following preliminary guidelines for human service practitioners interested in developing on-line support systems or referring clients to existing on-line groups.

1. Moderators should be active in reviewing messages, maintaining group norms, and preventing harm. In some cases, moderating an on-line support group will require considerable time, expertise, and some technical knowledge. In the groups we observed, moderators were volunteers. Peer volunteers are effective leaders of self-help groups (Wasserman & Danforth, 1988), but they may lack the qualifications necessary to handle some on-line situations. Interestingly, without the contextual cues of live groups, on-line moderators may be perceived as the voice of authority. The moderator's credentials or level of expertise should be made clear to members.

2. Users of electronic social support should be educated about its potential pitfalls. The potential for on-line "addiction," excessive time investment, idealization, emotional magnification, privacy violation, and the other types of harm identified previously, should be part of the user education process.

3. Mediated support groups should develop operating guidelines and communication rules. Procedures for reporting violations should be considered. We found little evidence that they are widely used in the groups we observed, but the fact that moderators in these groups failed to "catch" some harmful messages indicates to us that they may need help from members. Members should be encouraged to share their observations about the effectiveness of the group communication process, in addition to commenting on the content of the discussion.

4. Based on our observations of these groups, it seems clear to us that computer-mediated groups may be very useful for clients seeking information and advice, social support, and an expanded network of friends. We are less certain about the usefulness of the groups for emotionally vulnerable clients, particularly those

who traditionally would receive private therapy in a highly protective environment. Arguably, it is these clients who are most likely to be harmed by the practices we described previously. Human service professionals who are close to the clients are in the best position to match client needs with the features of on-line groups.

5. Designers of electronic self-help groups should establish clear purposes and "member profiles." The types of needs that will and will not be addressed by the group should be clarified so members can self-select the support environment that best suits their situations. For example, those seeking to discuss psychological challenges might require a different group than those concerned with physical disability. Although these criteria probably cannot be enforced, they may steer more vulnerable participants away from potentially harmful situations and give the group focus.

6. Procedures for contacting experts and therapists should be established. The moderators and members should be made aware of situations that require professional intervention rather than peer support. The system designers may need to develop "safety mechanisms" for situations that require rapid intervention.

7. Members should be encouraged to seek multiple sources of information, expertise, and support, so that the mediated support group supplements and enhances, rather than replaces members' face-to-face support networks.

8. When referring clients, human service professionals should consider the client's technical expertise and potential sources of training. Members should receive adequate technical training, so that they know how to use all features of the mediated support environment. Members of the groups we observed reported receiving training from senior citizen volunteers, social work students, and technologically-savvy family members. Technological roadblocks and the potential for members to get "lost" on the Internet should be minimized so that the positive features of electronic support can be fully realized. Procedures should be fully pilot-tested before they are implemented on a large scale.

CONCLUSION

Close analysis of the interactions on these three quite different on-line support environments confirms what many researchers have observed (Braithwaite et al., 1999; Dunham et al., 1998; Scheerhorn, 1997). Members of these groups share generous amounts of advice, emotional support, and companionship. Due to their participation, most members seem to experience an enriched and extended communication network. However, our analysis of this data also left us thinking that in our enthusiasm for its benefits, we must not overlook the potential for mediated support to cause harm. Some of the potentially harmful practices we observed can be dismissed as minor inconvenience. Brief communication delays caused by technical malfunctions come to mind. However, other practices we found genuinely troubling: the self-identified sex offender invading the conversation of sexual abuse survivors, the difficulty some members had in extracting themselves from the on-line groups, the rapid distribution of misinformation and poor advice. We believe that for the large majority of participants, the potential for harm is outweighed by the potential benefits of on-line support. Yet an aggressive agenda of research is needed on issues related to harm.

First on this agenda ought to be additional descriptive study of the mediated support phenomena. What kinds of mediated support groups currently exist? How do their functions, topics, rules, moderator roles, and communicative capabilities vary? How do these variations affect member participation and satisfaction? Of particular relevance to the current investigation would be studies that document the prevalence in other groups of the harmful and protective practices we observed. The degree to which protective features are actually used by members and their perceived effectiveness by members and moderators should be measured.

A second agenda item is research that documents the *effects* of the potentially harmful practices we have only illustrated in this study. This research can proceed along several paths. The perceptions of participants can be assessed to determine whether they are distressed by the violations of privacy, unrealistic expectations, limited access to expertise, and other practices we presumed to be harmful. A second approach would document harm by looking at the perceptions of family members and other members of the local network. Did they perceive harmful effects on the social behavior of the group member? Finally, more convincing measures of harm would be derived from studies that measured more concrete correlates of the social support process (as did Kraut et al., 1998). Depending on the purpose of the group, researchers could determine whether members experienced harmful (or beneficial) effects on such factors as their levels of drug use, work productivity, use of face-to-face therapy, or time spent in social activity. Comparative research with face-to-face groups would be helpful here.

Existing reports often describe the initial phases of mediated support systems. Intended purposes of the group, the population of users, and initial successes are typically well-documented (Brennan et al., 1992; Sharf, 1997; Scheerhorn, 1997). Most authors point to the need for longer-term investigation of these programs. Longitudinal research is rare (but see Kraut et al., 1998). However, basic data about group survival, the degree to which original members remain in the group, the effects of time on member satisfaction, and the changes in procedure that facilitate group evolution all remain underinvestigated. As these groups develop, moderators and members may confront new legal questions about liability, copyright infringements, and privacy violation. Published accounts of these problems and their solution will be useful to human service professionals and support group initiators.

Researchers attempting to describe the naturally-occurring communication practices of on-line support groups must confront a series of ethical questions. In presenting the data for this paper, we struggled with the best way to preserve the essence of what participants communicated in these quasi-public groups, while also protecting their rights and identities. Concerns about the copyright protections associated with e-mail and the difficulty of obtaining permission of all members (some of whom have since left the group, most of whom are known only through their cyber identities) eventually lead us to fictionalize the quoted material. A weakness of the study is that we can offer no guarantee that, despite our best efforts, we have accurately captured the original meaning. Continued dialogue about evolving legal requirements and the ethical responsibilities of researchers studying mediated communication is urgently needed if research is to continue in this area. In sum, the rapid development of mediated support groups raises ethical questions for researchers and practitioners alike. Both the implementation and the investigation of such groups should maximize the protections provided to members.

REFERENCES

Anderson, J. (1997). *Social work with groups: A process model.* New York: Longman.

Burleson, B. (1994). Comforting messages: Significance, approaches, and effects. In B. Burleson, T. Albrecht, & I. G. Sarason (Eds.), *Communication of social support* (pp. 3-28). Thousand Oaks, CA: Sage.

Braithwaite, D. O, Waldron, V. R., & Finn, J. (1999). Communication of social support in computer-mediated groups for people with disabilities. *Health Communication, 11,* 123-152.

Brashers, D. E, Adkins, M. & Meyers, R. E. (1994). Argumentation and computer-mediated group decision-making. In L. Frey (Ed.), *Group communication in context* (pp. 263-282). Hillsdale, NJ: Lawrence Erlbaum.

Brennan, P. F. & Fink, S. V. (1997). Health promotion, social support, and computer networks. In R. L. Street, W. R. Gold, & T. Manning (Eds.), *Health promotion and interactive technology* (pp. 157-170). Mahwah, NJ: Lawrence Erlbaum Associates

Brennan, P. F., Moore, S. M., & Smythe, K. A. (1992). ComputerLink: Electronic support for the home caregiver. *Advances in Nursing Science, 13,* 14-27.

Chesebro, J. W., & Bonsall, D. G. (1989). *Computer-mediated communication: Human relationships in a computerized world.* Tuscalloosa, AL: The University of Alabama Press.

Dunham, P., Hurshman, A., & Litwin, E., Gusslla, J. Elleworth, T, & Dodd, P. (1998). Computer-mediated social support: Single young mothers as a model system. *American Journal of Community Psychology, 26,* 281-306.

Finn, J. & Lavitt, M. (1994). Computer-based self-help groups for sexual abuse survivors. *Social Work with Groups, 17,* 21-46.

Granovetter, M. (1973). The strength of weak ties. *American Journal of Sociology, 73,* 1361-1380.

Green, H., & Himelstein, L. (October 19, 1998). A cyber revolt in health care. *Business Week,* p. 154.

Katz, J. E. & Aspden, P. (1997). A nation of strangers? *Communications of the ACM, 40,* 81-86.

Krackhardt, D. (1994). The strength of strong ties: The importance of Philos in organizations. In N. Nohria & R. Eccles (Eds.), *Networks and organizations: Structure, form, and action.* Boston, MA: Harvard Business School Press.

Kraut, R., Patterson., M., Lundmark, V., Kiesler, S., Mukhopadhyay, T., & Scherlis, W. (1998). Internet paradox: A social technology that reduces social involvement and psychological well-being? *American Psychologist, 53,* 1017-1031.

Kurtz, L. F. (1997). *Self-help and support groups: A handbook for practitioners.* Thousand Oaks, CA: Sage.

Lamberg, L. (1997). Computers enter mainstream psychiatry. *Journal of the American Medical Association, 278,* 799-801.

Leets, L. & Giles, H. (1997). Words as weapons: When do they wound? Investigations of harmful speech. *Human Communication Research, 24,* 260-301.

Madara, E. J. (1995, May). *On-line self-help: National and world-wide networks.* Paper presented given at Harvard University Conference, "The Computer as a Patient's Assistant," Cambridge, MA.

Mickelson, K. (1998). Seeking social support: Parents in electronic support groups.

In S. Kiesler (Ed.), *Culture of the Internet*, (pp. 157-178). Mahwah, NJ: Lawrence Erlbaum Associates.

Parks, M. R., & Floyd, K. (1995). Making friends in cyberspace. *Online Journal of Computer Mediated Communication, 1*, 4.

Scheerhorn, D. (1997). Creating illness-related communities in cyberspace. In R. L. Street, W. R. Gold, & T. Manning (Eds.), *Health promotion and interactive technology* (pp. 171-186). Mahwah, NJ: Lawrence Erlbaum Associates.

Sharf, B. (1997). Communicating breast cancer on-line: Support and empowerment on the Internet. *Women & Health, 26*, 65-84.

Street, R. L., Gold, W. R., & Manning, T. (Eds.) (1997). *Health promotion and interactive technology*. Mahwah, NJ: Lawrence Erlbaum Associates.

Thomas, H. (1995). From AA to A/CDFA: An innovative 12-step model for adult children from dysfunctional family backgrounds. In R. Kurland & R. Salmon (Eds.), *Group work practice in a troubled society*, (pp. 243-358). New York: The Haworth Press, Inc.

Tracy, K. (1991). Discourse. In B. Montgomery & S. Duck (Eds.), *Studying interpersonal interaction* (pp. 179-196). New York: The Guilford Press.

Walther, J. (1994). Anticipated ongoing interaction versus channel effects on relational communication in computer-mediated interaction. *Human Communication Research, 40*, 473-501.

Walther, J. (1995). Relational aspects of computer-mediated communication: Experimental observations over time. *Organization Science, 6*, 186-203.

Walther, J. (1996). Computer-mediated communication: Impersonal, interpersonal, and hyperpersonal interaction. *Communication Research, 23*, 3-43.

Walther, J. (1997). Group and interpersonal effects in international computer-mediated communication. *Human Communication Research, 23*, 342-369.

Walther, J. B., Anderson, J. F., & Park, D. W. (1994). Interpersonal effects in computer-mediated interaction: A meta-analysis of social and antisocial communication. *Communication Research, 21*, 460-487.

Wasserman, H., & Danforth, H. E. (1988). *The human bond: Support groups and mutual aid*. New York: Springer Publishing.

Conclusion

Gary Holden
Jerry Finn

The contents of this volume reveal that a variety of human service agencies are online for diverse purposes, including direct services, inter-agency coordination and collaboration, community education, fundraising, volunteer recruitment, and professional development. As the expansion of the use of the Internet continues and Internet functionality increases, there will be concomitant growth in online human service applications. The nature of human service delivery will necessarily change. While locally based services will continue to be important, the Internet will promote changes in the time/space/method in which services are delivered. Geography and service delivery need no longer be connected. The direction and efficacy of these changes, however, remains unclear. What *is* certain is that we are in a "start-up" phase of human service Internet development. Professionals must learn to integrate the technology while maintaining a firm grasp on their mission and their ethical standards. At the same time, they must understand and respond to potentially new social problems that may stem from increased use of the Internet by consumers, including harm from participation in online relationships or self-help groups, "cyberstalking" and online harassment, online addictions, and weakening of ties with face-to-face support systems.

Gary Holden, DSW, is Associate Professor at New York University, Ehrenkranz School of Social Work.

Jerry Finn, PhD, is Professor, Department of Social Work, University of New Hampshire.

[Haworth co-indexing entry note]: "Conclusion." Holden, Gary, and Jerry Finn. Co-published simultaneously in *Journal of Technology in Human Services* (The Haworth Press, Inc.) Vol. 17, No. 2/3, 2000, pp. 295-297; and: *Human Services Online: A New Arena for Service Delivery* (ed: Jerry Finn, and Gary Holden) The Haworth Press, Inc., 2000, pp. 295-297. Single or multiple copies of this article are available for a fee from The Haworth Document Delivery Service [1-800-342-9678, 9:00 a.m. - 5:00 p.m. (EST). E-mail address: getinfo@ haworthpressinc.com].

Reflecting on what our colleagues and we have written, the need for research becomes clearer. While descriptive studies dominate this area–we still need more of them. Models of effective online practices and cautions from lessons learned are much needed as human service agencies increasingly join the online community. As more agencies must decide whether to use scarce resources to engage in online practice, issues of effectiveness will quickly come to the fore. We have demonstrated in this series of articles that agencies can provide online assistance, education, and support. However, we need outcome studies. We especially need to determine for whom, for what outcomes, in what form, and under what circumstances, online practices are effective, as well as the cost-effectiveness of such interventions (McBride & Rimer, 1999).

How will professional development activities evolve on the Internet? Will listservs, distance learning, and distance supervision play an expanding role? Our own experiences with this book provide an example of professional development and collaboration. We have met face-to-face only three times and had fewer than 10 phone calls to complete this book. We did however exchange more than 300 e-mail messages and more than one hundred attached files. We also received electronic submissions for this volume from throughout the world. Further research is needed to document the extent and effectiveness of online professional development activities. Our experiences support those who claim that the Internet has prompted an explosion of collaborative opportunities.

This volume described one meta-site that organizes and provides information for human service professionals. Such meta-indexes of social work relevant information will be needed until the major search engines, or some alternative tool, can provide more complete coverage of the WWW (Lawrence & Giles, 1999) and return a more selective array of relevant information from searches. Further research is needed to examine the types and quality (e.g., Rippen et al., 1998) of information provided by online sources, the effectiveness of various models of information organization and delivery, and the outcomes of providing information to human service professionals as an integral part of their service delivery.

Given the rapid rate of development of services on the Internet, the time lag between change and documentation of such change emerging in the scholarly literature, and the limited space of printed volumes compared to the voluminous submissions that we received, a number of important areas are insufficiently covered in this volume. Telehealth and telebehavioral health, including video-consultation and treatment, are evolving areas in which some social workers are already involved. Advocacy and policy development are being used by a variety of groups seeking to facilitate systems change, but are not represented in this volume. Finally, issues related to online diversity and access for disenfranchised groups are topics deserving more coverage.

The "experts" have never been very accurate in predicting the future of technology. No doubt the Internet and its future developments will create changes that cannot be imagined today, and our current Internet-based human services may seem like an early telephone or phonograph might be viewed from today's vantage point. More than the emergence of mainframe computing that changed human service record keeping, and more than the emergence of personal computers that empowered individual line workers, the Internet will change the life of social workers. Just as today no agency would be without a telephone, the day is rapidly approaching when no agency will be without Internet access. While widespread telephone use occurred over fifty years, Internet use will likely occur in twenty. We have only begun to understand the changes that will result from this rapid move to online human services. We hope this volume has helped you to get ready for the journey.

REFERENCES

Lawrence, S. & Giles, C. L. (1999). Accessibility of information on the web. *Nature, 400*, 107-10.

McBride, C. & Rimer, B. K. (1999). Using the telephone to improve health behavior and health service delivery. *Patient Education and Counseling, 37*, 3-18.

Rippen, H. [Chair], Guard, R., Byrns, P., Silberr, D. & Cleland, R. [Leads] + Abbott, P. A., Ambre, J., Anderson, S., Arcari, R., Basler, T. G., Buckovich, S., Carnerio, J. T. M.,, Chang, B., Decker, W., Deering, M. J., Dragovich, C., Eng, T., Fitzmaurice, J. M., Fourcroy, J., J. M., Frydman, G. J., Golodner, L., Hay, G., Hoey, D., Holden, G., Hudgings, Johnson, M., Kerlin, B. D., Kimbrough, C. A., Lazar, A., Linden, T., Lloyd, D. S., Mark, D., Mazzaschi, A., Molloy-Hubbard, S., Morgan, R. E., Perveiler, F. M., Probyn, S., Renner, J., Rodbard, D., Rozen, M. J., Rucker, N. L., Ruggiero, L., Saba, V., Savage, M., Scolamiero, S. J., Shannon, T., Siemers, L., Silberg, W., Talley, C. R., Thurn, A., Tierny, J., Valentino, J. G. [Contributors] (1998). Criteria for assessing the quality of health information on the Internet. A Health Summit Group Policy Paper. Available at: *http://hitiweb.mitretek.org/hswg/documents/default.asp*

Index

Abell, M.D., 42
Abuse, spouse. *See under* Domestic
 violence
Access Project, 205
Acquired immune deficiency
 syndrome (AIDS)
 fatality rate of, 9
 history of, 8-9
 incidence of, 9
Advocacy, domestic violence services
 online and, 86,96-97
Agency(ies)
 Internet use by, primary functions
  of, 84
 role in computer technology
  utilization by
  community-based AIDS
  organizations, 112-114
 virtual volunteers for, 129-130
 visibility of, domestic violence
  services online and, 84-85
Agency for Health Care Policy and
 Research, 30
Aggression, displaced, in
 technology-mediated
 self-help settings, 280-281
AHEC Community Partners of
 Massachusetts, 196
AIDS. *See* Acquired immune
 deficiency syndrome
AIDS organizations,
  community-based, computer
  technology utilization and,
  103-117. *See also*
  Community-based AIDS
  organizations, computer
  technology utilization and
Alcoholics Anonymous, 241,285
Alliance of Information & Retrieval
 Systems (AIRS), 78

Altavista search engine, 85,87
American Association of Fundraising
 Counsel Trust for
 Philanthropy, "Annual
 Survey of State Laws
 Regulating Charitable
 Solicitations" by, 147
American Management Association,
 179
American Psychological Association,
 155
American Public Health Association,
 204,205
America's Promise, 120
Ameritech, 231
Amnesty International, 141
Amnesty International USA, 144
Anheuser-Busch Inc., 149
"Annual Survey of State Laws
 Regulating Charitable
 Solicitations," by American
 Association of Fundraising
 Counsel Trust for
 Philanthropy, 147
Anonymity
 CMCs and, 219-220
 loss of, in technology-mediated
  self-help settings, 277-278
Anxiety, in children, effect of
 computer network on, 27-47.
 See also under
 STARBRIGHT WORLD
 study of, 31-44. *See also*
 STARBRIGHT WORLD,
 effect on pediatric pain and
 anxiety, study of
Aronstein, 9
"Artrock Auction," 144
Assessment(s), accuracy of, liability
 and, 161-162